Yoruba-Speaking Peoples

of the Slave Coast of West Africa

Their Culture, History, Religion, Manners,
Customs, Laws, Language, Etc.

By Alfred Burdon Ellis

PANTIANOS
CLASSICS

Published by Pantianos Classics

ISBN-13: 978-1-78987-265-1

First published in 1894

Contents

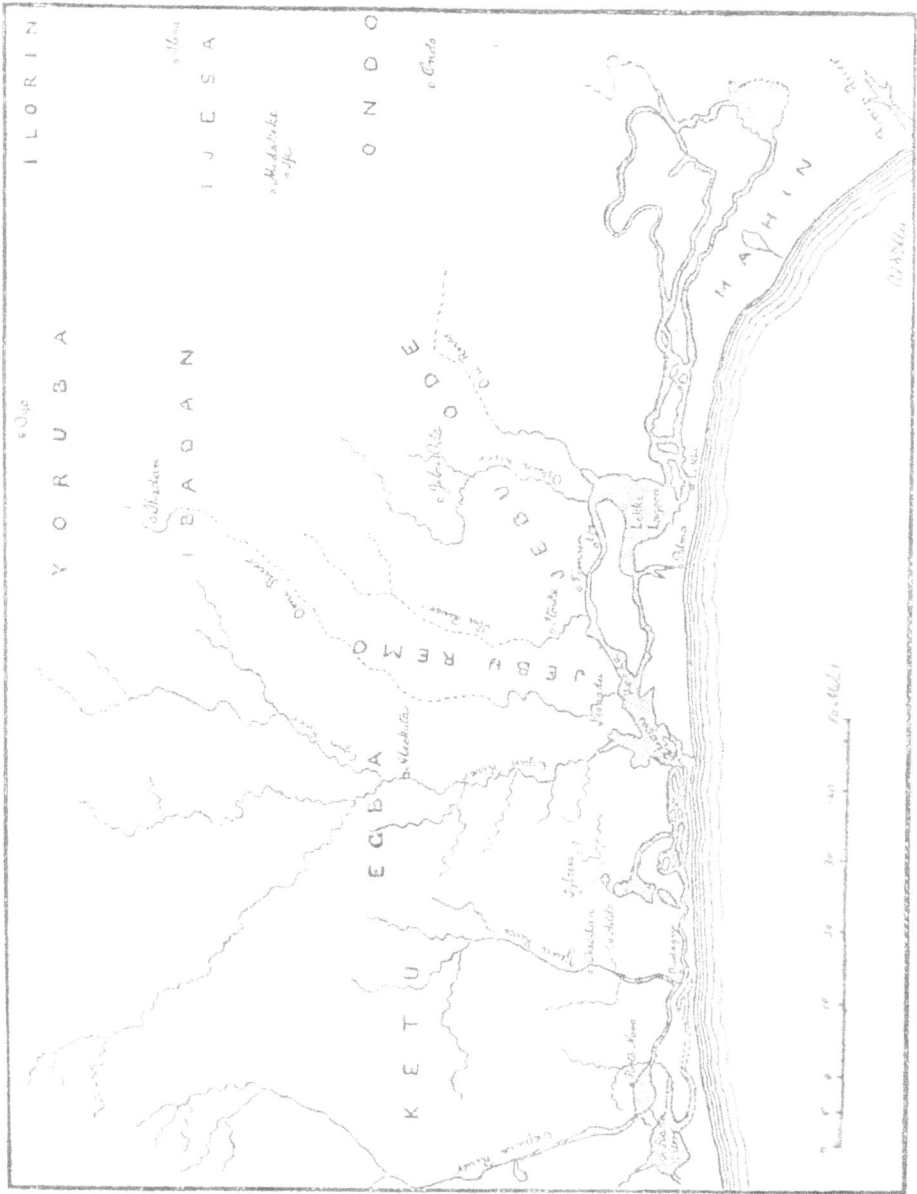

Chapter One - Introductory

THE portion of the West African coast occupied by the Yoruba-speaking peoples is situated in the eastern half of the Slave Coast, and lies between

Badagry, on the west, and the Benin River, on the east. The extent of sea-board held by them is thus smaller than that occupied either by the Tshi or by the Ewe tribes; but the Yorubas are really an inland people, and it was not until the beginning of the present century that they moved to the south and colonised Lagos and the adjacent littoral.

The territory now inhabited by the Yoruba tribes is bounded on the west by Dahomi, on the south-west by Porto Novo and Appa, on the south by the sea, on the east by Benin, and on the north by the Mohammedan tribes from the interior, who have within recent times conquered and annexed the Yoru-ba province of Ilorin, and whose territory may now be said to extend south-ward to about 8º 30' N. latitude. The aggressions of these Mohammedan tribes commenced very early in the present century, and it was no doubt this pressure from the north that caused the Yorubas to move to the south and colonise the seaboard.

Yoruba country at present comprises the following states, or political units:--

(1) The British colony of Lagos, which covers the whole sea-front between the meridian of the Ajarra Creek and the Benin River, and has absorbed the former native kingdoms of Appa, Pokra, Badagry, Lagos, Palma, Lekki, Ala, hin, Ogbo, and Jakri.

(2) Ketu. This is the western state. It is bounded on the west by Dahomi, on the south by Porto Novo, and on the east by Egba. Its northern limits are un-defined.

(3) Egba. It lies east of Ketu and south-west of Yoruba proper. Its capital is Abeokuta, "Under the Rock."

(4) Jebu. This is the south-eastern kingdom, and is divided into two prov-inces, called Jebu Remo and Jebu Ode. Jebu Ode has for its capital a town of the same name, that of Jebu Remo is called Offin. The river Odo Omi is con-sidered the north-western boundary of Jebu, and, roughly speaking, the terri-tory of the Jebus may be said to extend inland to a distance of some fifty miles from the lagoon.

(5) Ekiti Tribes. These tribes, which form a confederation, lie to the north-east of Jebu Ode.

(6) Ibadan. It lies north of Jebu Ode.

(7) Yoruba proper. This kingdom, whose capital is Oyo, lies to the north of Ibadan and Egglxt, and towards the west its boundary trends southward to within some twenty-five miles of Abeokuta.

(8) Ijesa, capital Ilesa. This state is situated to the sbuth-east of Yoruba proper.

(9) Ife, capital of the same name, lies south-west of Ijesa.

(10) Ondo. This kingdom, capital Ondo, is situated south-east of Ife.

In addition there are several small states, or rather independent town-ships, consisting of a town and a few outlying villages. The principal are Eg-bado, Okeodan, Ado, Awori, and Igbessa, all of which lie south of Egba. Their inhabitants are Egbados, or Southern Egbas (*Egba-odo*, Egbas of the coast).

The inhabitants of all these states speak one language, the, Yoruba. They are called Nagos by the French, and by the English are named after their political divisions, as Egbas, Ibadans, Jebus, &c.

The lagoon system, which in the last volume of this series was noted as commencing a short distance to the west of the Volta River, on the Gold Coast, extends along the whole sea-front of the territory occupied by the Yoruba-speaking tribes, and affords a continuous waterway from Porto Novo to Benin. The extension of the continent in a southerly direction, which was mentioned in the last volume as typical of the western half of the Slave Coast, and which may doubtless be attributed to the action of the Guinea current in closing with sand the openings to former indentations which existed in the coast-line, is also equally noticeable in this the eastern half of the Slave Coast; and, generally speaking, the country is open, flat, and devoid of stones. Jebu is an excep tion, being thickly forested; but it appears that less territory has been won from the sea south of Jebu, and cast of Lagos generally, than in the districts to the west, between Lagos and Dahomi. To the east of Lagos the old coast-line seems to have been almost conterminous with the northern shores of the Kradu and Lekki lagoons, and the water-way which connects them by way of Epi, while to the west it appears to have trended back northwards bevond the lagoons of Oluge and Porto Novo. It is only after crossing the narrow lagoon or creek called the Ajarra Creek, which runs in a convex curve from the Porto Novo lagoon to the Okpara, that stones are found in the soil; and about twenty miles to the west of this there appears to have been at one time a great bay, the northern limit of which was the Ko, or Great Marsh, of Dahomi, thirty-five iniles from the present coastline. The dotted line in the accompanying map shows the probable position of the ancient coast-line between the Volta River and Lekki.

Northward of the old coast-line the Yoruba country rises very gradually in a succession of low-lying plateans. traversed by a few lines of low hills, or undulations in the groand; but a chain of mountains, whose general direction is east and west, extends, at about eight degrees north latitude, from Dahomi to the northern border of Ijesa, where the country is rugged and difficult. Isolated and densely-wooded hills, from 800 to 1,200 feet high, are also found in Ife and Ondo.

In some parts, as at Sakiti, north of Ajarra, and at Abeokuta, isolated masses of granite afford evidence of great denudation. In fact the whole western coast of Africa, between the Isles de Los, seventy miles north of Sierra Leone, and Lagos, and probably beyond those limits, shows traces of an enormous denudation. The table-topped Kofiu Mountain, which rises sheer from the plain north of the.-Melikuri River to a height of 2,000 feet, is the sole remnant of a vast cap of sandstone that doubtless at one time covered the whole of that part of the country; and the Krobo Mountain, an isolated and precipitous mass, 800 feet high, situated in the Krobo plain on the Gold Coast, together with the table-topped mountains with vertical cliffs in the Ataklu district, to the north of the Quittah (Keta) lagoon, will probably, when geologically examined, prove to be other vestiges of the same sandstone formation.

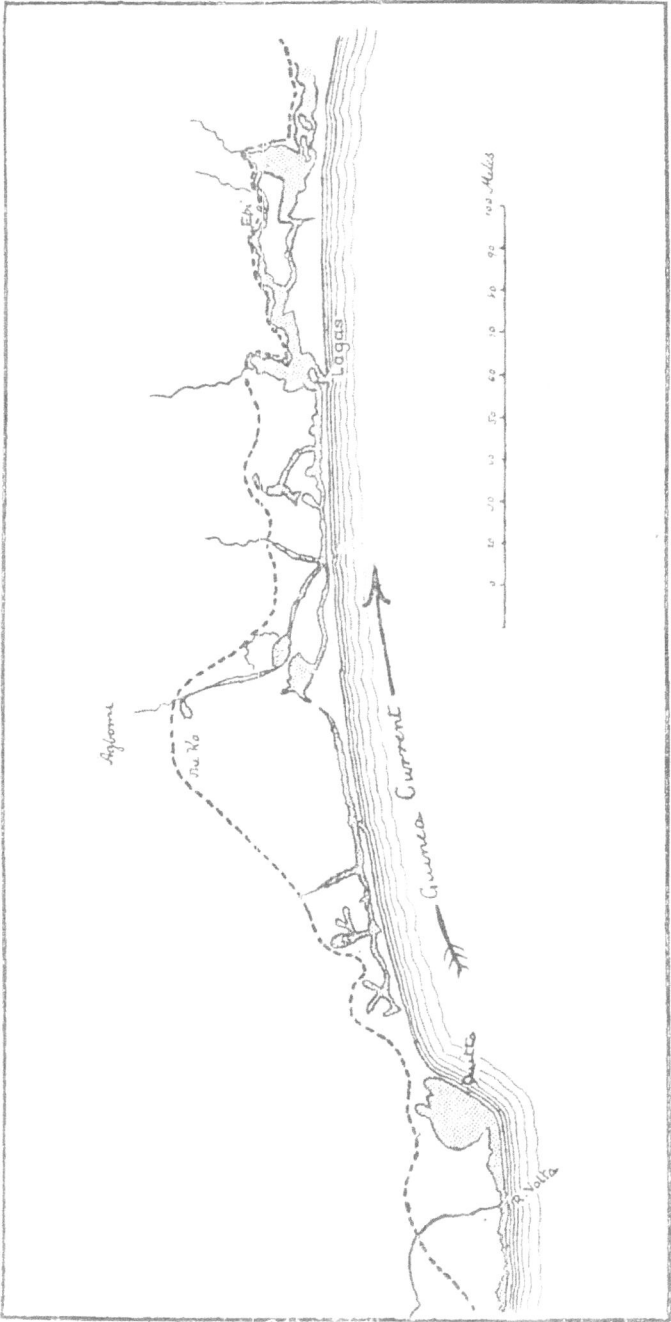

Of the early history of the Yoruba-speakino, peoples nothing is known, except what can be gleaned from Dalzel's "History of Dahomey," 1793, from which it would appear that, at the beginning of the eighteenth century, all the different tribes were united, and were ruled by a king who resided at Old Oyo, sometimes called Katunga. The kingdom of Yoruba also seems to have been more powerful than the other two great African kingdoms, Dahomi and Ashanti. Between 1724 and 1725 the King of Yoruba espoused the quarrel of the King of Ardra, whose kingdom had been overthrown by Dahomi, and sent a large army, chiefly consisting of cavalry, to invade Dahomi. By a stratagem [1] the Yorubas were routed, and the king of Dahomi then diplomatically sued for peace, which was granted; but about September, 1728, a new quarrel having arisen, this time in the interests of the King of Whydah, a Yoruba army again invaded Dahomi, and a desultory war lasted until 1730, wlien peace was once inore made. In 1738 another Yoruba army invaded Dahomi, defeated the king, and captured and burnt Agbomi, Kalia, and Zassa [2] and from that time forward the Yorubas annually raided into Dahomi, ravaging the country, and retiring again at the commeucement of the rains. This state of affairs was brought to an end by a treaty of peace inade in 1747, by which the King of Dahomi undertook to pay a heavy annual tribute to the King of Yoruba. After this we hear no more of the Yorubas in Dalzel's History, which is only carried to 1791, except that, in 1786, they interfered to prevent the Dahomis from attacking Porto -Novo; but the tribute appears to have been paid up to the days of King Gezo of Dahomi (1818).

Governor Dalzel informs us, however, that when the "Eyeos"[3] (Yorubas) were dissatisfied with a king, they sent a deputation to him with a present of parrot's eggs, and a message that they considered he must be fatigued with the cares of government, and that it was time for him to rest and take a little sleep. Upon receiving this inessage, the king forth with retired to his apartment, as if to sleep, and then gave directions to his women to strangle him, which they accordingly did. [4] In 1774, the then king declined to take the hint, and returned the parrot's eggs. The chiefs tried to support the custom by force, and Ochemi, the prime minister headed a rebellion, which was, however, crushed, and Ochemi, and all his numerous family were put to death.

The reason of our having such meagre information of this great West African kingdom is that the Yorubas did not inhabit the territories on the sea-coast, the Ewe tribes occupying the coast-line as far east as Badagry, and the Benin tribes the portion from Badagry to Benin. The Ewe tribes had in fact spread along the sea-shore from west to east, and the Benin tribes from east to west, till they met, and covered all the sea frontage of the inland territory occupied by the Yorubas. This neglect on the part of the Yorubas to push down to the sea may have been partly due to superstition, for Dalzel says that "the fetiche of the Eyeos was the sea," and that they and their king were threatened with death by their priests if they ever dared to look upon it. Slave traders and others, who frequented the Slave Coast during the last century, were thus not brought into contact with the Yorubas, and consequently we hear but little of them; while the literature concerning Ashanti and Dahomi, which, like Yoruba, were originally inland powers, but whose invasions of the coast kingdoms brought them into contact with Europeans, is ample.

As far as can be ascertained, the chief strength of Yoruba lay in its cavalry, which was said to number 100,000, a manifest exaggeration, for horses have never been numerous in the few districts of West Africa in which it is possible for them to live. The report as to the number of cavalry reached the traders through the coast tribe, who owned no horses, and who were no doubt greatly impressed by the spectacle of a few score of mounted men. According to tradition, the following was the method of determining the number of men required for a military expedition. An ox-hide was pegged down in front of the general's tent, and the horsemen made to ride over it in succession between two spears. When, by this process,. a hole had been worn in the hide, the number of men was thought sufficient for an ordinary campaign. For serious operations two ox-hides were used, one placed over the other.

Although as we know from Dalzel's History, Oyo, or Yoruba, was a powerful kingdom at least as early as 1724, Yoruba traditional history carries us back no further than the end of the eighteenth century, a fact which shows what little reliance can be placed upon the traditions of nations who are unacquainted with the art of -writing. The first king of whom the arokbi, or chroniclers, have any knowledge is Ajagbo, who appears to have reigned soon after 1780, and whose name is preserved in the metrical sentence which fixes the rhythm of the *ogidigbo* drum, as follows: *Gbo, Ajagbo, gbo oba gbo, ki emi, ki osi gbo.* [5]

In the days of Ajagbo the kingdom of Yoruba consisted of the four following states.

(1) Yoruba proper, whose capital, Old Oyo, or Katunga, was situated some ninety miles to the north of the present town of Oyo. The king of this state, whose title was *Alafin*, or *Alawofin*, literally "One who owns the entering of the palace," was the ruler over all the Yoruba-speaking tribes.

(2) Egba, which lay to the south and west of the above kingdom. Its chief town was Ake, and from it the chief took his title of *Alake*, "One who owns Ake."

(3) Ketu. This was then, as now, the western province. Its capital was Ketu, and from it the chief took his title of *Alaketu*, "One who owns Ketu."

(4) Jebu, which lay south and east of Yoruba proper. It was divided into Jebu Remu and Jebu Ode, each having its own chief, but the ruler of the latter, called the *Awujale*, was considered the chief of the whole.

The rulers of Yoruba, Egba, and Ketu styled each other "brother."

Ajagbo was succeeded by Abiodun, who is said to have enjoyed a long and peaceful reign, so that the reign of his brother and successor, Arogangan, can scarcely have commenced before 1800. It was during the reign of Arogangan that the Yoruba kingdom commenced to break up. The Fulas, it seems, overran the territory of the Hausas, and the latter, driven southward, sought refuge in the northern provinces of Yoruba. Arogangan had appointed his nephew, Afunja, governor of Ilorin, the north-eastern province, which contained a large number of Hausa refugees, and Afunja, being ambitious, conceived the project of utilising the Hausas in order to dethrone his uncle and make himself *Alafin*. His plans being matured, he raised an insurrection, which met with a measure of success, for Oyo was besieged, and Arogangan, in order to avoid falling into the hands of his nephew, poisoned himself; but Afunja was not able to secure the throne, as the elders of Oyo elected to the monarchy Adebo, the brother of Arogangan, and Afunja had to retire to Ilorin, where he maintained a semi-independent position. These events are supposed to have taken place about 1807, and it was about the same time that some of the Yorubas first pushed to the south and colonised Lagros. The first chief of Lagos was named Ashipa, and is said to have belonged to the family of the *Alafin*.

Adebo only reigned about four months, and died suddenly, from which it was supposed that he was poisoned. He was succeeded by Maku, who endeavoured to make head against the Mohammedan tribes who were now pressing in from the north, but he was defeated in a great battle, and committed suicide, after a reign of about only three months. An interregnum now ensued, during which the reins of power were held by the *Oba-shorun*, or prime minister, and it was not until five years had elapsed that a new king, named Majotu, was elected. He reigned about seven or eight years, committed suicide on account, tradition says, of the misbehaviour of his son, and was succeeded by Amodo.

Afunja had, since 1807, remained in possession of Ilorin, where he had sought to strengthen himself by encouraging Mohammedans to settle, and, about 1825, while Amodo was engaged with the invading tribes from the north, he again made war upon Yoruba. He captured and destroyed a number of towns, and was apparently about to carry all before him, when, for some reason that has never transpired, he was conveyed back to the town of Ilorin by those very Hausa mercenaries through whose aid he had hoped to become Alafin, and publicly burned alive. The Mohammedan party had for some years been dominant in Ilorin, and now, declaring that it would no longer recognise a pagan king, it elected a Mohammedan to the supreme power, and severed the connection with Yoruba.

Ilorin now took the lead in the Mohammedan invasion of Yoruba, and the Yorubas seem to have been invariably worsted. In 1830, when it was visited by Lander., Old Oyo was still the capital of Yoruba, but between 1833 and 1835 it was captured and destroyed by the Mohammedans, and the Yorubas, flying southwards, founded their present capital Oyo, about ninety miles south of the old one. The Egbas, taking advantage of the overthrow of Yoruba, declared themselves independent, but the Yorubas, as soon as they were settled in their new territory, attacked them with vigour, and drove them out of all their northern towns. A desultory war then lingered till about 1838, when the Egbas abandoned their territory, and moving to the south, founded their present capital, Abeokuta. The new town was divided into several distinct quarters, or townships, which were named after an equal number of towns that had been destroyed in the war, and one of them, Ake, still preserves the name of the old Egba capital. Although these events occurred so recently, they have already become clothed with myth; and Lishabe, the chief who led them to Abeokuta, is believed by the Egbas to have been a giant and a demi-god.

About the same time, Ibadan, a town of the old province of Egba, situated some thirty-five miles south of Oyo, declared itself independent of Egba; the original Egba inhabitants having been driven out by the Jebus, and the latter, in their turn, by Yoruba refugees. Other secessions took place, and by 1840 the Yoruba kingdom had split up into the following independent states.

(1) Yoruba, south of Old Yoruba, capital Oyo.

(2) Egba, south and west of Old Egba, capital Abeokuta.

(3) Ketu.

(4) Jebu.

(5) Ibadan, a small state south of Oyo. It owned a nominal allegiance to the Alafin, because its inhabitants were Yoruba refugees, but was really independent.

(6) Ijesa, a small state south of Ilorin. The ruler was styled the *Owa*.

(7) Ife, a small state south-west of Ijesa. The ruler was styled the *Oni*.

The former Yoruba province of Ilorin was now inhabited by Fulas, Bornus, and Hausas, and was said to have a population of 300,000, 80,000 of whom were in the town of Ilorin. The Fulas were the dominant race, and the government was in their hands.

Shortly after 1840 the Ekiti tribes, as they were afterwards termed, that is, the inhabitants of the various towns lying between lbadan and Ijesa, and the adjoining territory to the south, formed a, confederation, which was soon joined by Ife and Ijesa, the ruler of the latter state being elected bead of the confederation. The Mohammedans of Ilorin were the first to take alarm at this coalition, and attacked the confederates, destroying or annexing several towns while Ibadan soon followed suit, and after a time succeeded in conquering and annexing Ijesa. The result of these various conflicts was that the confederation was entirely subdued, one half passing under the rule of Ilorin and the other under that of Ibadan. Before long, however, the inhabitants of the towns which had been annexed to Ilorin applied to Ibadan for assistance, and another war ensued, which resulted in the expulsion of the Ilorins, and the establishment of the rule of Ibadan over the whole Ekiti confederation. This was about 1858.

While these events were taking place in the interior, Lagos, which, as we have seen, was colonised from Yoruba at the beginning of the century, had become a place of some note as a slave emporium. The wars in the north, which had been almost incessant since the rebellion of Afunja about 1807, had resulted in the capture of many thousands of prisoners of war, of both sexes and all ages, and the dregs of these, the men who were of no local importance, and the women who were no longer attractive, were, in accordance with the usual practice, sold to the slave-traders. Lagos was the most convenient port, and they were therefore inarched. down there in gangs to await shipment. This traffic in slaves, which brought Lagos into some notoriety commenced about the year 1815, and soon attained very large dimensions.

In 1836 a struggle for the succession broke out in Lagos, and resulted in Kosoko, the legitimate pretender, being expelled the kingdom by his rival Oluwole, who secured the throne for himself. Oluwole died in 18{???}, and was succeeded by Akitoye, who was foolish enough to invite Kosoko, who was still alive and in banishment, to come and live in Lagos. Kosoko readily accepted the invitation, soon began conspiring, and before long found himself sufficiently well supported to rebel. In the struggle which ensued the town of Lagos was burned, and Akitoye driven into banishment. He found a refuge at Badagry, and, in order to induce the English to espouse his cause, promised that, if he were reinstated at Lagos, he would help to suppress the slave-trade. This negotiation coming to the knowledge of Kosoko, he despatched a force to Badagry to attack Akitoye, which burned the town, killed an English trader named Gee, and destroyed a great deal of property belonging to British subjects. The senior naval officer upon the station thereupon determined to support Akitoye against Kosoko, and H.M. sloops *Philomel*, *Harlequin*, *Niger*, and *Waterwitch*, with the gun vessels *Bloodhound* and *Volcano*, assembled off the Lagos bar in -November, 1851, and on the 25th all the ships' boats, towed by the Bloodhound, entered the lagoon and proceeded towards Lagos Island. As the British Consul, who was with the flotilla, had hopes that Kosoko would submit to a display of force, flags of truce were kept flying; and although, on rounding the first point, a heavy musketry fire was opened by the natives, the fire was not returned, and the flags were not lowered till the boats were within a mile of the town. At this point several guns opened on the boats, so the flags of truce were hauled down and the fire returned. The fire from the boats had, however, but little effect on the natives, who were well covered by stockades and mud walls, and a party of one hundred and sixty men was accordingly landed. They found themselves in a maze of narrow streets, from every corner of wh_ich they were fired upon by concealed enemies, and after losing two officers killed and several men wounded, they were compelled to retreat to the boats.

This failure led to a more determined attack in December, on the 26th of which month a considerable force, under the command of Commodore H. W. Bruce, entered the lagoon in boats. The natives offered a stubborn resistance, and had in position several guns, which were exceedingly well served. The *Teazer* got aground abreast of a battery, upon which her own gun could not be brought to bear, and to save her from destruction it became necessary to land a party and carry the battery by assault. This was done in gallant style, but with the heavy loss of one officer and thirteen inen killed, and four officers and fifty-eight men wounded. The other vessels and boats had in the meantime kept up a vigorous bombardment, which was maintained all that day, and continued next morning from daybreak until about 11 a.m., when a magazine on shore blew up and set fire to the town. The flames, fanned by the sea-breeze, spread with remarkable rapidity, and the heat was so intense that the fire of the natives gradually slackened and then finally stopped. Next morning, Kosoko and his followers havinu abandoned the place, the British landed. They found the beach strongly stockaded, and an enfilading piece of ordnance at every promontory. Fifty-two guns were captured, but the victory was dearly purchased, as the total loss during the two days' operations amounted to two officers and fifteen men killed, four officers and sixty-eight men wounded, many of them very severely.

Akitoye was now reinstated, and on January 1st, 1852, signed a treaty, undertaking to suppress the export slave trade, and to expel all Europeans engaged in the traffic. About September of the same year some Portuguese slave traders, who had been expelled under this treaty, returned to Lagos, and, with the assistance of some of the chiefs, secretly renewed the traffic. Akitoye, being informed of what was going on, strove to stop it, whereupon the Portuguese incited the chiefs to rebel, and in August, 1853, Kosoko returned from Epi, where he had taken refuge, to head the movement. The British naval autborities again interfered in favour of Akitoye; a party of seamen and marines was landed to support him, and on the 13th of August, after a sharp skirmish, defeated Kosoko and his adherents, who once more fled to the east.

Akitoye died in September, poisoned, it was said, by the slave trade party, and his son Docemo was, through British influence, appointed his successor. Kosoko, who had again found an asylum with the chief of Epi, refused to accept this arrangement, and continued to harass Docemo and the Lagos people until by an agreement made in January, 1854, he was recognised as King of Palma and Lekki, on condition of renouncing all claim to the sovereignty of Lagos. In August, 1861, Docemo ceded Lagos to the British in consiaeration of a pension of £1,000 a year, and Lagos thus became a British possession; but it is doubtful if the cession was altogether voluntary on Docemo's part, for during the first few years succeeding the signature of the treaty he made several protests against it.

In 1860 a new war broke out in the interior. Ijaye, an important town of Yoruba, declared itself independent of the *Alafin*, who called upon the Ibadans to assist him in reducing it to allegiance. The Ibadans complied, whereupon the Egbas sided with Ijaye; but these allies sustained a severe defeat at the hands of the Yorubas and lbadans, losing, it is said, 40,000 in killed and prisoners, and Ijaye was destroyed on March 17th, 1862.

Up to this time the Egbas had been considered the protéges of the British, and great interest had been taken in the welfare of Abeokuta, which was regarded as the bulwark of Christianity in West Africa. This interest dated from about 1838, when a number of Egba slaves, who had been liberated at Sierra Leone from captured slave vessels, returned to Abeokuta and asked that missionaries might be sent to them. A Protestant mission was established there in 1848, and when an attack on the town was threatened by Gezo, King of

Dahomi, in 1850, Mr. Beecroft, the British Consul for the Bights, and Commander Forbes, R.N., were sent to Agbomi to endeavour to persuade the king to abandon his design. The mission completely failed, and Gezo attacked Abeokuta on March 3rd, 1851, but was repulsed with some loss. [6] The British occupation of Lagos in 1861 put an end to the friendly feelings of the Egbas, who resented the protection granted by the colonial authorities to fugitive slaves from Abeokuta, and objected to the stoppage of the export slave trade, in which they had been largely engaged. They seem also to have had some suspicion that their independence was threatened, for when in May, 1861, it was proposed to send some trained gunners of the 2nd West India Regiment to Abeokuta to instruct the people in the use of some guns that had been presented by the British Government, and to lend aid during another attack that was now threatened by Dahomi, the Egbas made excuse after excuse, and finally declined to receive them. In 1862 they further displayed their ill-will by molesting, and plundering several native traders from Lagos, and, as they refused reparation, the Governor of Lagos, in 1863, blockaded all the roads leading to Abeokuta.

In 1863, Kosoko, chief of Palma and Lekki, desired to return to Lagos, and, in order to obtain permission, ceded Palma and Lekki to the British. The Possu, or chief of Epi, raised objections to this cession. He had, it appeared, certain territorial rights over these places, and their cession, moreover, shut him off from the sea. As he refused to cede his rights, an expedition, consisting of three officers and 124 men of the 2nd and 3rd West India Regiments, proceeded in H.M.S. *Investigator* to Epi, where the troops and a rocket party of one officer and fourteen seamen landed. The natives offered a strenuous resistance, and the expeditionary force suffered a loss of three men killed and three officers and twenty-eight men wounded, but the town was destroyed. After this the chief renounced all further claim to territory south of the lagoon. In July, 1863, the chiefs of Badagry likewise ceded all their territory to the British.

The war between the Egbas and Ibadans caused by the affair of Ijaye had been carried on in a desultory manner since 1862; but in 1864, after the repulse of the Dahomis from before Abeokuta on March 15th, [7] the Jebus, who had hitherto adopted the policy of excluding all strangers from their territory, and had lived in complete isolation, shut off by their forests from the rest of the tribes, joined the Egbas, and the war was prosecuted with more vigour. The Jebus of Ikoradu, a town at the northern extremity of the Lagos lagoon, refused to join their fellow-tribesmen in the alliance with the Egbas, their reason being that their interests were identified with those of the people of Lagos, and that they had suffered equally with them from the cessation of trade caused by the maltreatment of traders by the Egbas. In revenge, the Egbas, early in 1865, despatched to Ikoradu an army of 12,000 men, which besieged the town, and, after the native fashion, threw up two entrenched camps against it. The Colonial Government, alarmed at the near approach of this force, and appealed to by the Ikoradus for aid, warned the

Egbas to desist, and ordered them to return to their own country. The Egbas sent insulting messages in reply, and a force of some 280 men, consisting of the 5th West India Reaiment and the Lagos Police, was accordingly sent against them, which stormed the camps and routed the Egbas with heavy loss, on March 29th, 1865. This affair of course only served to widen the breach between the British and the Egbas, the latter, besides, conceived that the Colonial Government encouraged the annual raids of Dahomi upon Egba territory; and, in 1867, they expelled all the missionaries from Abeokuta, and cut off all relations with the British.

It seems that a letter, purporting to be signed by a hostile chief, fell into the hands of the Egbas, who knew that the chief could not write, and fancied they recognised the handwriting as that of a Protestant missionary who had formerly lived in Abeokuta. The missionaries in Abeokuta were thereupon accused of betraying the Egbas to their enemies; there was a popular tumult, and the mob howled for their blood. It was only with great difficulty that the chiefs and elders succeeded in saving the lives of the accused, who were immediately expelled from the town, and their houses and churches destroyed. In 1880, the French Roman Catholic missionaries obtained leave to establish a mission in Abeokuta, which thenceforward fell more under the influence of the French.

The interior continued to be disturbed by inter-tribal wars until about, 1870, when affairs calmed down, but in 1877 the Egbas plundered some Ibadan traders, and the Ibadans sent an army to avenge the outrage. Upon this the Jebus renewed their former alliance with the Egbas, and Ijesa and the Ekiti tribes, which had now been under the rule of Ibadan since 1858, seized the opportunity for rebellion, a step which was soon followed by a declaration of war against Ibadan by Ilorin. The Mohammedans of Ilorin rapidly invaded the country and laid siege to Ofa, a town situated some twenty miles to the northeast of the city of Ibadan, and the Ibadans were obliged to withdraw their army of invasion from Egba in order to defend their own territory, which was now threatened from three sides. The Egbas, however, did not follow up the retreating force, and, indeed, took no further part in the war, they being held in check by the fear of leaving Abeokuta unprotected against Dahomi, which power had been in the habit of making annual demonstrations in its vicinity for some years past; and the struggle was continued between Ibadan, on the one side, and Ilorin, Ijesa, the Ekiti tribes, and Jebu, on the other.

Ibadan secured the support of Modakeke and Ife, two populous towns situated on hills on the opposite sides of a small stream, to the south-west of Ijesa, and the war continued for some years without any great advantage being gained by either side. The Modakekes were staunch allies of the Ibadans, but the sympathies of the Ifes were rather with the Ijesa and the Ekiti tribes, with whom they had been in alliance during the war which terminated in 1858. Their situation, however, made them afraid of coming to an open rupture with Ibadin, so, in response to the demand of the Ibadans, they sent a contingent to the Ibadan camp, but at the same time also secretly sent an equal force to the camp of the Ijesas and Ekitis. This double game could not long escape detection, and in 1882 the Modakekes, assisted by a force of Ibadans, attacked Ife, and the town, which was regarded as holy, and the cradle of the Yoruba race, was destroyed. The Ifes now openly joined the enemies of Ibadan, but most of the tribes had by this time become heartily sick of the prolonged struggle, and in 1883 a body of Jebus who were encamped on the Omi River made peace with the Ibadans on their own account, and returned home. The Awujale of Jebu Ode, paramount chief of the two Jebu provinces, was so alarmed at this event that he fled from the town of Jebu Ode, which he was by law forbidden to leave, and took refuge at Epi. Here he was invited by the Jebu elders to commit suicide; he proved docile, and a new *Awujale* was elected by the peace party. His election, however, was not approved by the war party, and a strong force of Jebus, under the *seriki*, or second war chief, still kept the field against Ibadan.

The war, which was really only a succession of skirmishes at long intervals, dragged on till 1884, when the Governor of Lagos was asked to mediate and secure a peace. In 1886 this request was renewed by all the combatants except Ilorin, and the Governor accordingly acted as mediator, with the result that representatives from the different tribes assembled at Lagos, and on June 4th an agreement was signed, of which the following were the chief points:

(1) Ibadan, Ijesa, and the Ekiti tribes to respectively retain their independence.

(2) The four Ekiti towns of Otan, Tresi, Ada, and Igbajo to be ceded to Ibadan, on the understanding that the present inhabitants Were at liberty to leave them.

(3) The town of Modakeke to be reconstructed on territory, between the Oshun and Oba rivers, to the north of its then situation; such of the inhabitants as elected to pass under the rule of Ibadan moving to the new site, and those who preferred to become subject to Ife living in Ife territory, but not in Modakeke, which was to be dealt with by the Ifes as they thought fit.

The belligerents were at this time established in six large camps, the chief being those at Kiji and Oke Afesi, situated about a mile apart upon opposite sides of a mountainous valley in the north of Ijesa, the former occupied by the Ibadans and the latter by the Ijesas and Ekiti tribes. The Ibadalis had another camp at Ikirun, about fifteen miles west of Kiji, between the two arms of the Erinle River, where they confronted the Ilorins, who were encamped at Ofa, eighteen miles to the north. The Modakekes, with an Ibadan contingent, were at Alodakeke watching

the Ifes, who, with the Jebu force under the *Serikei*, were encamped about two miles to the south. In accordance with the terms of the agreement, Commissioners were sent to the interior by the Government of Lagos to take steps to break up the camps. These proved to be towns rather than camps, since they consisted of the ordinary mud-walled houses of the natives, were defended by loop-holed mud walls, and contained many thousands of women and children. The Ibadan camp at Kiji, which had been in existence for seven years, was estimated to contain between 50,000 and 60,000 inhabitants, at least two-thirds of whom were non-combatants, and the Oke Mesi camp 40,000. These two camps were evacuated and burned on September 28th, 1886, their occupants returning to their former homes; but an unexpected obstacle was now offered by the Modakekes, who first asked for a delay, and then positively refused to carry out the agreement and quit their town, alleging that they could not leave the spot where their forefathers were buried. The fact was they feared that if they remained on the soil of Ife, the Ifes would revenge themselves upon them for the destruction of the holy city, and that if they moved to Ibadan territory the Ibadans would enslave them; and after some further delay, the Commissioners, finding there was no prospect of the Modakekes keeping their promise, returned to Lagos. The Ilorins had not been parties to the agreement of June 4th, but the Commissioners endeavoured to arrange a peace between them and the Ibadans, and induce them to abandon their camps at Ofa and Ikirun; this, however, did not succeed, and the war between these two tribes continued.

In the meantime, while the interior had been disturbed by these protracted native wars, the colony of Lagos had received further extensions, Ketonu, a district on the eastern shores of Lake Denham Waters, having at the request of the natives, who feared French aggression, been declared British in January, 1880; while Appa, which lies between Ketonii and Badagry, was placed within the British jurisdiction in 1883. By Letters Patent, dated 13th January, 1886, Lagos was made a separate colony, independent of the government of the Gold Coast.

In 1888, in consequence of the reported intrigues of the French in Abeokuta, who were said to have offered to tolerate slavery, and to pay an annual subsidy, if the Egbas would place themselves under French protection, efforts were made to have the limits of British and French territory and spheres of influence defined, with the result that articles of arrangement for the delimitation of the English and French possessions on the West Coast of Africa were signed at Paris, on August 10th, 1889. The fourth article defined the territories and spheres of influence on the Slave Coast, the line of demarcation being the meridian which intersects the territory of Porto Novo at the Ajarra Creek, and extending from the sea to the ninth degree of north latitude. By this arrangement the eastern half of Appa, with its capital, and Pokra, became British, while the western half of Appa, together with Ketonu, became French. Egba and Okeodan fell within the British sphere of influence, and Ketu within that of the French.

The war between Ibadan and Ilorin still lingered on, and, in 1889, Mr. Millson, the. Assistant Colonial Secretary, was sent to the interior to endeavour to arrange a meeting between the Governor of Lagos and the belligerents in order to bring these hostilities to an end, but, as the chiefs declined to enter into any negotiations with the Commissioner, the mission failed.

Although Abeokuta had now been definitely placed within the British sphere of influence there was no improvement in the relations between the Egbas and the Lagos government. In January, 1891, a great political meeting was held at Abeokuta, at which the old charge that the government connived at or encouraged the annual inroads of Dahomi was revived, and some European missionaries were expelled. A Commissioner from the government was sent to Abeokuta in August, but achieved no results, and in January, 1892, the Egbas declared all their trade routes, both to the coast and to the interior, closed, and ceased all commercial relations with the colony. A further attempt on the part of the government to open negotiations was made in the following month, but completely failed, and at a meeting of Egba chiefs, held on the 13th of April, the proposal to reopen the trade routes to Lagos was unanimously negatived.

While affairs had been in this unsatisfactory state in the western portion of the sphere of British influence, a dispute with the Jebus had sprung up in the east. The Ejinrin market, situated about ten miles east of Epi, was closed by the Awujale of Jebu Ode on account of some disagreement with the people of Lagos; and though, in October, 1890, in consequence of representations made by the government of Lagos, it was formally opened by the Governor and representatives sent by the Awujale, the Jebus made this concession unwillingly, and had no intention whatever of departing from their policy of excluding foreigners from the interior of their country. Consequently, when, in May, 1891, the Acting Governor, Captain Denton, C.M.G., left Lagos with an escort of Hausas to proceed on a mission to Jebu Ode, with the object of coming to some agreement for the opening of the country to commerce, the Jebus refused to allow the party to enter their territory, on the plea that they feared hostile action. The Awujale not only refused to treat, but rejected the presents offered on behalf of the British Government, fearing, no doubt, that to accept them would entail some concession on his part.

Upon this affair being referred to the Home Government, the Governor was instructed to demand an apology from the Jebus for the so-called insult offered to the Acting Governor, and to insist upon a free right of way through Jebu country. The Awujale was to be informed that, if these terms were not complied with, force would be used. In December, 1891, this ultimatum was conveyed to the Awujale by an officer of the Lagos Constabulary, and the Awujale then consented to send to Lagos representatives fully empowered to make the apology and sign a treaty.

In January, 1892, the representatives arrived, and on the 21st made a formal apology, and signed an agreement to maintain a free and unrestricted right-of-way for persons and goods through Jebu territory; the Government of the Colony undertaking to pay the Jebus an annual sum of £500 in compensation for the duties they had been accustomed to levy on goods.

For a short time the Jebus observed their treaty engagements, and one member of the Church Missionary Society was allowed to pass through Jebu Ode on his way to the interior; but when, soon afterwards, in the month of

February, another missionary attempted to pass through the capital he was ill-used and sent back. A party of Ibadan carriers, who sought to pass through from the north, was also turned back. The Awujale asserted that the Ibadans had been insolent, but it was evident that the young men of the tribe were determined to maintain the old Jebu policy of isolation. The Jebus were a turbulent and proud nation, and they considered it disgraceful to observe engagements which had been extorted from them by threats. In consequence of these breaches of the treaty, the Inspector- General of the Lagos Constabulary was sent to the Awujale to ask for explanations. He landed at Itoike, but was not allowed to proceed any further, the Awujale sending to say that he did not wish "to palaver" with the Lagos Government.

The Home Government now authorised the employment of force. Special-service officers were sent out from England, two officers and 155 men of the Gold Coast Constabulary were ordered from Accra, and three officers and ninety-nine men of the 1st Battalion West India Regiment were despatched from Sierra Leone. These, with 165 of the Lagos Constabulary, and an Ibadan Contingent of 100 men, making a total combatant force of about 500, left Lagos, under the command of Colonel F.C. Scott, C.B., on the 12th of May, and disembarked at Epi without opposition on the day following. On the 16th the column advanced from Epi; there was a slight skirmish at Pobo on the same day, another at Kpashida next day, and on the 18th the force encamped at Majoda.

Next morning the Jebus were found in position, ready to defend the passage of the Oshun River, and an action commenced at 7 a.m. The fire of the Jebus not only swept the ford, which they had deepened by digging out the bed of the stream, but also the narrow bush-track which led to it, and was exceedingly heavy and well sustained. It was reported that they had offered a human sacrifice to the goddess of the river, to enlist her aid against the invaders, and this had so powerful an effect upon the superstitious minds of the constabulary, that for a full hour they could not be induced to enter the stream; and it was not until the West Indians, who had been held in reserve, were ordered up to lead the way across the Oshun, that the enemy's position was carried. Between the river and the village of Magbon, which the victors entered shortly after 10 a.m., was found the camp which the Jebus had occupied the previous night. It was estimated to have accommodated from 5,000 to 6,000 persons, and as about half the occupants of a native camp are women and non-combatants, the passage of the river was probably disputed by about 3,000 men. The Jebu losses were supposed to be severe, but the British force lost only three killed and twenty-four wounded, exclusive of carriers.

On the 20th of May the advance was resumed soon after daybreak, and, being met by a flag of truce, the force occupied the town of Jebu Ode the same day without resistance. It was about four miles in circumference, defended by a mud wall, and contained in time of peace about 15,000 inhabitants, all of whom, with the exception of the Awujale and his immediate following, had now fled. On the 25th, the Governor arrived from Lagos to conduct the negotiations with the Awujale, who made complete submission, alleging that the young men had fought contrary to his wishes and orders; and, on the 30th and 31st, the expeditionary force, with the exception of three officers and 140 men of the Constabulary, who remained in occupation of Jebu Ode, left for Lagos, one column marching through Sagamu and Ikoradu, and another through Itoike.

The trade routes on the east were now opened, but those through Egba country still remained closed, and for some time it was thought that a military expedition against Abeokuta would be necessary. The ease with which the Jebus, who were considered a very powerful tribe, had been punished, had, however, made a profound impression upon the native mind, and many British subjects of Egba descent at Lagos, fearing that, if the chiefs of Abeokuta maintained their unfriendly attitude, the independence of Egba would be lost, strongly impressed upon their compatriots the necessity of coming to terms. In consequence, the Egbas declared their willingness to receive the Governor, Mr. Carter, and come to some arrangement, with the result that oil the 18th of January, 1893, a treaty was signed at Abeokuta. The Egbas undertook to refer all disputes between themselves and British subjects to the Governor for settlement, to establish complete freedom of trade between Egba country and Lagos, and to close no trade route without the consent of the Governor. They also promised to abolish human sacrifice, and not to cede any portion of Egba territory to a foreign power without the consent of the British. On the other hand, Great Britain guaranteed that the independence of Egba should be fully recognised, and no annexation of any portion of it be made without the consent of the Egba authorities.

There is a considerable difference between the Yoruba-speaking Peoples and the Ewe-speaking Peoples. We still find the characteristics which were dominant among the latter, namely, indolence, improvidence, and duplicity, but they are no longer so pronounced, probably, almost certainly, because life and property are more secure. The Yoruba has more independence of character tban the Tshis, Gas, or Ewes, and servility is rare, He even has the sentiments of nationality and patriotism, and though these are regarded with disfavour by the Colonial Government, they are none the less tokens of superiority. He is a keener trader, is more sociable, and is in all respects socially higher than the tribes of the other three cognate groups. This is in a great measure due to the physical characteristics of the country. There being but little forest, except in the eastern districts, communication is easy, and the territory is moreover opened up by several rivers. Instead, then, of being dispersed in a number of inconsiderable hamlets, which are mere specks in a vast and impenetrable forest, the Yorubas have been able to live in towns, each of which is within easy communication of others. No doubt their superior social instincts first caused them to congregate in towns, and now many generations of town life has further developed them. There is even a certain amount of loyalty in the Yoruba, a quality for which one might look in vain among the Ewe tribes. Without saying that the Yorubas are more intelligent, we can safely say that their intellect is more cultivated; the asperities of savage life are softened, the sharper angles are worn down by frequent intercourse with their fellowmen, and at the present day they are certainly the leading people in West Africa.

[1] Ewe-speaking Peoples," p. 285.
[2] Ewe-speaking Peoples," p. 294.
[3] The Yorubas were called Eyeos or Oyos by old writers, after the name of their capital, Oyo.]
[4] This custom remained in force until quite recent times, if, indeed, it is yet altogether extinct.
[5] "Grow old, Ajagbo, grow old king, grow old, may I also grow old." Each drum has its own measure or rhythm, which is proper to it, and, in order to preserve this rhythm, sentences are invented to call it to mind. In this case the rhythm is-- *Gbo | Ajegbo | - | gbo | oba gbo | - | ki emi ki osi | gbo.*
[6] "Ewe-speaking Peoples," pp. 315-6.
[7] "Ewe speaking Peoples," pp. 322-324.

Chapter Two - Chief Gods

THE tendency which we noted in the case of the Ewe speaking peoples to replace gods which were purely local, and only worshipped by those dwelling in the vicinity, by tribal gods, and by gods worshipped by an entire people, has in the case of the Yoruba tribes been very fully developed, and all the gods possessing any importance are known to and worshipped by the Yoruba-speaking peoples as a whole. The effect of increasing the number of general objects of worship has been to diminish the importance of the local objects of worship, the *genii loci*, who, except in Jebu and in some of the remoter districts, have been so shorn of their power as now to- be scarcely above the level of the fairies and water-sprites of mediæval England, or, which is perhaps a closer parallel, of the Naiads and Hama-dryads of ancient Greece. This of course is what was to be expected, for the general objects of worship govern, between them, all the phenomena which most nearly affect mankind; and the special function of each *genius loci* is thus now vested in some other god, who is believed to be more powerful, because he is worshipped over a larger axea and has a more numerous following. Gods, however, which are purely tutelar have not been so much affected, and tutelary dieties of towns and of individuals are still common, because the native, while enrolling himself as a follower of a general god, likes also to have a protector whose sole business is to guard his interests; and who, though his power may be limited, is not likely to be distracted by the claims of others to his attention.

The term used by the Yoruba tribes to express a superhuman being, or god, is *orisha*, and as it is used equally to express the images and sacred objects, and also as an adjective with the meaning of sacred or holy, it answers exactly to the Tshi term bohszon, the Gã *wong*, and the Ewe *vodu*. The word *orisha* seems to be compounded of *ori* (summit, top, head) and *sha* (to select, choose); though some natives prefer to derive it from *ri* (to see) and *isha* (selection, choice), and thus to make it mean "One who sees the cult."

(1) OLORUN.

Olorun is the sky-god of the Yorubas, that is, he is the deified firmament, or personal sky, just as Nyankupon is to the Tshis, Nyonmo to the Gas, and Mawu to the Ewes. As was mentioned in the last volume, the general bias of the negro mind has been in favour of selecting the firmament for the chief Nature god, instead of the Sun, Moon, or Earth; and in this respect the natives resemble the Aryan Hindus, Greeks, and Romans, with whom Dyaus pitar, Zeus, and Jupiter equally represented the firmament.

The Tshis and Gas use the words Nyankupon and Nyonmo to express sky, rain, or thunder and lightning, and the Ewes andYorubas, the words Mawn and Olorun to express the two former. The Tshi peoples say *Nyankupon lom* (Nyankupon knocks); "It is thundering"; *Nyankupon aba* (Nyankupon has come), "It is raining"; and the Gã peoples, Nyonmo, knocks (thunders), Nyonmo pours, Nyonmo drizzles, &c., while in just the same way the Ancient Greeks ascribed these phenomena to Zeus, who snowed, rained, hailed, gathered clouds, and thundered. Nyankupon has for epithets the following: *Amosu* (Giver of Rain); *Amovua* (Giver of Sunshine); *Tetereboensu* (Wide-speading Creator of Water), and *Tyoduampon*, which seems to mean "Stretched-out Roof" (*Tyo*, to draw or drag, *dua*, wood, and *pon*, flat surface).

Nyankupon and Nyonmo thunder and lighten as well as pour out rain, but Olorun, like the Ewe Mawu, does not wield the thunderbolt, which has become the function of a special thunder-god, and he consequently has suffered some reduction in importance. The name Olorun means "Owner of the Sky" (*oni*, one who possesses, *orun*, sky, firmament, cloud [1]), and the sky is believed to be a solid body, curving over the earth so as to cover it with a vaulted roof.

Like Nyankupon, Nyonmo, and Mawu, Olorun is considered too distant, or too indifferent, to interfere in the affairs of the world. The natives say that he enjoys a life of complete idleness and repose, a blissful condition according to their ideas, and passes his time dozing or sleeping. Since he is too lazy or too indifferent to exercise any control over earthly affairs, man on his side does not waste time in endeavouring to propitiate him, but reserves his worship and sacrifice for more active agents. Hence Olorun has no priests, symbols, images, or temples, and though, in times of calamity, or affliction, whjen the other gods have turned a deaf ear to his supplications, a native will, perhaps, as a last resource, invoke Olorun, such occasions are rare, and as a general rule the god is not worshipped or appealed to. The name Olorun, however, occurs in one or two set phrasesor sentences, which appear to show that at one time greater regard was paid to him. For instance, the proper reply to the morning salutation, "Have you risen well?" is *O yin Olorun*, "Thanks to

Olorun;" and the phrase "May Olorun protect you" is sometimes heard as an evening salutation. The former seems to mean that thanks are due to the sky for letting the sun enter it; and the latter to be an invocation of the firmament, the roof of the world, to remain above and protect the earth during the night. Sometimes natives will raise their hands and cry, "Olorun, Olorun!" just as we say, "Heaven forbid!" and with an equal absence of literal meaning.

Olorun has the following epithets:--

(1) *Oga-ogo* (*Oga*, distinguished or brave person; *ogo*, wonder, praise).

(2) *Olowo* (*ni-owo*) "Venerable one."

(3) *Eleda* (*da*, to cease from raining), "He who controls the rain."

(4) *Elemi*, "a living man," literally "he who possesses breath." It is a title applied to a servant or slave, because his master's breath is at his mercy; and it is in this sense also that it is used to Olorun, because, if he were evilly, disposed, he could let fall the solid firmament and crush the world.

(5) *Olodumaye* or *Olodumare*. The derivation of this epithet is obscure, but it probably means "Replenisher of brooks" (*Olodo*, possessing brooks). We find the same termination in *Oshumaye* or *Oshumare*, Rainbow, and in *Osamaye* or *Osamare*, Water Lily, and it is perhaps compounded of *omi*, water, and *aye*, a state of being.alive.

It may be mentioned that, just as the missionaries have caused Nyankupon, Nyonmo, and Mawu to be confused with the Jehovah of the Christians, by translating these names as "God," so have they done with Olorun, whom they consider to be a survival from a primitive revelation, made to all mankind, in the childhood of the world. But Olorun is merely a nature-god, the personally divine sky, and he only controls phenomena connected in the native mind with the roof of the world. He is not in any sense an omnipotent being. This is well exemplified by the proverb which says, "A man cannot cause rain to fall, and Olorun cannot give you a child," which means that, just as a man cannot perform the functions of Olorun and cause rain to fall, so Olorun cannot form a child in the womb, that being the function of the god Obatala, whom we shall next describe. In fact, each god, Olorun included, has, as it were, his own duties; and while he is perfectly independent in his own domain, he cannot trespass upon the rights of others.

(2) OBATALA.

Obatala is the chief god of the Yorubas. The name means "Lord of the White Cloth" (*Oba-ti-ala*.), and is explained by the fact that white is the colour sacred to Obatala, whose temples, images, and paraphernalia are always painted white, and whose followers wear white cloths. Another derivation is Oba-ti-ala, "Lord of Visions," and this gains some probability from the fact that Obatala has the epithets of Orisha *oj'enia*, "The Orisha who enters man," and Alabalese (*Al-ba-ni-ase*), [2] "He who predicts the future," because he inspires the oracles and priests, and unveils futurity by means of visions. "Lord of the White Cloth," however, is the translation most commonly adopted, and appears to be the correct one. The god is always represented as wearing a white cloth.

Obatala, say the priests, was made by Olorun, who then handed over to him the management of the firmament and the world, and himself retired to rest. Obatala is thus also a sky-god, but is a more anthropomorphic conception than Olorun, and performs functions which are not in the least connected with the firmament. According to a myth, which is, however, contradicted by another, Obatala made the first man and woman out of clay, on which account he has the title of *Alamorere*, "Owner of the best clay;" and because he kneaded the clay himself he is called Orisha *kpokpo*, "The Orisha who kneads clay" (*kpo*, to knead or temper clay). Though this point is disputed by some natives, all are agreed that Obatala forms the child in the mother's womb, and women who desire to become mothers address their prayers to him; while albinoism and congenital deformities are regarded as his handiwork, done either to punish some neglect towards him on the part of the parents, or to remind his worshippers of his power.

Obatala is also styled "Protector of the Town Gates," and in this capacity is represented as mounted on a horse, and armed with a spear. On the panels of the temple doors rude carvings are frequently seen of a horseman with a spear, surrounded by a leopard, tortoise, fish, and serpent. Another epithet of Obatala is *Obatala gbingbiniki*, "The enormous Obatala." His special offerings are edible snails.

Amongst the Ewe-speaking Peoples at Porto Novo, Obatala determines the guilt or innocence of accused persons by means of an oracle termed *Onshe* or *Onishe* (messenger, ambassador). It consists of a hollow cylinder of wood, about 31/2 feet in length and 2 feet in diameter, one end of which is covered with draperies and the other closed with shells of the edible snail. This cylinder is placed on the head of the accused, who kneels on the ground, holding it firmly on his head with a hand at each side. The god, being then invoked by the priests, causes the cylinder to rock backwards and forwards, and finally to fall to the ground. If it should fall forward the accused is innocent, if backward guilty. The priests say that Obatala, or a subordinate spirit to whom he deputes the duty, strikes the accused, so as to make the cylinder fall in the required direction; but sceptics and native Christians say that a child is concealed in the cylinder and overbalances it in front or behind, according to instructions given beforehand by the priests. They add that when a child has served for a year or two and grown too big for the cylinder he is put to death, in order that the secret may be preserved; and is succeeded by another, who, in his turn, undergoes the same fate-but all this is mere conjecture.

(3) ODUDUA.

Odudua, or Odua, who has the title of Iya agbe, The mother who receives," is the chief goddess of the Yorubas. The name means "Black One" (dit, to be black; dudit, black), and the negroes consider a smooth, glossy, black skin a great beauty, and far superior to one of the ordinary cigar-colour. She is always represented as a woman sitting down, and nursing a child.

Odudua is the wife of Obatala, but she was coeval with Olorun, and not made by him, as was her husband. Other natives, however, say that she came from Ife, the holy city, in common with most of the other gods, as described in a myth which we shall come to shortly. Odudua represents the earth, married to the anthropomorphic sky-god. Obatala and Odudua, or Heaven and Earth, resemble, say the priests, two large cut-calabashes, which, when once shut, can never be opened. This is symbolised in the temples by two whitened saucer-shaped calabashes, placed one covering the other; the upper one of which represents the concave firmament stretching over and meeting the earth, the lower one, at the horizon.

According to some priests, Obatala and Odudua represent one androgynous divinity; and they say that an image which is sufficiently common, of a human being with one arm and leg, and a tail terminating in a sphere, symbolises this. This notion, however, is not one commonly held, Obutala and Odudua being generally, and almost universally, regarded as two distinct persons. The phallus and yoni in juxtaposition are often seen carved on the doors of the temples both of Obatala and Odudua; but this does not seem to have any reference to androgyny, since they are also found similarly depicted in other places which are in no way connected with either of these deities.

According to a myth Odudua is blind. In the beginning of the world she and her husband Obatala were shut up in darkness in a large, closed calabash, Obatala being in the upper part and Odudua in the lower. The myth does not state how they came to be in this situation, but they remained there for many days, cramped, hungry, and uncomfortable. Then Odudua began complaining, blaming her husband for the confinement; and a violent quarrel ensued, in the course of which, in a frenzy of rage, Obatala tore out her eyes, because she would not bridle her tongue. In return she cursed him, saying "Naught shalt thou eat but snails," which is the reason why snails are now offered to Obatala. As the myth does not make Odudua recover her sight, she must be supposed to have remained sightless, but no native regards her as being blind.

Odudua is patroness of love, and many stories are told of her adventures and amours. Her chief temple is in Ado, the principal town of the state of the same name, situated about fifteen miles to the north of Badagry. The word *Ado* means a lewd person of eithersex, and its selection for the name of this town is accounted for by the following legend. Odudua was once walking alone in the forest when she met a hunter, who was so handsome that the ardent temperament of the goddess at once took fire. The advances which she made to him were favourably received, and they forthwith mutually gratified their passion on the spot. After this, the goddess became still mora enamoured, and, unable to tear herself away from her lover, she lived with him for some weeks in a hut, which they constructed of branches at the foot of a large silk-cotton tree. At the end of this time her passion had burnt out, and having become weary of the hunter, she left him; but before doing so she promised to protect him and all others who might come and dwell in the favoured spot wliere she had passed so many pleasant hours. In consequence many people came and settled there, and a town gradually grew up, which was named Ado, to commemorate the circumstances of its origin. A temple was built for the protecting goddess; and there, on her feast days, sacrifices of cattle and sheep are made, and women abandon themselves indiscriminately to the male worshippers in her honour.

(4) AGANJU AND YEMAJA.

Before her amour with the hunter, Odudua bore to her husband, Obatala, a boy and a girl, named respectively Aganju. and Yemaja. The name Aganju means uninhabited tract of country, wilderness, plain, or forest, and Yemaja, "Mother of fish" (*yeye*, mother; *eja*, fish). The offspring of the union of Heaven and Earth, that is, of Obatala and Odudua, may thus be said to represent Land and Water. Yemaja is the goddess of brooks and streams, and presides over ordeals by water. She is represented by a female figure, yellow in colour, wearing blue beads and a white cloth. The worship of Aganju seems to have fallen into disuse, or to have become merged in that of his mother; but there is said to be an open space in front of the king's residence in Oyo where the god was formerly worshipped, which is still called *Oju-Aganju-*"Front of Aganju."

Yemaja married her brother Aganju, and bore a son named Orungan. This name is compounded of orun, sky, and gan, from ga, to be high; and appears to mean "In the height of the sky." It seems to answer to the *khekheme*, or "Free-air Region" of the Ewe peoples; and, like it, to mean the apparent space between the sky and the earth. The offspring of Land and Water would thus be what we call Air.

Orungan fell in love with his mother, and as she refused to listen to his guilty passion, he one day took advantage of his father's absence, and ravished her. Immediately after the act, Yemaja sprang to her feet and fled from the place wringing her hands and lamenting; and was pursued by Orungan, who strove to console her by saying that no one should know of what had occurred, and declared that he could not live without her. He held out to her the alluring prospect of living with two husbands, one acknowledged, and the other in secret; but she rejected all his proposals with loathing, and continued to run away. Orungan, however, rapidly gained upon her, and was just stretching out his hand to seize her, when she fell backward to the ground. Then her body immediately began to swell in a fearful manner, two streams of water gushed from her breasts, and her abdomen burst open. The streams from Yemaja's breasts joined and formed a lagoon, and from her gaping body came the following:--(1) Dada (god of vegetables), (2) Shango (god of lightning), (3) Ogun (god of iron and war), (4) Olokun (god of the sea), (5) Olosa (goddess of the lagoon), (6) Oya (goddess of the river Niger), (7) Oshun (goddess of the river Oshun), (8) Oba (goddess of the river Oba), (9) Orisha Oko (god of agriculture), (10) Oshosi (god of hunters), (11) Oke (god of mountains), (12) Aje Shaluga (god of wealth), (13) Shankpanna (god of small-pox), (14) Orun (the sun), and (15) Oshu (the moon). [3] To commemorate this event, a town which was given the name of Ife (distention, enlargement, or swelling up), was built on the spot where Yemaja's body burst open, and became the holy city of the Yoruba-speaking tribes. The place where her body fell used to be shown, and probably still is; but the town was destroyed in 1882, in the war between the Ifes on the one hand and the Ibadans and Modakekes on the other.

The myth of Yemaja thus accounts for the origin of several of the gods, by making them the grandchildren of Obatala and Odudua; but there are other gods, who do not belong to this family group, and whose genesis is not accounted for in any way. Two, at least, of the principal gods are in this category, and we therefore leave for the moment the minor deities who sprung from Yemaja, and proceed with the chief gods, irrespective of their origin.

(5) SHANGO.

Shango, the god of thunder and lightning, is, next to Obatala, the most powerful god of the Yorubas; he was the second to spring from the body of Yemaja. His name appears to be derived from *shan*, "to strike violently," and *go*, "to bewilder;" and to have reference to peals of thunder, which are supposed to be produced by violent blows. [4] He has the epithet of Jakuta, "Hurler of stones," or "Fighter with stones" (*Ja*, to hurl from aloft, or *ja*, to fight, and *okuta*, stone); and stone implements, which have long ceased to be used in West Africa, are believed to be his thunderbolts.

To wield the thunderbolt is certainly one of the proper functions of the sky-god, and the process by which he becomes deprived of it is not by any means clear. It does not appear to be the result of advancing culture, for the Zeus of the Greeks and the Jupiter of the Romans, who had respectively the epithets *Kerauneios* and *Tonans*, retained it; as do the Nyankupon of the Tshis and the Nyonmo of the Gas; while, like the Ewes and Yorubas, the Aryan Hindus made another god, namely, Indra, offspring of Dyaus, wield the lightning.

The notion we found amongst the Ewes that a birdlike creature was the animating entity of the thunderstorm has no parallel here, and Shango is purely anthropomorphic. He dwells in the clouds in an immense brazen palace, where he maintains a large retinue and keeps a great number of horses; for, besides being the thunder-god, he is also the god of the chase and of pillage. [5] From his palace, Shango hurls upon those who have offended him red-hot chains of iron, which are forged for him by his brother Ogun, god of the river Ogun, of iron and of war; but this, it should be observed, is seemingly a modern notion, and the red-hot chains furnished by Ogun have a suspicious resemblance to the thundefbolts of Jupiter, forged by Vulcan. The Yoruba word for lightning is *mana-mana* (*ma-ina*, a making of fire), and has no connection either with iron (*irin*) or a chain (*ewon*); while the name Jakuta shows that Shango is believed to hurl stones and not iron. The iron-chain notion, therefore, appears to have been borrowed from some foreign source, and, moreover, not to yet have made much progress. The Oni-Shango, or Priests of Shango, [6] in their chants always speak of Shango as hurling stones; and whenever a house is struck by lightning they rush in a body to pillage it and to find the stone, which, as they take it with them secretly, they

28

always succeed in doing. A chant of the Oni-Shango very commonly heard is, "Oh Shango, thou art the master. Thou takest in thy hand thy fiery stones, to punish the guilty and satisfy thine anger. Everything that they strike is destroyed. Their fire eats up the forest, the trees are broken down, and all living creatures are slain;" and the lay-worshippers of Shango flock into the streets during a thunderstorm crying, "Shango, Shango, Great King! Shango is the lord and master. In the storm he hurls his fiery stones against his enemies, and their track gleams in the midst of the darkness." "May Shango's stone strike you," is a very common imprecation.

According to some natives, Oshumare, the Rainbow, is the servant of Shango, his office being to take up water frorn the earth to the palace in the clouds. He has a messenger named Ara, "Thunder-clap," whom he sends out with a loud noise. A small bird called *papagori* is sacred to Shango, and his worshippers profess to be able to understand its cry.

Shango married three of his sisters: Oya, the Niger; Oshun, the river of the same name, which rises in Ijesa and flows into the water-way between Lagos and the Lekki lagoon, near Emina; and Oba, also a river, which rises in Ibadan and flows into the Kradu Water. All three accompany their husband when he goes out, Oya taking with her her messenger *Afefe* (the Wind, or Gale of Wind), and Oshun and Oba carrying his bow and sword. Shaugo's slave *Biri* (Darkness) goes in attendance.

The image of Shango generally represents him as a man standing, and is surrounded by images, smaller in size, of his three wives; who are also represented as standing up, with the palms of their hands joined together in front of the bosom. Oxen, sheep, and fowls are the offerings ordinarily made to Shango, and, on important occasions, human beings. His colours are red and white. He is consulted with sixteen cowries, which are thrown on the ground, those which he with the back uppermost being favourable, and those with the back downward the reverse. He usually goes armed with a club called oshe, made of the wood of the ayan tree, which is so hard that a proverb says, "The ayan tree resists the axe." In consequence of his club being made of this wood, the tree is sacred to him.

The priests and followers of Shango wear a wallet, emblematic of the plundering propensities of their lord, and the chief priest is called *Magba*, "The Receiver." As amongst the Ewe tribes, a house struck by lightning is at once invaded and plundered by the disciples of the god, and a fine imposed on the occupants, who, it is held, must have offended him. Persons who are killed by lightning may not, properly speaking, be buried; but if the relations of the deceased offer a sufficient payment, the priests usually allow the corpse to be redeemed and buried. Individuals rendered insensible by lightning are at once despatched by the priests, the accident being regarded as proof positive that Shango requires them. A common idea is that Shango is subject to frequent outbursts of ungovernable temper, during which he thumps and bangs overhead, and hurls down stones at those who have given him cause for offence.

The foregoing are, with the exception of the myth of the fiery chains, the old ideas respecting Shango; but on to them are now rapidly becoming grafted some later myths, which make Shango, an earthly king who afterwards became a god. This Shango was King of Oyo, capital of Yoruba, and became so unbearable through rapacity, cruelty, and tyranny, that the chiefs and people at last sent him a calabash of parrots' eggs, in accordance with the custom that has already been mentioned; with a message that he must be fatigued with the cares of government, and that it was time for him to go to sleep. On receiving this intimation, Shango, instead of allowing himself to be quietly strangled by his wives, defied public opinion and endeavoured to assemble his adherents; and, when this failed, sought safety in flight. He left the palace by night, intending to endeavour to reach Tapa, beyond the Niger, which was his mother's native place; and was accompanied only by one wife and one slave, the rest of his household having deserted him. During the night the wife repented of her hasty action, and also left him; so, when in the morning Shango found himself lost in the midst of a pathless forest, he had no one with him but his slave. They wandered about without food for some days, seeking in vain for a path which would lead them out of the forest, and at last Shango, left his slave, saying, "Wait here till I return, and we will then try further." After waiting a long time, the slave, as his master did not appear, went in search of him, and before long found his corpse hanging by the neck from an *ayan*-tree. Eventually the slave succeeded in extricating himself from the forest, and finding himself in a part of the country he knew, made his way towards Oyo, where he told the news.

When the chiefs and elders heard that Shango had hanged himself they were much alarmed, fearing that they would be held responsible for his death. They went, in company, with the priests, to the place where the slave had left the body, but were unable to find it, for it was no longer on the tree. They searched in every direction, and at last found a deep pit in the earth, from which the end of an iron chain protruded. They stooped over the pit and listened, and could hear Shango talking down in the earth. They at once erected a small temple over the pit, and leaving some priests there to propitiate the new god, and establish a worship, returned to Oyo, where they proclaimed: "Shango is not dead. He has become an *orisha*. He has descended into the earth, and lives among the dead people, with whom we have heard him conversing." Some of the townspeople, however, being ignorant and foolish, did not believe the story, and when the criers cried, "Shango is not dead," they laughed and shouted in return, "Shango is dead. Shango hanged himself." In consequence of this wicked conduct, Shango came in person, with a terrific thunderstorm, to punish them for their behaviour; and, in order to show his power, he killed many of the scoffers with his fiery stones, and set the town on fire. Then the priests and elders ran about -among the burning houses, shouting, "Shango did not hang himself. Shango has become an *orisha*. See what these bad men have brought upon you by their unbelief. He is angry because they laughed at him, and he has burned your houses with his fiery stones because you did not vindicate his honour." Then the populace fell upon the scoffers and beat them to death, so that Shango was appeased, and his anger turned away. The place where Shango descended into the earth was called Kuso, and soon became a town, for many people went to dwell there.

Perhaps this myth really does refer to some former King of Oyo, though why such a king should usurp the functions of the thunder-god, is not at all clear. It is inconsistent in part, for it makes the chiefs and elders alarmed at the suicide of Shango, because they feared to be held responsible for his death; yet they would have been equally responsible had he complied with established custom, and committed suicide when he received the parrots' eggs they sent him. The fact of the *ayan* being sacred to the god Shango, no doubt caused that tree to be selected for the legendary suicide of the king Shango; and the iron chain which protruded from the hole in the ground was probably suggested by the notion of red-hot chains of lightning. As we have said, this myth is rapidly becoming blended with the older ones, and, in consequence of these events having taken place at Kuso, Shango has the title of *Oba-Kuso,* "King of Kuso."

Another myth makes Shango the son of Obatala, and married to the three river goddesses Oya, Oshun, and Oba, but reigning as an earthly king at Oyo. The story relates that one day Shango obtained from his father Obatala a powerful charm, which, when eaten, would enable him to vanquish all who opposed him. Shango ate most of the medicament, and then gave the rest to Oya to keep for him; but she, as soon as his back was turned, ate the rest herself. Next morning the chiefs and elders assembled at the palace as usual, to judge the affairs of the people, and each spoke in his turn; but when it came to Shango's turn to speak, flames burst forth from his mouth, and all fled in terror. Oya, too, when she began to scold ber women in the palace, similarly belched forth flames, so that everybody ran away, and the palace was deserted. Shango now saw that he was, as a god, inferior to none; so calling his three wives to him, and taking in his hand a long iron-chain, he stamped on the earth till it opened under him, and descended into it with his wives. The earth closed again over them, after they had gone down, but the end of the chain was left protruding from the ground.

This myth well exemplifies the confusion that has now been created in men's minds between the thunder-god proper and the demi-god, the result being a kind of compound Shango, possessing attributes of each. The Shango of this story resembles in his marital relations the thunder-god, but the descent into the earth with the iron chain, the end of which is left above ground, is like the legendary descent of the deified king, and is probably only another version of the same event. It is probable that contact with Mohammedans has had something to do with the invention of this myth. The genii, as we read of them in the "Arabian Nights," are frequently described as breathing forth flames to destroy their opponents; and a descent into the earth, which opens when stamped upon, is a mode of exit often found in the same collection. These ideas do not appear to be ones at all likely to have arisen spontaneously in the negro mind, and we find nothing of the sort in the groups cognate to the Yoruba. Moreover, a thunder-god must, from the very nature of his being, live above the eaxth amongst the clouds; and to make him descend into the bowels of the earth, is to place him in a situation where he could not exercise the functions of his office. These remarks equally apply to the following myth.

Since his descent into the earth with his three wives at Oyo, Shango has often come back to the world. One day, when down in the earth, he quarrelled with Oya, who had stolen some of his "medicines;" and she, terrified at his violence, ran away, and took refuge with her brother the Sea-God (Olokun). As soon as Shango discovered where she had gone, he swore a great oath to beat her so that she would never forget it. Next morning he came up from below with the Sun, and, following him in his course all the day, arrived with him in the evening at the place where the sea and sky join, and so descended with him into the territories of his brother Olokun. The Sun had not knowingly shown Shango the road across the sky to Olokun's palace, for Shango had been careful to keep behind him all the time, nearly out of sight, and to hide when the Sun looked round.

When Shango reached Olokun's palace and saw his wife Oya there, he made a great noise and commotion. He rushed towards her to seize her, but Olokun held him; and while the two were struggling together Oya escaped, and ran to bide with her sister Olosa (the Lagoon). When Olokun saw that Oya had gone he released Shango, who, now more furious than ever, ran after his wife cursing and threatening her. In his rage he tore up the trees by their roots, as he ran along, tossing them here and there. Oya, looking out from her sister's house, saw him coming along the banks of the lagoon, and, knowing that Olosa could not protect her, ran out again, and fled along the shores towards the place where the Sun goes down. As she was running, and Shango coming behind, roaring and yelling, she saw a house near at hand, and, rushing into it, claimed protection of a man whom she found there, whose name was Huisi. She begged Huisi to defend her. Huisi asked what he, a man, could do against Shango; but Oya gave him to eat of the "medicines" she had stolen from her husband, and he, being thus made an *orisha*, promised to protect her. As Shango approached, Huisi ran from his house down to the banks of the lagoon, and tearing up a large tree by the roots, brandished it in the air, and defied Shango. There being no other tree there, Shango seized Huisi's canoe, shook it like a club, and the two weapons, striking together, were shattered to pieces. Then the two oiishas wrestled together. Flames burst from their mouths, and their feet tore great fissures in the earth as they dragged each other to and fro. This struggle lasted a long time without either being able to gain the mastery, and at last Shango, filled with fury at being baffled, and feeling his strength failing, stamped on the earth, which opened under him, and he descended into it, dragging Huisi down with him. At the commencement of the combat, Oya had fled to Lokoro; [7] she remained there, and the people built a temple in her honour. Huisi, who had become a god by virtue of the "medicine" he had eaten, also had a temple erected in his honour, on the spot where he had fought with Shango.

In this myth Oya steals the medicine and gives it to Huisi; in the former one she also stole it, but ate it herself. In each case it caused flames to burst from the mouth.

(6) IFA.

Ifa, god of divination, who is usually termed the God of Palm Nuts, because sixteen palm-nuts are used in the process of divination, comes after Shango in order of eminence. The name Ifa apparently means something scraped or wiped off: he has the title of Gbangba (explanation, demonstration, proof). Ifa's secondary attribute is to cause fecundity: he presides at births, and women pray to him to be made fruitful; while on this account offerings are always made to him before marriage, it being considered a disgrace not to bear children. To the native mind there is no conflict of function between Ifa and Obatala, for the former causes the woman to become pregnant, while the latter forms the child in the womb, which is supposed to be a different thing altogether.

Ifa first appeared on the earth at Ife, but he did not come from the body of Yemaja, and his parentage and origin are unexplained. He tried to teach the inhabitants of Ife how to foretell future events, but they would not listen to him, so he left the town and wandered about the world teaching mankind. After roaming about for a long time, and indulging in a variety of amours, Ifa fixed his residence at Ado, where he planted on a rock a palm-nut, from which sixteen palm-trees grew up at once.

Ifa has an attendant or companion named Odu (? One who emulates), and a messenger called Opele (*ope*, puzzle, or *ope*, palm-tree). The bandicoot (*okete*) is sacred to him, because it lives chiefly upon palm-nuts. The first day of the Yoruba week is Ifa's holy day, and is called *ajo awo*, "day of the secret." On this day sacrifices of pigeons, fowls, and goats are made to him, and no-body can perform any business before accomplishing this duty. On very important occasions a human victim is immolated.

A priest of Ifa is termed a *babalawo* (*baba-ni-awo*), "Father who has the secret," and the profession is very lucrative, as the natives never undertake anything of.importance without consulting the god, and always act in accordance with the answer returned. Hence a proverb says, "The priest who is more shrewd than another adopts the worship of Ifa." As Ifa knows all futurity, and reveals coming events to his faithful followers, he is considered the god of wisdom, and the benefactor of mankind. He also instructs man how to secure the goodwill of the other gods, and conveys to him their wishes, His priests pluck all the hair from their bodies and shave their heads, and always appear attired in white cloths.

The general belief is that Ifa possessed the faculty of divination from the beginning, but there is a myth which makes him acquire the art from the phallic god Elegba. In the early days of the world, says the myth, there were but few people on the earth, and the gods found themselves stinted in the matter of sacrifices to such an extent that, not obtaining enough to eat from the offerings made by their followers, [8] they were obliged to have recourse to various pursuits in order to obtain food. Ifa, who was in the same straits as the other gods, took to fishing, with, however, but small success; and one day, when he had failed to catch any fish at all, and was very hungry, he consulted the crafty Elegba, who was also in want, as to what they could do to improve their condition. Elegba replied that if he could only obtain the sixteen palm-nuts from the two palms -that Orungan [9] the chief man, had in his plantation, he would show Ifa how to forecast the future; and that he could then use his knowledge in the service of mankind, and so receive an abundance of offerings. He stipulated that in return for instructing Ifa in the art of divination, he should always be allowed the first choice of all offerings made. Ifa agreed to the bargain, and going to Orungan, asked for the sixteen palm-nuts, explaining to him what he proposed to do with them. *Orungan*, very eager to know what the future had in store for him, at once promised the nuts, and ran with his wife Orisha-bi, "Orisha-born," to get them. The trees, however, were too lofty for them to be able to reach the palm-nuts, and the stems too smooth to be climbed; so they retired to a little distance and drove some monkeys that were in the vicinity into the palms. No sooner were the monkeys in the trees than they seized the nuts, and, after eating the red pulp that covered them, threw the bard kernels down on the ground, where Orungan and his wife picked them up. Having collected the whole sixteen, Orisha-bi tied them up in a piece of cloth, and put the bundle under her waist-cloth, on her back, as if she were carryino, a child. Then they carried the palm-nuts to Ifa. Elegba kept his promise and taught Ifa the art of divination, and Ifa in his turn taught Oruno-an, who thus became the first *babalawo*, It is in memory of these events that when a man wishes to consult Ifa, he takes his wife with him, if he be married, and his mother if he be single, who carries the sixteen palm-nuts, tied up in a bundle, on her back, like a child; and that the *babalawo*, before consulting the god, always says, "*Orugan, ajuba oh. Orisha-bi ajuba oh.*" ("Orungan, I hold you in grateful remembrance. Orisha-bi, I hold you in grateful remembrance."

For the consultation of Ifa a whitened board is employed, exactly similar to those used by children in Moslem schools in lieu of slates, about two feet long and eight or nine inches broad, on which are marked sixteen figures. These figures are called "mothers." The sixteen palm-nuts are held loosely in the right hand, and thrown through the half-closed fingers into the left hand. If one nut remain in the right hand, two marks are made, thus | |; and if two remain. one mark, |.[10] In this way are formed the sixteen "mothers," one of which is declared by the *babalawo* to represent the inquirer; and from the order in which the others are produced he deduces certain results. The interpretation appears to be in accordance with established rule, but what that rule is is only known to the initiated. The following are the "mothers":

(1) *Buru Meji.*

(4) *Di Meji.*

(2) *Yekuro Meji.*

(5) *Losho Meji.*

(3) *Ode Meji.*

(6) *Oron Meji.*

(7) *Abila Meji.*

(12) *Ture Meji.*

(8) *Akala Meji.*

(13) *Leti Meji.*

(9) *Sa Meji.*

(14) *Ka Meji.*

(10) *Kuda Meji.*

(15) *Shi Meji.*

(11) *Durapin Meji.*

(16) *Fu Meji.*

35

No. 6 is No. 5 inverted; 8 is 7 inverted; 10, 9 inverted; 13, 12 inverted; and 14, 11 inverted. Meji means "two," or "a pair," and the following appears to be the meaning of the names:--(1) The close pair (*buru*, closely). (2) The removed pair (*Yekuro*, to remove). (3) The street pair (*Ode*, a street). (4) The closed-up pair (*Di*, to close up, make dense). (5) The squatting-dog pair (*losho*, to squat like a dog). (6) The cross-bow pair (*oron*, cross-bow). (7) The striped pair (*abila*, striped). (8)?Vulture-pair (*akala*, vulture). (9) The pointing pair (*sha*, to point). (10) The pair ending downward (*Ku*, to end, *da*, to upset on the ground). (11)?The top-heavy pair (*Dura*, to make an effort to recover from a stumble; *opin*, end, point). (12) The tattoo-mark pair (*ture*, name of certain tattoo-marks). (13) The edge pair (*leti*, on the edge of). (14) The folded-up pair (*Ka*, to fold or coil). (15) The opened pair (*shi*, to open). (16) The alternate pair (*fo*, to pass over, pass by, jump over, skip).

From these sixteen "mothers" a great many combinations can be made by taking a column from two different "mothers," and figures thus formed are called "children." Thus (13) and (2) and (11) and (10) make respectively:

As the figures are read from right to left, the system is probably derived from the Mobammedans. James Hamilton, indeed, describes [11] a very similar mode of divination which he saw in the oasis of Siwah, where it was called *Derb el ful*, or *Derb el raml*, according to whether beans or sand were used. He says: "Seven beans are held in the palm of the left hand, which is struck with a smart blow with the right half-closed fist, so that some of the beans jump into the right hand - if an odd number, one is marked; if even, two. The beans are replaced in the left hand, which is again struck with the right, and the result marked below the first. This being repeated four times gives the first figure, and the operation is performed until there are obtained four figures, which are placed side by side in a square; these are then read vertically and perpendicularly (*sic*), and also from corner to corner, thus giving in all ten figures. As each may contain four odd or four even numbers, they are capable of sixteen permutations, each of which has a separate signification, and a proper house, or part of the square in which it should appear."

The initiation fee paid to a priest for teaching the art of divination is, it is said, very heavy, and moreover does not cover the whole of the expense; for the Oracle is, like Oracles generally, ambiguous and obscure, and the neophyte finds that he constantly has to refer to the priests for explanations of its meaning, and on each such occasion he is required to pay a consultation fee. When a man is initiated the priest usually informs him that he must henceforward abstain from some particular article of food, which varies with the individual.

Ifa figures in connection with a legendary deluge, the story of which, now adapted to the Yoruba theology, was probably derived from the Mohammedans. Some time after settling at Ado, Ifa became tired of living in the world, and accordingly went to dwell in the firmament, with Obatala. After his departure, mankind, deprived of his assistance, was unable to properly interpret the desires of the gods, most of whom became in consequence annoyed. Olokun was the most angry, and in a fit of rage he destroyed nearly all the inhabitants of the world in a great flood, only a few being saved by Obatala, who drew them up into the sky by means of a long iron chain. After this ebullition of anger, Olokun retired once more to his own domains, but the world was nothing but mud, and quite unfit to live in, till Ifa came down from the sky, and, in conjunction with Odudua, once more made it habitable.

(7) ELEGBA.

Elegba, or Elegbara (Elegba-Bara), often called Esbu, is the same phallic divinity who was described in the volume on the Ewe-speaking Peoples. The name Elegba seems to mean, "He who seizes" (*Eni-gba*), and Bara is perhaps *Oba-ra*, "Lord of the rubbing" (*Ra*, to rub one thing against another). Eshu appears to be from *shu*, to emit, throw out, evacuate, The propensity to make mischief, which we noted as a minor characteristic of the Ewe Elegba, is much more prominent in the Yoruba god, who thus more nearly approaches a personification of evil. He is supposed always to carry a short knobbed club, which, originally intended to be a rude representation of the *phallus*, has, partly through want of skill on the part of the modellers of the images, and partly through the growing belief in Elegba's malevolence, come to be regarded as a weapon of offence. [12] Because he bears this club he has the title of *Agongo ogo*. *Ogo* is the name of the knobbed club, and is most probably a euphemism for the phallus; it is derived from *go*, to hide in a bending or stooping posture. The derivation of *agongo* is less easy to determine, but it seems to be from *gongo*, tip, extremity.

The image of Elegba, who is always represented naked, seated with his bands on his knees, and with an immensely, disproportionate *phallus*, is found in front of almost every house, protected by a small hut roofed with palm-leaves. It is with reference to this that the proverb says: "As Eshw has a malicious disposition, his house is made for him in the street" (instead of indoors). The rude wooden representation of the *phallus* is planted in the earth by the side of the hut, and is seen in almost every public place; while at certain festivals it is paraded in great pomp, and pointed towards the young girls, who dance round it.

Elegba, in consequence of the bargain he made with Ifa, receives a share of every sacrifice offered to the other gods. His own proper sacrifices are, as among the Ewe tribes, cocks, dogs and he-goats, chosen on account of their amorous propensities; but on very important occasions a human victim is

37

offered. In such a case, after the head has been struck off, the corpse is disembowelled, and the entrails placed in front of the image in a large calabash or wooden dish; after which the body is suspended from a tree, or, if no tree be at hand, from a scaffolding of poles. Turkeybuzzards are sacred to Elegba and are considered his messengers, no doubt because they devour the entrails and bodies of the sacrifices.

There is a noted temple Lo Elegba in a grove of palms near Wuru, a village situated about ten miles to the east of Badagry. The market of Wuru is under his protection, and each vendor throws a few cowries on the ground as a thank-offering. Once a year these cowries are swept up by the priests, and with the sum thus collected a slave is purchased to be sacrificed to the god. A slave is also sacrificed annually, towards the end of July, to Elegba in the town of Ondo, the capital of the state of the same name. Elegba's principal residence is said to be on a mountain named Igbeti, supposed to be situated near the Niger. Here he has a vast palace of brass, and a large number of attendants.

Circumcision among the Yorubas, as among the Ewes, is connected with the worship of Elegba, and appears to be a sacrifice of a portion of the organ which the god inspires, to ensure the well-being of the remainder. To circumcise is *dako (da-oko) da*, to be acceptable as a sacrifice, and *oko*, the foreskin. Circumcision is *ileyika*, or *ikola*, the former of which means "the circular cutting" (*ike*, the act of cutting, and *ikeya*, a circuit), and the latter, "the cutting that saves" (*ike*, the act of cutting, and *ola*, that which saves). Except among the Mohammedans there is no special time for performing the rite of circumcision, it being fixed for each individual by Ifa, after consultation, but usually it is done early in life. No woman would have connection with an uncircumcised man. A similar operation is performed on girls, who are excised, by women operators, shortly before puberty, that is, between the ages of ten and twelve years.

As is the case in the western half of the Slave Coast, erotic dreams are attributed to Elegba, who, either as a female or male, consorts sexually with men and women during their sleep, and so fulfils in his own person the functions of the *incubi* and *succubi* of mediaeval Europe.

(8) OGUN.

Ogun is the god of iron and of war, and, like Shango, is also a patron of hunters. Iron is sacred to him, and when swearing by Ogun it is usual to touch an iron implement with the Ilorgue. The name Ogun seems to mean "One who pierces" (*gun*, to pierce, or thrust with something pointed). He is specially worshipped by blacksmiths, and by those who make use of iron weapons or tools. Any piece of iron can be used as a symbol of Ogun, and the ground is sacred to him because iron ore is found in it. He is one of those who sprang from the body of Yemaja.

The usual sacrifice offered to Ogun is a dog, together with fowls, palm oil, and minor articles of food. A proverb says, "An old dog must be sacrificed to Ogun," meaning that Ogun claims the best; and a dog's head, emblematic of this sacrifice, is always to be seen fastened up in some conspicuous part of the workshops of blacksmiths. On very important occasions, however, a human victim is offered, and, as in the case of a sacrifice to Elegba, the entrails are exposed before the image and the body suspended from a tree. The victim is slain by having his head struck off upon the stool of Ogun, over which the blood is made to gush. The reason of this is that the blood is believed to contain the vital principle, and therefore to be an offering, particularly acceptable to the gods.

This belief appears to be common to most barbarons peoples; the Israelites held it, [13] and blood was considered to be so peculiarly the portion of their national god, that the blood of all animals slain, whether for sacrifice or food, had to be presented as an offering, no one being allowed to eat it under pain of death. [14]

When war has been decided upon, a slave is purchased at the expense of the town, or tribe, and offered as a sacrifice to Ogun, to ensure success. The day before that on which he is to be immolated, the victim is led with great ceremony through the principal thoroughfares, and paraded in the market, where he is allowed to say or do anything he pleases (short of escaping his impending fate), may gratify his desire with any woman who takes his fancy, and give his tongue every licence. The reason of his being thus honoured for the twenty-four hours before being sacrificed, is that it is believed he will be born again and become a king; and, after the head has been struck off, the corpse is treated with the greatest respect by all. In order for this sacrifice to be effective, it is necessary that the war leaders should take the field before the body begins to become offensive. The Ibadans, who appear to be rather averse to human sacrifice, always used to perform this duty by deputy, paying the priests of Ife to sacrifice for them a slave in that town. When the war of 1877 began they omitted to do this, thinking that the affair would not be serious; and, attributing their subsequent want of success to the omission, they afterwards sacrificed a slave to Ogun in their camp at Kiji in 1885, they having been prevented from doing it earlier by their leader, a Mohammedan, who died in that year.

The priests of Ogun usually take out the hearts of human victims, which are dried, reduced to powder, then mixed with rum, and sold to persons who wish to be endowed with great courage, and who drink the mixture. The reason of this is that the heart is believed to be the seat of courage and to inherently possess that quality; and that when the heart is devoured or swallowed the quality with which it is inspired is also taken into the system.

[1] The *n* in *oni*, or *ni*, always changes to *l* before the vowels *a*, *e*, *o*, and *u*. See Chapter on Language, Verbs (6).
[2] *Al-oni* (one who. has); *ba* (to overtake); *ni* (to have); *ase* (a coming to pass), "One who overtakes the coming to pass."
[3] The order, according to some, was Olokun, Oloss, Shango, Oye, Oshun, Oba, Ogun, Dada, and the remainder as above.

[4] For the same notion among the Tshis and Gas, *see* Note at p. 36.

[5] Hunting and thunder were likewise the functions of the Aztec god, or goddess, Mixcoatl. (Nadaillac, "Prehistoric America," p. 298.)

[6] Oni, one who possesses or gets.

[7] Near Porto Novo.

[8] Compare this with Lucian, "Zeus in Tragedy," where Zeus complains that the sea captain Mnesitheus had, only sacrificed one cock to entertain sixteen gods.

[9] The son and ravisher of Yemaja is also so named]

[10] This process is repeated eight times, and the marks are made in succession in two columns of four each.

[11] "Wanderings in North Africa," pp. 264-65.

[12] In the case of Priapus we find a similar connection between the phallus and a cudgel. See Catullus, xx., "The Garden God."]

[13] Genesis ix. 4; Leviticus xvii. 11, 14.

[14] Leviticus xvii. 3,4; iii. 16,17; vii. 28-27.

Chapter Three - Minor Gods

(1) OLOKUN.

OLOKUN (*oni-okun*, he who owns the sea), "Lord of the Sea," is the sea-god of the Yorubas. He is one of those who came from the body of Yemaja.

As man worships that from which he has most to fear, or from which he hopes to receive the greatest benefits, the inland tribes pay little or no attention to Olokun, who is, however, the chief god of fishermen and of all others whose avocations take them upon the sea. When Olokun is angry he causes the sea to be rough and stirs up a raging surf upon the shore; and it is he who drowns men, upsets boats or canoes, and causes shipwrecks.

Olokun is not the personally divine sea but an anthropomorphic conception. He is of human shape and black in colour, but with long flowing hair, and resides in a vast palace under the sea, where he is served by a number of sea-spirits, some of whom are human in shape, while others partake more or less of the nature of fish. On ordinary occasions animals are sacrificed to Olokun, but when the condition of the surf prevents canoes from putting to sea for many days at a time, a human victim is offered to appease him. It is said that such sacrifices have been made in recent times, even at Lagos, by the people of the Isaleko quarter, who are chiefly worshippers of Olokun. The sacrifice was of course secret, and according to native report the canoemen used to watch by night till they caught some solitary wayfarer, whom they gagged and conveyed across the lagoon to the sea-shore, where they struck off his head and threw the body into the surf.

A myth says that Olokun, becoming enraged with mankind on account of their neglect of him, endeavoured to destroy them by overflowing the land; and had drowned large numbers when Obatala interfered to save the remainder, and forced Olokun back to his palace, where he bound him with seven iron chains till he promised to abandon his design. This, perhaps, has reference to some former encroachment of the sea upon the low-lying sandy shores, which are even now liable to be submerged at spring-tides. [1]

Olokun has a wife named Olokun-su, or Elusu, who lives in the harbour bar at Lagos. She is white in colour and human in shape, but is covered with fish-scales from below the breasts to the hips. The fish in the waters of the bar are sacred to her, and should anyone catch them, she takes vengeance by up-setting canoes and drowning the occupants. A man who should be so ill-advised as to attempt to fish on the bar would run a great risk of being thrown overboard by the other canoemen. Olokunsu is an example of a local sea-goddess, originally, as on the Gold Coast at the present day, considered quite independent, being attached to the general god of the sea, and account-ed for as belonging to him.

(2) OLOSA.

Olosa (*oni-osa*, owner of the laaoon) is the goddess of the Lagos Lagoon, and the principal wife of her brother Olokim, the sea-god. Like her husband she is long-haired. She sprang from the body of Yemaja.

Olosa supplies her votaries with fish, and there are several temples dedi-cated to her along the shores of the lagoon, where offerings of fowls and sheep are made to her to render her propitious. When the lagoon is swollen by rain and overflows its banks she is angry, and if the inundation be serious a human victim is offered to her-, to induce her to return within her proper limits.

Crocodiles ate Olosa's messengers, and may not be molested. They are supposed to bear to the goddess the offerings which the faithful deposit on the shores of the lagoon or throw into the sedge. Some crocodiles, selected by the priests on account of certain marks borne by them, are treated with great veneration; and have rude sheds, thatched with palm leaves, erected for their accommodation near the water's edge. Food is regagularly supplied to these reptiles every fifth day, or festival, and many of them become suffi-ciently tame to come for the offering as soon as they see or hear the wor-shippers gathering on the bank.

(3) SHANKPANNA.

Shankpanna, or Shakpana, who also came from the body of Yemaja, is the Small-pox god. The name appears to be derived from *shan*, to daub, smear, or plaster, which probably has reference to the pustules with which a small-pox patient is covered, and *akpania*, [2] a man-killer, homicide. He is accompa-nied by an assistant named Buku, [3] who kills those attacked by small-pox by wringing their necks.

Shan-kpanna is old and lame, and is depicted as limping along with the aid of a stick. According to a myth he has a withered leg. One day, when the gods were all assembled at the palace of Obatala, and were dancing and making merry, Shankpanna endeavoured to join in the dance, but, owing to his de-formity, stumbled and fell. All the gods and goddesses thereupon burst out laughing, and Shankpanna, in revenge, strove to infect them with small-pox, but Obatala came to the rescue, and, seizing his spear, drove Shankpanna away. From that day Shankpanna was forbidden to associate with the other gods, and he became an outcast who has since lived in desolate and uninhabited tracts of country.

Temples dedicated to Shankpanna are always built in the bush, at some little distance from a town or village, with a view to keeping him away from habitations. He is much dreaded, and when there is an epidemic of small-pox the priests who serve him are able to impose almost any terms they please upon the terrified people, as the price of their mediation, To whistle by night near one of Shankpanna's haunts is believed to be a certain way of attracting his notice and contracting the disease. As is the case with Sapatan, the small-pox god of the Ewe tribes, who have perhaps adopted the notion from the Yorubas, flies and mosquitos are the messengers of Sbankpanna, and his emblem is a stick covered with red and white blotches, symbolic, it seems, of the marks he makes on the bodies of his victims.

(4) SHIGIDI.

Shigidi, or Shugudu, is deified nightmare. The name appears to mean "something short and bulky," and the god, or demon, is represented by a broad and short head, made of clay, or, more commonly, by a thick, blunted cone of clay, which is ornamented with cowries, and is no doubt emblematic of the head.

Shigidi is an evil god, and enables man to gratify his hate in secret and without risk to himself. When a man wishes to revenge himself upon another he offers a sacrifice to Shigidi, who thereupon proceeds at night to the house of the person indicated and kills him. His mode of procedure is to squat upon the breast of his victim and "press out his breath;" but it often happens that the tutelary deity of the sufferer comes to the rescue and wakes him, uponwhich Sbigidi leaps off, falls upon the earthen floor, and disappears, for he only has power over man dur ing sleep. This superstition still lingers among the negroes of the Bahamas of Yoruba descent, who talk of being "hagged," and believe that nightmare is caused by a demon that crouches upon the breast of the sleeper. The word nightmare is itself a survival from a similar belief once held by ourselves, *mare* being the Anglo-Saxon *mære*, elf or goblin.

The person -who employs Shigidi, and sends him out to kill, must remain awake till the god returns, for if he were to fall asleep Shigidi would at that moment turn back, and the mission would fail. Shigidi either travels on the wind, or raises a wind to waft him along; on this point opinions differ. The first symptom of being attacked by Shigidi, is a feeling of heat and oppression at the pit of the stomach, "like hot, boiled rice," said a native. If a man experiences this when he is falling asleep, it behoves him to get up at once and seek the protection of the god he usually serves.

Houses and enclosed yards can be placed under the guardianship of Shigidi. In order to do this a hole is dug in the earth and a fowl, sheep, or, in exceptional cases, a human victim is slaughtered, so that the blood drains into the hole, and is then buried. A short, conical mound of red earth is next built over the spot, and an earthen saucer placed on the summit to receive occasional sacrifices. When a site has thus been placed under the protection of Shigidi, he kills, in his typical manner, those who injure the buildings, or who trespass there with bad intentions.

(5) OLAROSA.

Olarosa (?*Alarense*, helper) is the tutelary deity of Houses. He is represented as armed with a stick or sword, and his image is found in almost every household guarding the entrance. His office is to drive away sorcerers and evil spirits, and to keep Elegba from entering the house.

(6) DADA.

Dada, more properly Eda, or Ida, is the god of New-born Babes and Vegetables. The name appears to mean natural production, anything produced or brought forth by natural process. Dada is repre. sented by a calabash ornamented with cowries, on which is placed a ball of indigo. He is one of those who came from the body of Yemaja.

(7) OYA.

Oya is the goddess of the Niger, which is called *Odo Oya*, the river of Oya. She is the chief wife of the thunder-god, Shango, and, as has already been said, her messenger is Afefe, the Wind. At Lokoro, near Porto Novo, there is said to be a temple of Oya containing an image of the goddess with eight heads surrounding a central head. This is supposed to be symbolical of the numerous outfalls of the Niger through its delta. Oya, and the two following sprang from Yemaja.

(8) OSHUN.

Oshun, goddess of the river of the same name, which is the sacred river of Jebu Ode, is the second wife of Shango. Crocodiles which bear certain marks are sacred to her, and are considered her messengers. Human sacrifices are made to Oshun in time of need.

(9) OBA.

Oba, the third wife of Shango, is the goddess of the River Ibu, or Oba.

(10) AJE SHALUGA.

Aje Shaluga is the god of Wealth, and confers riches on his worshippers. The name appears to mean either "the gainer who makes to recur," or "the sorcerer who makes to recur." (*Aje*, sorcerer; *aje*, earner, or gainer, and *shalu*, to recur.) His emblem is a large cowry. One proverb says, "Aje Shaluga often passes by the first caravan as it comes to the market, and loads the last with benefits;" and another, "He who while walking finds a cowry is favoured by Aje Shaluga." The large cowry, emblematic of Aje Shaluga, has no value as. a medium of exchange, the small white cowries being alone used for that purpose. He is the patron of dyes and of colours generally. He came from the body of Yemaja.

(11) ORISRA OKO.

Orisha Oko (*oko*, farm, garden, plantation) is the god of Agriculture, and is one of those who sprang from the body of Yemaja. As the natives chiefly depend upon the fruits of the earth for their food, Orisha Oko is much honoured. There is scarcely a town or village that has not a temple dedicated to him, and he has a large number of priests and priestesses in his service.

Although his first care is to promote the fertility of the earth, he is also -the god of natural fertility in general, for he is a phallic divinity, and his image is always provided with an enormous *phallus*. He thus resembles Priapus, who, although a phallic deity, was, apparently, primarily a garden-god, who fostered and protected crops. (Catullus, xix. xx.; Tibullus, I. i.)

An emblem of Orisha Oko is an iron rod, and honey bees are his messengers. It is probably with reference to his phallic attributes that he has the title of *Eni-duru-* "the erect personage." One of his functions is to cure malarial fevers, to which those who disturb the soil in the process of cultivation are particularly liable.

There is an annual festival to Orisha Oko, held when the yam crop is ripe, and all then partake of new yams. At this festival general licence prevails, the priestesses give themselves indiscriminately to all the male worshippers of the god, and, theoretically, every man has a right to sexual intercourse with every woman he may meet abroad. Social prejudices have, however, restricted the application of this privilege, and it is now only slave-girls, or women of the lowest order, who are really at the disposal of the public, and then only if they are consenting parties. At this festival all kinds of vegetable productions are cooked and placed in vessels in the streets, for general use.

(12) OSANHIN.

Osanhin (*san*, to benefit) is the god of Medicine, and, as he is always applied to in cases of sickness, his worship is very general. His emblem is the figure of a bird perched upon an iron bar.

(13) ARONI.

Aroni is the Forest-god, and, like the last, has a knowledge of medicine, though the cure of disease is not his special function. The name means "One having a withered limb," and Aroni is always represented as of human shape but with only one leg, the head of a dog, and a dog's tail.

Aroni seizes and devours those who meet him in the forest and attempt to run away when they see him; but if a man faces him boldly and shows no sign 'of fear, he leads him to his dwelling in the fastnesses of the forest, and keeps him there for two or three months, during which time he teaches him the secrets of the plants and their medicinal properties. When the pupil has no more to learn Aroni dismisses him, giving him a hair from his tail to prove to the incredulous that he has really been initiated.

An eddy of wind, rushing through the forest and swirling up the dead leaves, is considered a manifestation of Aroni.

(14) AJA.

Aja, whose name appears to mean a wild vine, is a deity somewhat similar to Aroni. Like Aroni, she carries off persons who meet her into the depths of the forest, and teaches them the medicinal properties of plants; but she never harms anyone. Aja is of human shape, but very diminutive, she being only from one to two feet high. The aja vine is used by women to cure enflamed breasts.

(15) OYE.

Oye, the god of the Harmattan wind, is a giant who, according to some, lives in a cavern to the north of Ilorin, while others say that 'he resides on the mountain named Igbeti, where Elegba is supposed to have his palace.

(16) IBEJI.

Ibeji, Twins (*bi*, to beget, *eji*, two) is the tutelary deity of twins, and answers to the god Hoho of the Ewe-tribes. A small black monkey, generally found amongst mangrove trees, is sacred to Ibeji. Offerings of fruit are made to it, and its flesh may not be eaten by twins or the parents of twins. This monkey is called *Edon dudu*, or *Edun oriokun*, and one of twin children is generally named after it *Edon*, or *Edun*.

When one of twins dies, the mother carries with the surviving child, to keep it from pining for its lost comrade, and also to give the spirit of the deceased child something to enter without disturbing the living child, a small wooden figure, seven or eight inches long, roughly fashioned in human shape, and of the sex of the dead child. Such figures are nude, as an infant would be, with beads round the waist.

At Erapo, a village on the Lagoon between Lagos and Badagry, there is a celebrated temple to Ibeji, to which all twins, and the parents of twins, from a long distance round make pilgrimages.

It is said to be usual in Ondo to destroy one of twins. This is contrary to the practice of the Yorubas, and, if true, the custom has probably been borrowed from the Benin tribes to the east.

(17) OSHUMARE.

Oshumare is the Rainbow-god, the Great Snake of the Underneath, who comes up at times above the edge of the earth to drink water from the sky. The name is compounded of *shu*, to gather in dark clouds, to become gloomy, and the word *mare*, or *maye*, which occurs in one of the epithets of Olorun, and the meaning of which is uncertain. This god is also common to the Ewe-tribes, under the name of Anyiewo, and has been described in "The Ewe-Speaking People of the Slave Coast of West Africa." A variety of the python, called by the Yorubas *ere*, is the messenger of the rainbow-god, and is sacred to him.

(18) OKE.

Oke, mountain, or hill, is the god of Mountains, and is worshipped by those who live in mountainous or rocky country. If neglected, he is apt to roll down huge masses of rock upon the habitations of those who have been forgetful of his wants, or to sweep them away by a landslip. When any great mishap of this nature occurs, a human victim is offered up to turn away his anger. The falling of boulders or detached pieces of rock is always considered the handiwork of Oke and a sign that something is required. The emblem of Oke is a stone or fragment of rock. He is one of those who sprang from Yemaja.

At Abeokuta there is a rocky cavern in which Oke is worshipped. It is popularly believed by the other tribes that the Egbas, when defeated in war, can retire into this cavern, which then hermetically seats itself till the danger is past.

(19) OSHOSI.

Oshosi, who is also one of those who came from Yemaja, is the patron of Hunters. He resides in the forest, and drives the game into the snares and pitfalls of his faithful followers, whom he also protects from beasts of prey. He is represented as a man armed with a bow, or frequently by a bow alone. Offerings are made to him of the fruits of the chase, chiefly of antelopes.

(20) AND (21) THE SUN AND THE MOON.

According to the myth, the sun, moon, and stars came from the body of Yemaja. Orun, the Sun, and Oshu, the Moon, are gods, but the stars do not seem to have been deified. The worship of the sun and moon is, moreover, now very nearly obsolete, and sacrifices are no longer offered to them, though the appearance of the -new moon is commonly celebrated by a festival.

The stars are the daughters of the sun and moon. The boys, or young suns, on growing up tried to follow their father in his course across the sky to where the sea and the sky meet, and which, say the Yorubas, is the place where the white men go and find all the things with which they fill their ships; but he, jealous of his power, turned upon them and tried to kill them. Some of them sought refuge with Olosa, some with Olokun, and the remainder with their grandmother, Yemaja, who turned them into fish. Thus all the sons were driven out of the sky, but the daughters remained with their mother and still accompany her by night. This myth is virtually the same as that current among the eastern Ewe-tribes, who have almost certainly learnt it from their Yoruba neighbours.

To see the new moon is lucky, and, just as in England, people wish when they first see it. As amongst the Ewe-tribes, an eclipse of the Moon is supposed to indicate that the Sun is beating her, and steps are taken to drive him away, similar to those described in "The Ewe-Speaking People."

The Yorubas pay some attention to the heavenly bodies. The planet Venus, when near the Moon, is called Aja-Oshu, the Moon's Dog, becauseshe travels with it. When a morning star she is called Ofere, or Ofe, which seems to mean a pale blue colour. When an evening star she is called Irawo-ale, Star of the Evening. Sirius is called Irawo-oko, Canoe Star, because it is believed to be a guide to canoemen. A proverbial saying likens the stars to chickens following a hen, the Moon; and the Milky Way is called the group of chickens."

(23) OLORI-MERIN.

Olori-merin, possessor of four heads, is another god whose worship is nearly, if not quite, obsolete. He was the tutelary deity of towns, and was represented by a hillock, or, if no hillock existed within the precincts of the town, by an artificial mound.

Sacrifice was made to Olori-merin every three months, or four times a year, and always consisted of a new-born child not more than three or four days' old

. The child's throat was cut by a priest, and the blood, caught in a calabash or earthen vessel, was placed on the summit of the mound, after which the flesh was sliced up into small pieces and buried in the mound. During this dreadful scene the mother had to be present. This sacrifice was called Ejodun (Eje-odun), "The season of blood."

Olori-merin had, as his name betokens, four heads, with which he watched the four points of the compass from the top of his mound, and it was believed that no war or pestilence could attack a town under his protection. He had the legs and feet of a goat. Sometimes, at -night, he appeared in the shape of a venomous serpent.

[1] Another myth of this nature has been mentioned in Chapter II., under Ifa.
[2] *Akpania*, *kpa*, to kill, and *enia*, a person.
[3] Perhaps *bu*, to rot, emit a.stench, and *iku*, death.

Chapter Four - Remarks on the Foregoing

IN the myths of the origin of the various gods described in the last two chapters we probably see the result of the indwelling-spirit theory having been lost sight of. As long as a god was accepted to be the animating principle or spiritual entity of some natural object or feature, his origin required no explanation, for his existence was bound up with the feature or object, and, if the question was thought of at all, he must have been, in the native mind, co-eval with the origin of the world. When, however, as has been the case with most of the deities worshipped by the Yoruba tribes as a whole, the gods ceased to be identified with local objects or natural phenomena, some other explanation of their origin became necessary; for man, however low he may be in the scale of civilisation, is always desirous of knowing the reasons for everything, and the West African negro in particular is of a very inquisitive turn of mind. Then, in order to satisfy the natural desire to know who the gods were and whence they came, the myths we have already recounted grew up, and the numerous discrepancies in them appear to show that the process was comparatively recent. It looks as if the stories had not yet had sufficient time to become generally known in a commonly accepted version.

The deities Obatala and Odudua represent, say the priests, Heaven and Earth. Oloran is the real Heaven-god, or Sky-god, answering to the Ewe Mawu, but he is now almost pushed out of sight, and Obatala, a more active agent, acts for him. The difference between Olorun and Obatala appears to be that the former is the personal divine firmament, and the latter an anthropomorphic sky-god, a later conception; and we perhaps here see a repetition of the process by which in the religion of ancient Greece Kronos supplanted Uranus. Obatala, or Heaven, marries Odudua, or Earth, [1] and has two children, named Aganju and Yemaja, who, according to the priests, represent Land and Water. These two intermarry and have a son, Orungan, "Air," the region between the solid firmament, and the earth. Orungan ravishes his mother Yemaja, who, while endeavouring to escape from further outrage, falls and bursts open, whereupon a number of gods emerge from her gaping body.

The gods whose origin is thus accounted for as the offspring of Yemaja, are of various types. The Sea-god (Olokun), the Thunder-god (Shango), the Sun, the Moon, the Lagoon (Olosa), the three river-goddesses Oya, Oshun, and Oba, the god of Mountains (Oke), and Ogun, god of iron and war and of the River Ogun, are all the product of Nature-worship, but are not of one type, for the Sun and Moon belong to the old order of things, to the same religious system as Olorun, and are personally divine, while the others belong to the new order, and are anthropomorphic. Shankpanna, god of small-pox, is personified pestilence, and belongs to another type; while Dada, Oshosi, Aje Shaluga, and Orisha Oko, as the respective patrons of vegetable productions, hunters, wealth, and agriculture, may be regarded as the tutelary deities of industries, and as belonging to a third class of religious conceptions. The myth thus assigns a common origin alike to the ancient gods and to those which are more modern.

There are, however, other gods who do not belong to this family circle; that is, they are not descendants of Obatala and Odudua, so the mythological scheme is incomplete, no attempt being made to account for their origin. These gods are the God of Divination (Ifa), the Forest-god (Aroni), the Phallic-god (Elegba), the Harmattan Wind (Oye), the Rainbow (Oshumare), the tutelary deity of households (Olarosa), the god of Medicine (Osanhin), and Shigidi. These also are of various types. The Harmattan Wind and the Rainbow are Nature-gods of the old order, and Aroni, god of forests, of the new. Olarosa and Osanhin are tutelary deities, and Shigidi is personified nightmare. Ifa was probably originally the God of fecundation, though now his chief function is to foretell the future. Elegba, primarily a phallic divinity, seems to be gradually becoming a personification of evil, and here we perhaps see a tendency towards Dualism, which in the future might, if undisturbed, result in Elegba becoming the Evil Deity, and Obatala or Ifa the Good.

The incompleteness of the scheme seems, as has been said, to show that the myth of Yemaja is comparatively recent, and this is supported by the fact that the myth itself is not universally accepted in its entirety. Shango, for example, is said by some to be of independent origin, like Ifa; and Odudua, the mother of Yemaja, according to the myth, is by others included in the number of those who sprang from Yemaja's body. No general consensus of opinion has yet been arrived at, but the myth of Yemaja is the only one that holds the field, and no doubt in course of time the gods whose origin is as yet unexplained would also be held to have come from the daugliter of Obatala, and Odudua.

We find the same want of accord in the myths of the origin of man. According to some, Obatala made the first man and woman out of clay or mud, whence he has obtained his titles of Alamorere and Orisha Kpokpo; while, according to others, the first pair came, with the gods, from the body of Yemaja. Although the first story somewhat resembles the account of the origin of man given in the Book of Genesis, there is no reason for supposing it to be borrowed. When uncivilised man, after speculating about the origin of mankind, has come to the conclusion that there must have been a first pair, and has accounted for that first pair by the theory that they were made by a superior being out of something; the material which he would be most likely to select for their manufacture is clay or mud, because it is with these that he makes his own first rude attempts to model the human form. To make a rude imitation of the figure of a man in clay requires far less skill and far less labour than to carve one out of a block of wood, whence it is that most of the images of the gods are made of clay. Clay figures being primordial, and images being ordinarily made of clay even when the arts have somewhat advanced, this would be the substance which the myth-makers would introduce into their myths describing the origin of the first pair, a connection of ideas between clay and the human form already existing. [2]

The second story, which cannot be any older than the myth of Yemaja, of which it is a part, is sufficiently precise to give the name of the first couple, that of the man being Obalofun (Lord of Speech), and that of the woman Iya (Mother). After coming out of the goddess at Ife, they settled there, and had a numerous progeny, which increased and multiplied till the whole earth was populated, hence it is that Ife is considered the cradle of the human race. Of course Obalofun and Iya were Yorubas, for it is a peculiarity of every uucivilised people to believe that the first man and woman were of their race.

Another tradition, though it makes Ife the place of origin of the Yoruba tribes, represents it as being colonised by persons migrating from the interior. This tradition is perhaps a dim recollection of a historical fact, historical, that is, in so far that the Yoruba tribes probably did in the remote past come down from the interior, and occupy the territory in which they were found at the commencement of the present century; for the cognate Tshi tribes of the Gold Coast also have a tradition of a migration from the interior. Most probably the two traditions refer to a great southward movement of the original stock from which the Tshi, Gã, Ewe, and Yomba tribes are descended, and which, starting from some central point in the interior, spread out in fan-shape till it reached the sea-coast. The tradition of the Yoruba migration is as follows.

Long ago a certain person living in the far interior sent fifteen people from his country to go to the south, and with them came, of his own free will, one named Okambi, [3] who afterwards became the first King of Yoruba. When they were leaving, the person who sent them gave Okambi a slave, a trumpeter named Okinkin, [4] a fowl, and something tied up in a piece of black cloth. They journeyed for some time, and when they opened the gate of the south and passed into the unknown country, they found nothing but water spread out before them. At first they thought of returning, but fearing the anger of the person who had sent them, they entered the water; and, finding it quite shallow, waded on through it. This they did for some time until Okinkin the trumpeter sounded his trumpet, in accordance with the instructions the person had given, and thereby reminded Okambi of the something tied up in black cloth, which was to be opened when the trumpet sounded. The cloth was accordingly untied, and a palm-nut, with some earth fell into the water from it. The nut immediately began to grow, and shot up so rapidly that in a few minutes it had become a tall palm with sixteen branches. [5] All the party, being very tired from their long wading climbed up into the tree and rested on the branches till next morning, in which position a certain person named Okiki [6] saw them from the country from which they had been sent out. When he saw them, Okiki reminded Okinkin the trumpeter that it was his duty to sound the trumpet again, whereupon he sounded it, and Okambi untied the piece of black cloth a second time. When it was opened, earth fell from it, and, drying up the water, made a small mound. The fowl that the personage had given Okambi then flew on to the mound and scratched the earth here and there, and wherever the earth fell it dried up the water. When there was a good space covered with earth, Okambi came down from the tree, bringing with him his trumpeter Okinkin and his slave Tetu. [7] The other persons wished to come down also, but Okambi would not allow them to do so until they had promised to pay him, at stipulated periods of time, a tribute of 200 cowries apiece. The place where the palm sprung up from the water afterwards became Ife, and, some time after, three brothers set out from there in different directions, to make fresh discoveries. When they went away they left a slave, named Adimu, [8] to rule Ife during their absence.

This tradition is vague and meagre of detail, the only points brought out being that a certain number of persons migrated southward from the interior, and found a region covered with water. This latter detail, however, strongly supports the theory that a real migration took place; for the large stretches of shallow water of the lagoon system, which during the rainy season are enormously extended by the inundation of the low-lying portions of the surrounding country, could scarcely have failed to excite the wonder of a people accustomed to the plateaus and mountain ranges of the interior, and to leave a lasting impression upon their memories.

[1] Rhea, bride of Kronos, to some extent represented the earth in Grecian mythology.
[2] According to one Greek myth, Pandora, the first woman, was ruade by Hepæestus out of earth, and, according to anotlier, Prometheus made man out of earth and water. See also Lucian, "Dialogues of the Gods," i.

[3] This name means "an only child." *Okan*, one, and *bi*, to bear.

[4] Okinkin appears to mean "owner of a very small portion."

[5] This number often recurs in Yoruba myths. There were sixteen palm-nuts on the two palms in the garden of Orungan, the chief man, which Ifa obtained for the purpose of divination, and sixteen palm trees grew up from the palm-nut that Ifa planted on the rock at Ado. Sixteen persons, viz. fifteen and Okambi, commence the journey to the south.

[6] This name is sometimes given as Okiki-shi. Okiki means rumour, or report, and Okiki-sbi, "borrowed from report." There is an unintelligible Gã proverb, "Nobody knows who has born Okaikoi," which perhaps refers to the same personage.

[7] Tetu means "executioner."

[8] Adimu, a tight grasp, hold-fast.

Chapter Five - Priests and Worship

THE Yoruba priesthood is divided into recognised orders, but before describing them it will be necessary to give some account of a secret society which is inseparably connected with the priesthood, and which, except in Jebu, Where it is called Oshogbo, is known as the Ogboni Society.

The Ogboni Society really holds the reins of government, and kings themselves are obliged to submit to its decrees. The members are popularly believed to possess a secret from which they derive their power, but their only secret appears to be that of a powerful and unscrupulous organisation, each member of which is bound to assist every other, while all are bound to carry out, and if necessary enforce, the decrees of the body. Each town and village has its Ogboni "lodge," and the members recognise each other by conventional signs and passwords.. At their meetings, which are held with a great affectation of mystery, they deliberate upon all matters which interest the tribe or community. The decisions of the Ogboni are final, and nothing of importance can be done without their consent When the missionaries wished to establish theniselves at Abeokuta, the king could not grant the necessary permission till the Ogbonis had considered the matter and signified their consent. The power of the Ogbonis, however, varies in different states, and in Ibadan they seem to be little more than public executioners.

Of course, since the organization is secret, little can really be known about it. Death is said to be the penalty for betraying the secrets of the order. According to native report, a member who has been convicted of such an offence is placed in a narrow cell, with his legs protruding through two holes in the wall into an adjoining cell, where they are fastened to two stakes driven into the earthen floor. The executioner sits in this adjoining cell, and the offender is tortured to death by having the flesh scraped from his legs with sharp-edged shells. Whether this is true or not it is impossible to say.

According to some natives the Ogboni Society has for its chief object the preservation of established religious customs, while according to others it is principally occupied with the civil power. It really appears to concern itself with every matter of public interest, and seems to resemble in all important particulars a very similar society, called Porro, which is found among the Timnis of Sierra Leone. What is quite certain is that the protecting deity of the Ogboni is the goddess Odudua, who is generally spoken of by members by her title Ile (Earth). It seems probable that the society was originally intended for the initiation to manhood of youths who had arrived at puberty, like the Boguera of the Beebuanas, the Niamwali of the Manganja, and the ceremony of the Mpongwe, described by Mr. Winwood Reade, [1] and that its civil and judicial functions are later usurpations. If this were so, it would to some extent be connected with phallic worship, and phallic emblems are very commonly seen carved on the doors of Ogboni lodges. The name Ogboni is probably derived from Ogba, "Companion."

The Alafin of Yoruba is the chief of all the Ogboni, and he thus is able to exert influence beyond the limits of his own kingdom. In most states the chief of the Ogboni is the head of the priesthood, and is styled *Ekeji Orisha*, "Next to the Gods." He convokes councils of priests on extraordinary occasions, and decides disputed points. In Jebu every man of rank is an Oshogbo, but in Ibadan, as has been said, the Ogboni seem chiefly to exercise the functions of executioners. Criminals are delivered to them for execution and are put to death secretly in the Ogboni lodge. The heads are afterwards fixed to a tree in the market-place, but the bodies are never seen again, and the relatives are thus unable to give them the rites of sepulture, which is considered a great disgrace.

The Yoruba priesthood (*Olorisha*, priest) is divided into three orders, each of which is further subdivided into ranks or classes.

The first order comprises three ranks, viz. (1) the *Babalawo*, or priests of Ifa; (2) priests who practise medicine, and who serve Osanhin and Aroni, gods of medicine; (3) priests of Obatala and Odudua. White is the distinguishing colour of this order, and all priests belonging to it invariably wear white cloths. The *Babalawo* wear armlets made of palm-fibre, and carry a cow-tail (*iruke*), while priests of Obatala are distinguished by necklaces of white beads. There are two high priests of this order, one of whom resides at Ife and the other at Ika, some distance to the north.

The second order comprises (1) the Oni-Shango, or priests of Shango; and (2) priests of all other gods not before mentioned, except Orisha Oko. Red and white are the distinguishing colours of this order, and all members of it shave the crown of the head. Priests of Shango wear necklaces of black, red, and white beads; those of Ogun an iron bracelet on the left arm; and those of Oshun, one of Shango's wives, brass armlets and anklets.

The third order consists of (1) priests of Orisha Oko, god of Agriculture, and (2) priests of demi-gods, or deified men, such as Huisi, who defended

Oya against Shango. Priests of this order are distinguished by a small white mark painted on the forehead.

The reason of the *Babalawo* taking the highest place in the priesthood is that it is through his agency, as the priest of Ifa, the god of divination, that man learns what is necessary to be done to please the other gods. The priests of Ifa thus, to a certain extent, control and direct the worship of the other gods, and in time of calamity, war, or pestilence it is their business to declare what ought to be done to make the gods propitious.

The Magba, or chief priest of Shango, has twelve assistants, who are termed, in order of authority, right-hand (*Oton*), left-hand (*Osin*), third, fourth, fifth, and so on. They reside near Kuso, the spot at which Shango is said to have descended into the earth.

The priests, besides acting as intermediaries between the gods and men, preside at all trials by ordeal, and prepare and sell charms, amulets, &c. The priests of Ifa are diviners proper, but other priests also practise divination, though not with palm-nuts and the board peculiar to Ifa. The methods are various; one, called *keke*, is a casting of lots by means of small sticks or stalks of grass, each of which represents a particular individual; another, called *gogo*, is a drawing of lots. A certain number of grass stalks, one of which is bent, are held in the band or wrapped in a piece of cloth, so that the ends only show; and each person in turn draws one, the bent stalk indicating the one who is in fault. The person of a priest is sacred, and violence offered to one is severely punished.

The office of priest is hereditary in the families of priests, but members are recruited in other modes. Seminaries for youths and girls, like those of the *kosio* of the Ewe tribes, are a regular institution, and in them applicants for the priestly office undergo a novitiate of two or three years, at the end of which they are consecrated and take a new name. The ceremony of consecration is very similar to that described in the last volume. [2]

The ordinary service of the temples is performed by the dependents of the priesthood, the affiliated youths, and the "wives" of the gods, who keep the vessels filled with water, and every fifth day sweep out the temples. In the vicinity the affiliated young people practise the religious dances and songs, and for hours together may be heard repeating chants of only two or three notes, till they work themselves up into a state of frenzy, and break out into loud shrieks and cries.

Temples are ordinarily circular huts built of clay, with conical roofs thatched with grass; the interior is usually painted with the colour sacred to the god, and the doors and shutters, and the posts which support the overhanging eaves, are carved. The temples of the chief gods are usually situated in groves of fine trees, amongst which one or two large silk-cotton trees (*Bombaces*), which seem to be regarded with veneration throughout all West Africa, tower above the rest. From the summits of the trees, or from tall bamboos, long streamers flutter in the wind and testify to the sanctity of the locality. Sometimes there is a grove only, without any temple, but more frequently the grove or avenue adjoins a shrine. These groves are regarded with superstitious reverence, and have proper names; a grove sacred to Ifa and his companion Odu is, for instance, called an Igbodu. Near the western entrance of the town of Ode Ondo is a celebrated grove or sacred avenue, to one side of which, in the adjoining bush, the sacrifice of human victims and the execution of criminals takes place. Persons approaching each other in opposite directions are not allowed to pass each other in this avenue, one of them being required to turn back and wait till the path is clear.

The temples of tutelary deities of towns are usually to be found in the central square of the town, or near the principal gate, and those of the tutelary deities of families or households near the house-door or in the yard. In shape and construction they resemble the temples of the chief gods, but those of the pro. tecting deities of households are mere miniatures, and are sometimes only small sheds, open at the ends and sides. Besides these structures, which are seen in every street, one often finds larger huts, circular in shape, thatched with grass, and larcre enough to contain a seated man. These, which might be mistaken for temples but for the fact that they contain no images, are built for the accommodation of pious persons who wish to meditate and pray. A temple is called *Ile Orisha*, "House of the Orisha."

The Yoruba gods are almost invariably represented by images in human form, which appear grotesque, but are not meant to be so, the grotesqueness being merely the result of want of skill. These images are regarded as emblems of absent gods. They themselves are not worshipped, and there is no idolatry in the proper sense of the word, though no doubt there is a tendency to confuse the symbol with the god. Likewise, through a confusion of objective and subjective connection, there is an idea that the god enters into the image to receive the sacrifices offered by his faithful followers, and to listen to their adoration and prayers. Earthen vessels receive the libations of blood -and palm-oil, while the yolks of eggs, which here, as elsewhere in West Africa, are regarded as offerings peculiarly proper to the gods, are smeared upon the posts, door-sills, and threshold. [3] In important temples, and also in the houses of kings and chiefs of high rank, a tall drum, called a *gbedu*, is kept. It is usually covered with carvings representing animals and birds, and the *phallus*. This drum is only beaten at religious fetes and public ceremonies, and a portion of the blood of the victims immolated is always sprinkled upon the symbolic carvings, upon which palm-wine, the yolks of eggs, and the feathers of sacrificed chickens are also smeared. In this case the offering is to the protecting spirit of the drum, which is that of a slave who has been sacrificed on it. This plan of supplying an artificial guardian-spirit for objects, other than natural objects, which are considered of importance, is a development of ghostworship, and on the Gold Coast such guardians are provided for the "stools" of kings and chiefs, as well as for temple and state drums.

Sacrifice is the most important part of ceremonial worship, and no god can be consulted without it, the value of the offering varying with the importance of the occasion. Besides the offerings thus made for special purposes, or on special occasions, persons who are the followers of a god-that is, those who wear his distinguishing badge and are believed to be under his protection-make, as a rule, daily offerings of small value, such as a few cowries, or a little maize-flour, palm-oil, or palm-wine.

As has already been mentioned, each god has certain animals which it is proper to sacrifice to him; to use the phraseology of the Old Testament, every god has his "clean" and his "unclean" animals. Some sacrifices are "unclean" to all the gods, as the turkey-buzzard (*gunu-gunu*), the vulture (*akala*), and the grey parrot (*ofe*). As the two former devour offal and carrion, and are, in fact, scavengers, we can see a reason for considering them unclean; but why the grey parrot should also be so considered is not evident. The natives endeavour to account for the "uncleanliness" of these birds by two popular sayings, which run as follows:--

"The turkey-buzzard was required to offer sacrifice, but he refused to do so; the vulture was required to offer sacrifice, but he also refused. When the pigeon was required to offer sacrifice, he did so."

"The grey parrot being required to offer sacrifice, refused to offer it; but the green parrot took the sacrifice and offered it. After all, the grey parrot is a citizen of Oyo (the capital of Yoruba) and the green parrot an inhabitant of the country, and yet people thoughit that the grey parrot was not wise."

As the turkey-buzzard, vulture, and grey parrot refused to offer sacrifice, they became "unclean," while the pigeon and the green parrot, which offered it, remained "clean." The latter part of the second saying appears to be ironical, for the grey parrot, in consequence of its uncleanliness, is never offered up, while the green parrot is sacrificed.

On important occasions the priest designates to the suppliants the sacrifice which he thinks necessary to induce the god to lend a favourable ear. They prostrate themselves before the shrine with cries of "*Toto, toto-huu*," an exclamation which denotes humiliation and submission, while the priest, in a long harangue, presents their petition, or case, to the god. He usually begins his address by flattering the god, dwelling upon his fame and power, and showing how his humble servitors are entirely dependent upon his good-will. Then he calls attention to the self-abasement of the god's faithful followers "So-and-so," to the value of the victim which they have brought him, and begs him to be propitious and listen to their humble prayer. He then sacrifices the victim, sprinkles some of the blood on the image, pours the remainder on the ground, [4] and places the head and entrails in a shallow earthen vessel in front of the temple.

Sacrifices are thus offered in the presence of the god, that is, before his image, which he is supposed to animate for the time being, but there is one exception to this general rule. This is, on occasions when sacrifice is made at cross-roads, or at a point where several roads meet, in order to avert an impending calamity. In this case the sacrifice is probably made to the legion of spirits, mostly evil, who are supposed to haunt the forests and uninhabited tracts of country; and the general belief is that the approaching danger is diverted from the proper road., and turned away from the community which it threatened. In reference to this practice a proverb says, "The cross-roads do not dread sacrifices." [5]

Sometimes, in response to the appeal of the priest, the god answers in a bird-like, twittering voice, first heard whispering at a little distance and then comingnearer. When this occurs, the worshippers lie prone with their faces to the ground, awe-stricken, while the priest carries on a conversation with the spirit voice, and subsequently interprets it to the auditors. This conception that a spirit-voice should be a twittering, chirping, or whistling sound is very wide-spread; as Dr. Tyler has shown, it used to exist ainong the Greeks and Romans, and it may at the present day be found aniong the Indian tribes of North America, the Zulus, and the Polynesians. [6] The spirit-voice is no doubt produced by a confederate priest, by incans of a blade of grass, or a leaf, placed between the teeth.

The image of a god which is merely tutelar to one individual is only treated with respect during the life of that individual, after which it is thrown away. Since the god is personal to the individual, and has no other purpose than to protect him, the image is only of use as a vehicle of communication between them so long as the man lives. After his death the god no longer enters or animates the image, which in consequelice loses its sacred character, and becomes an ordinary object of no value. Thus, whenever a man dies, his tutelary god, if he had one, is thrown away by the surviving members of the household, and the extraordinary belief, held by some Europeans, that the negro makes and breaks his gods at will, may probably be accounted for as a misconception of this practice.

Although human sacrifices occur amongst the Yoruba tribes, we find among them no parallel to the wholesale slaughters which take place, or rather used to take place, in Ashanti and Dahoini. The reason no doubt is, that the Yoruba kings and chiefs are not sufficiently powerful to be able to sacrifice life on a large scale; for the more powerful the monarch, the more he can afford to disregard public opinion, and since the masses supply the victims, human sacrifices are never regarded by them with favour. Whether, when Yoruba was a homogeneous and powerful state, human sacrifices were a state institution, as they were in Dahomi, we have no means of ascertaining, but all the probabilities point in that direction.

During the period that the Yorubas have been known to Europeans no large number of victims has been put to death even on the occasion of the death of a king. A king of Oyo died on April 27th, 1859, and only four men were sacrificed, but forty-two of his wives poisoned themselves in order to accompany him to the Land of the Dead. In Ondo about twenty persons were sacrificed when a king died, and there was an established procedure, one victim having to be immolated when the corpse was washed, four at different entrances to the palace, and a sixth in the market-place. On the day of the burial from eight to ten victims, with a cat, were either killed and interred with the corpse or buried alive, and during the three months which are re-

56

quired to elapse before a new king can be installed there were occasional sacrifices. In 1882 the king of Ondo entered into an engagement with the government of Lagos to put an end to human sacrifices, but he does not appear to have kept it. At the present day, amongst all the tribes, when a king or chief dies it is usual for two of his wives to commit suicide, and should no volunteers be forthcoming, two are selected and put to death. Horses are often killed and buried with their owners.

There was until very recently, and perhaps still is, an annual human sacrifice at Abeokuta, called the "basket-sacrifice," a euphemism designed to conceal the real nature of the ceremony. The victim was enclosed in a long basket, as in Dabomi, from whence perhaps the custom was adopted, thrown down from a height, and despatched by a mob armed with clubs. It was a national offering, but when times were prosperous the victim was often spared and dedicated to a god, whose temple-slave be then became. There used also to be an annual sacrifice of one human victim at Ikoradu, and a similar offering every sixth year to the god Ogun at Ikriku.

In times of great urgency human sacrifices are offered to some of the gods, for example, to Shango, Ifa, Elegba, Ogun, Olokun, and Olosa; but they are nearly always made at night, and the people are required to remain in their houses. There is none of the publicity and display which we found in Ashanti and Dahoini, and so the people escape the brutalising effect which the frequent spectacle of scenes of bloodshed must produce. Even the priests, always the last to be influenced by a change of public opinion, seem to regard human sacrifice as something to be deplored, but occasionally necessary. The victim is slaughtered almost in secret, and the sound of the temple-drunis and the mournful chants of the assistants alone inform the people of what is taking place. The natives avoid any direct reference to the subject. "The night is bad," they say. As on the Gold Coast, the victim is always decapitated in front of the image, so that the blood from the severed arteries may spurt over it. For Elegba the body is opened and the entrails placed before him in a shallow dish. The body of a man sacrificed to the sea-god Olokun is thrown into the sea, and that of a man offered to Olosa into the lagoon.

The Commissioners who were sent to the interior in 1886 to break up the camps of the belligerent tribes, succeeded in inducing the rulers of Ijesa and Ekiti to sign an enactment abolishing human sacrifices, both to the gods and at the funeral obsequies of men of rank. They endeavoured to obtain a similar undertaking from the Ifes, but here they met with some difficulty, Ife being the home of human sacrifice, and though the chief men promised to put an end to the practice, only four of the eighteen persons who composed the Ife Counoil signed the agreement. The Oni of Ife said that sacrifice was made at Ife for the whole human race, the white man not excepted; and that if the sacrifice made on his behalf were to be discontinued, his superior knowled, and the arts derived therefrom, would depart from him.

[1] "Savage Africa," p. 246.

[2] Ewe-Speaking Peoples," p. 143.

[3] A purificatory egg was used to propitiate the goddess Isis (Juvenal, Sat. vi. 518).

[4] Whence it is that tbe verb *da*, "to be poured out," has also the meaniug "to be acceptable as a sacrifice."

[5] The ancients offered sacrifices -it the cross-roads to Hekate, Goddess of Night. (Lucian, "Dialogues of the Dead," I.).

[6] "Primitive Culture," vol. i. p. 452.

Chapter Six - Egungun, Oro, Abiku, and Various Superstitions

EGUNGUN

EGUNGUN really means "bone," hence "skeleton," and Egungun himself is supposed to be a man risen from the dead. The part is acted by a man disguised in a long robe, usually made of grass, and a mask of wood, which generally represents a hideous human face, with a long pointed nose and thin lips, but sometimes the head of an animal.

Egungun appears in the streets by day or night indifferently, leaping, dancing, or walking grotesquely, and uttering loud cries. He is supposed to have returned from the land of the dead in order to ascertain what is going on in the land of the living, and his function is to carry away those persons who are troublesome to their neighbors. He may thus be considered a kind of supernatitral inquisitor who appears from time to time to inquire into the general domestic conduct of people, particularly of women, and to punish misdeeds. Although it is very well known that Egungun is only a disguised man, yet it is popularly believed that to touch him, even by accident, causes death.

A crowd always stands round watching, at a respectful distance, the gambols of an Egungun, and one of the chief amusements of the performer is to rush suddenly towards the spectators, who fly before him in every direction in great disorder, to avoid the fatal touch. To raise the hand against Egungun is punished with death, and women are forbidden, on pain of death, to laugh at him, speak disparagingly of him, or say he is not one who has risen from the dead. "May Egungun cut you in pieces," is an imprecation often heard.

Egungun is thus at the present day a sort of "bogey," or make-believe demon, whose chief business is to frighten termagants, busybodies, scandalmongers, and others, but it seems probable that originally he was regarded as the incarnation of the dead, and that the whole custom is connected with manes-worship. In June there is an annual feast for Egungun lasting seven days, during which lamentations are made for those who have died within the last few years. It is a kind of All-Souls festival, and resembles the *Affirah-*

bi festival of the Tshi tribes, described in the first volume of this series. [1] Moreover, Egungun also appears in connection with funeral ceremonies. A few days after the funeral an Egungun, accompanied by masked and disguised men, parades the streets of the town at night, and, as in the Roman *conclainatio*, calls upon the deceased loudly by name. A superstitious and half -frightened crowd follows, listening for any response that may be given to the weird cries of the Egungun. A few days later the Egungun, again accompanied by several followers, proceeds to the house in which the death took place, and brings to the relatives news of the deceased, usually that he has arrived in Deadland safely, and is quite well. In return for the good news the family set food, rum, and palm-wine in a room of the house, and inviting the Egungun to partake of it, themselves retire, for to see Egungun eating is death. When Egungun and his followers have consumed everything loud groans are heard to issue from the room, and, this being a sign that be is about to depart, the family re-enter and entrust him with messages for the deceased.

A large proportion of the slaves landed at Sierra Leone, at the beginning of the present century, from slave-ships that had been captured by British cruisers, were Yorubas, and their Christian descendants have preserved the practice of Egungun, who may often be seen performing his antics in the streets of Freetown. There, however, his disguise is less elaborate than in Yoruba country, and he appears in a long robe of cotton-print, with a piece of cloth, having apertures for the eyes, covering the face and head. Spectators soon gather round him, and though, if asked, they will tell you that it is only "play," many of them are half-doubtful, and whenever the Egungun makes a rush forward the crowd flees before him to escape his touch.

ORO

The word Oro means fierceness, tempest, or provocation, and Oro himself appears to be personified executive power.

Oro is supposed to haunt the forest in the neighbourhood of towns, and he makes his approach known by a strange, whirring, roaring noise. As soon as this is heard, all women must shut themselves up in their houses, and refrain from looking out on pain of death. The voice of Oro is produced by whirling round and round a thin strip of wood, some 21/2 inches broad, 12 inches long, and tapering at both ends, which is fastened to a stick by a long string. It is, in fact, the instrument known to English boys as the "bull-roarer," and which Mr. Andrew Lang has shown to have been used in the mysteries of Ancient Greece, Australia, New Mexico, New Zealand, and South Africa. [2] No women may see the "bullroarer" and live, and all women are obliged, under pain of death, to say that they believe Oro to be a powerful Orisha, and to act up to that belief.

In Yoruba country Oro is manipulated by the Ogboni Society. Criminals condemned to death are sometimes given to Oro, in which case they are ordinarily never seen again, but their clothes are shown entangled in the branches of a lofty tree, where Oro is said to have left them when flying through the air. In such a case Oro is said to have devoured the bodies. Sometimes, however, the headless corpse of the criminal is discovered in the forest on the outskirts of the town, but nobody is allowed to bury it. Unlike Egungun, Oro only appears on his feast-days, or, to use the native expression, when a town has an Oro-day. The voice of Oro heard from morning to night, - and all women are closely confined to their houses, while Oro himself, in a long robe hung with shells, and a wooden mask painted white, with the lips smeared with blood, parades the town with a numerous following.

In Ondo there is an annual festival to Oro, called Oro Doko. It lasts for three lunar months, and every ninth dav women are obliged to remain within their houses from daybreak till noon, while the men parade the streets, whirling the bull-roarer, dancing, singing and beating druims and killing all stray dogs and fowls, on which tbev afterwards feast. A large boulder of granite, cailed Olumo, on the summit of a hill in Abeokuta, is sacred to Oro, and no one may ascend it.

Just as Egungun is now used for social purposes, and to preserve order in private life, so is Oro used for political purposes, to preserve order in the communitv at large; yet, from. the analogy of other peoples, and from the fact that it is death for a woman to see the instrument which produces the voice of Oro, there can be no doubt that originally Oro was the spirit that presided at the celebration of male mysteries, such as are found among the Kurnai of Australia, and he has perhaps been diverted from his proper purpose by the influence of the Ogboni.

ABIKU

Abiku, abi, "that which possesses *iku*," "death"; hence, "predestined to death" is a word used to mean the spirits of children who die before reaching puberty, and also a class of evil spirits who cause children to die; a child who dies before twelve years of age being called an Abiku, and the spirit, or spirits, who caused the death being also called Abiku.

The general idea seems to be that the uninhabited tracts of country abound with numbers of evil spirits or demons, who suffer from hunger, thirst, and cold, since nobody offers sacrifice to them and they have no temples, and who are constantly endeavouring to improve their condition by entering the bodies of new-born babes. Only one Abiku can enter and dwell in the body of the same child, and, as there is great competition amongst the Abikus for such a position, an Abiku is only suffered by his companions to enter peaceably, and, in fact, to be recognised as having vested rights in a child, on condition of his promising them a share of the comforts he is about to obtain.

When an Abiku has entered a child he takes for his own use, and for the - use of his companions, the greater part of the food that the child eats, who in consequence begins to pine away and become emaciated. If an Abiku who had entered a child were not bound to supply the wants of other Abikus who had not succeeded in obtaining human tenements, no great harm would ensue, since the sustenance taken could be made sufficient both for the child and his tenant. It is the incessant demands that are made by the hungry

Abikus outside, and which the indwelling Abiku has to satisfy, that destroy the child, for the whole of his food is insufficient for their requirements. When a child is peevish and fretful it is believed that the outside Abikus are hurting him in order to make the indwelling Abiku give them more to eat; for everything done to the child is felt by his Abiku. The indwelling Abiku is thus, to a great extent, identified with the child himself, and it is possible that the whole superstition may be a corruption of the Gold Coast belief in the *sisa*. [3]

A mother who sees her child gradually wasting away without apparent cause, concludes that an Abiku has entered it, or, as the natives frequently express it, that she has given birth to an Abiku, and that it is being starved because the Abiku is stealing all its nourishment. To get rid of the indwelling Abiku, and its companions outside, the anxious mother offers a sacrifice of food; and while the Abikus are supposed to be devouring the spiritual part of the food, and to have their attention diverted, she attaches iron rings and small bells to the ankles of the child, and hangs iron chains round his neck. The jingling of the iron and the tinkling of the bells is supposed to keep the Abikus at a distance, hence the number of children that are to be seen with their feet weighed down with iron ornaments.

Sometimes the child recovers its health, and it is then believed that this procedure has been effective, and that the Abikus have been driven away. If, however, no improvement takes place, or the child grows worse, the mother endeavours to drive out the Abiku by making small incisions in the body of the child, and putting therein green peppers or spices, believing that she will thereby cause pain to the Abiku and make him depart. The poor child screams with pain, but the mother hardens her heart in the belief that the Abiku is suffering equally.

Should the child die it is, if buried at all, buried without any funeral ceremony, beyond the precincts of the town or village, in the bush; most other interments being made in the floors of the dwellinghouses. Often the corpse is simply thrown into the bush, to punish the Abiku, say the natives. Sometimes a mother, to deter the Abiku which has destroyed her child from entering the body of any other infant she may bear in the future, will beat, pound, and mutilate the little corpse, while threatening and invoking every evil upon the Abiku which has caused the calamity. The indwelling, Abiku is believed to feel the blows and wounds inflicted on the body, and to hear and be terrified by the threats and curses.

TREE-SPIRITS

Several varieties of trees are believed to be inhabited by indwelling spirits, which are not exactly gods, but answer more to the hama-dryads of Ancient Greece, or to the elves of mediaeval Europe. From the analogy of the Tshi tribes there is little doubt but that these tree-spirits were once gods of the Srahmantin type, *i.e.*, of the type of those which on the Gold Coast are believed to animate the gigantic silk-cotton trees; but now, owing to the great increase in the number of general objects of worship, which makes the propitiation of the local object a matter of less importance, they have been shorn of a great deal of their power, and pushed more into the background.

The *Ashorin* tree is, one which is inhabited by a spirit who, it is believed, would, if its attention were not diverted, drive away anyone who attempted to fell the tree. The woodman therefore places a little palm-oil on the ground as a lure, and when the spirit leaves the tree to lick up the delicacy, proceeds to cut down its late abode.

The *Apa*, frequently called the African mahogany, is inhabited by an evil spirit, and is commonly seen encircled with palm-leaves, and with an earthen pot at its foot to receive the offerings of woodcutters. It is believed to emit a phosphorescent light by night. The wood of this tree is in some demand for the construction of drums, which are hollow wooden cylinders covered with hide at one end; but before it can be out down the spirit must be propitiated by an offering, usually consisting of a fowl and some palm-oil. The *Apa* is the emblem of vengeance.

The *Iroko* (silk-cotton tree) is also inhabited by a spirit, but it is not very powerful or malicious, and when a man desires to fell such a tree it is sufficient protection for him to invoke the indwelling spirit of his own head by rubbing a little palm-oil on his forehead. The *Iroko* is used chiefly for building, whence probably it comes to be the emblem of refuge.

A proverb, referring to the risks a man runs in cutting down trees inhabited by spirits, says "The axe that cuts the tree is not afraid, but the woodman covers his head with *etu*" (a magic powder).

These customs may be compared with those of the modern Greeks of Siphinos, one of the Cyclades. Mr. Bent says [4] that when the woodcutters have to cut down a tree they suppose to be inhabited by a spirit (hamadryad), they are exceedingly careful when it falls to prostrate themselves humbly and in silence, lest the spirit should chastise them as it escapes. Cato also [5] instructs a woodcutter that, in order to escape the consequences of thinning a sacred grove, he must sacrifice a hog, and beg permission to thin the grove in order to restrain its overgrowth.

As is the case among the Ewe tribes of the Slave Coast, wizards and witches are by the Yorubas believed to hold nocturnal meetinus at the foot of trees tenanted by spirits, more especially the *Apa*, whose indwelling spirit is believed to assist them in their malpractices. Here, too, the owl again appears, but now, instead of the bird being the messenger or agent of the tree spirit, it is the wizard (*Aje*) himself, who metamorphoses himself into an owl and proceeds on the mission of death.

Witchcraft is, in the minds of the natives, the chief cause of sickness and death. They cannot, they think, attribute these evils to the gods, unless they occur in some way special to a god; as, for instance, when a man is struck by lightning, in which case the event would be attributed to Shango-or contracts small-pox, when the disease would be attributed to Shanpanna; for they are very careful to keep on good terms with the gods, by scrupulously observing their religious duties. They consequently attribute sickness and death, other than death resulting from injury or violence, to persons who have for bad purposes enlisted the services of evil spirits, that is to say, to wizards and witches. Witches are more common than wizards, and here, as elsewhere in the world, it is the oldest and most hideous of their sex who are accused of the crime.

Properly speaking, a person charged with witchcraft should be subjected to trial by ordeal, and then, if found guilty, immediately executed; but the excited populace, filled with superstitious terror, frequently acts without waiting for proof, and puts the accused to death without trial. Curiously enough, the phenomenon that so frequently occurred in England, when a belief in witchcraft was an article of faith, appears here also; and old women, accused of being witches, very often acknowledge that they are, and charge themselves with deaths which may have recently occurred in the community.

Amulets and charms (*onde*) are numerous and of various kinds. Some, like the *vo-sesao* of the Ewe tribes, are really the badges of different gods, such as the *ajude*, or iron armlet worn by hunters, who are the servitors of Ogun, god of iron, and possess no virtue of themselves, being merely useful as serving to remind the gods that the wearers are under their protection. Others are amulets proper, and are believed to derive a protecting power from the gods, from whom they have, through the agency of the priests, been obtained. Amulets are generally sewn up in leather cases; those obtained from Mohammedans, and which usually consist of a verse from the Koran, always are.

The name *onde* means "one in bondage," and is compounded of *eni*, "a person," or "one who," and *ide*, "the act of being confined." This name seems to point to the former existence of a belief similar to that now held by the Tshi-tribes in regard to the *Suhman*; namely, that the amulet is animated by an indwelling spirit, who has been confined therein by a superior power. At the present time, however, the onde cannot be regarded in any way as being animated, or an orisha. Prayers are never addressed to it, nor are offerings presented to it; it is merely the instrument or vehicle through which the god from whom it was obtained acts, and by means of which events which affect the wearer of the *onde* are brought to the knowledge of the god.

An *onde* for the protection of the person is worn on the body, being tied round the wrist, neck, or ankle, or placed in the hair. Others, for the protection of property, are fastened to houses, or tied to sticks and stumps of trees in cultivated plots of ground. In consequence of their being tied on to the person or object they protect, the word *edi*, which really means the act of tying or binding, has now the meaning of amulet or charm, just as in Ewe the word *vo-sesa* (amulet) is derived from *vo* and *sa*, to tie or bind. Another word sometimes used to express amulet is *ogun*, which, however, more properly means medicinal preparation, poison, or magical drug.

The following are some examples of current superstitions.

(1) The fur of the *choro*, a kind of hare, is a charm which protects the house from fire.

(2) A house fumigated with the bark of the *crun* tree is purged of evil spirits and, consequently, of sickness. Charcoal made from the wood of this tree is largelyused as a medicine.

(3) Powder made of the leaves of the sensitive plant, is a charm to make the inmates of a house fall into a deep sleep, and is used by thieves.

(4) To kill an *ajako*, a kind of jackal, brings misfortune upon the slayer. A proverb says, "He who kills an *ajako* will suffer for it."

(5) The flocking of vultures denotes impending war. These birds prey on the slain, and so, by an inversion of ideas, are supposed to cause war.

(6) To break the bones of the crane called *agufon* causes calamity.

(7) Whoever touches the nest of the bird called *ogarodo* will die.

The Yorubas have the same superstitions in regard to the hooded crow, porcupine, tortoise, and wild cat (ogboya) as have the Ewe tribes. [6]

By country-custom no Yoruba may milk a cow, and in consequence cows are always tended by foreignborn slaves, usually Fulani.

We find a curious example of the manner in which objective and subjective connection are confused in the expression, *Abede ni ti okira*-" Right through is the cutting of the sword-fish." This saying is used as a charm by warriors, and is believed to ensure success, because it is supposed that the sword-fish (*okira*) cuts in two all its foes in the sea.

The Yorubas have a superstition which has close points of resemblance to the "changeling" superstition of Northern Europe. It is referred to in many folk-lore tales, and the following is an example.

"There lived at Otta" (a village on the River Ibo, which is a tributary of the Ogun) "a woman named Bola, who had a male child. When the child was small the mother carried him on her back when she went to market, but when he became about nine months old she used to lay him down on a mat in her house, fasten the door, and go to market by herself. After this it always happened that when she returned from the market she found that all the food she had left in the house had disappeared. This seemed to her very strange, and she at first suspected her neighbours, but she always found the doorfastening untouched, and was unable to fathom the mystery.

"One day a neighbour came to her and said, 'I am going to the market at Orichi to-morrow morning early, and therefore must ask you to repay me the string of cowries that you sent your little boy to borrow from me.' Bola, much astonished, declared that she had borrowed no cowries from the woman, and had sent no one to her; but the neighbour persisted that Bola's child had come to her, and had borrowed a string of cowries in the name of his mother. 'Come, then,' said Bola, 'and see my child.'

"The two women went into the house where the child was sleeping on his mat. 'You see him,' said Bola, 'there he is, sleeping. Do you not see that be is yet too young, to walk? How then could he come to you? And how could he ask you for cowries, seeing that he cannot yet talk?

"The neighbour looked closely at the child, and then solemnly declared that it was really he who had come to her, but that when he came he was much

64

big er than he was now, and had the appearance of a child of about ten years of age. "When Bola, heard this she was much distressed. She could not doubt her neighbour's word, and she feared that her child must be possessed by an evil spirit. She paid the neighbour the string of cowries, and begged her to say, nothing; then, when the child's father came to the house, she told him the whole story.

"The father and mother decided to search into the mystery. The father, therefore, carefully hid himself in the house, one day while the mother and child were out. Then Bola returned to the house with the child, put him down on the mat, said to him, 'Sleep good while I go to the market,' and then went out, and fastened the door as usual.

"Scarcely had Bola gone, than the father, from his hiding-place, saw the baby stand up, and begin to grow till he became a big boy. Then he went to the calabashes where the food was kept, and was beginning to eat it, when the father came out from his hiding-place.

"Immediately the child saw his father he became a little baby again, and lay on the floor crying. He was possessed by a spirit. His mother came back, and they beat him to drive the spirit out, so that the spirit fled."

The parallel between this tale and the changeling stories of Northern Europe is close. In the latter, as in the Yoruba version, the changeling, while in the presence of its foster-mother and others, affects to be an infant, but throws off his disguise as soon as he imagines himself to be alone. See, for instance, the tale called "The Father of Eighteen Elves," in Arnason's collection of Icelandic legends. [7] The only difference-an important one, it is true-is in the genesis of the changeling. In Europe it is an elfin child, who is substituted for a stolen human child, but here it is the child himself who is possessed by an evil spirit, just as an Abiku possesses a child, though with different results.

We also find a superstition which recalls that of the were-wolf, for the hyena (*Kpelekpe*) is often supposed to be a man who assumes that disguise at night, to prey upon sheep and cattle, and, if the opportunity offers, upon human beings. Such man-hyenas are believed to be able, by means of certain howls and cries, to compel people to go out to them in the dark forest to be devoured. A similar belief is found in Abyssinia. [8] The weird "laugh" of the hyena, and its nocturnal habits, no doubt account for this superstition, just as similar causes have led to the owl being universally regarded as a bird of ill omen.

A belief in metamorphosis is universal, and is not limited to a change to an animal form, since men and women are sometimes transformed into trees, shrubs, rocks, or natural features. The shrub *buje*, whose fruit is used to stain the skin in imitation of tattoo marks, was a Yoruba belle of that name, who was metamorphosed. Her story will be found among the Tortoise Stories in the chapter on Folklore.

The Iyewa lagoon is also said to have been a woman. The story runs that a poor woman, named Iyewa, had two children, whom she had a hard struggle to support; but she used every day to go with them into the forest to gather firewood, which she carried to the town and sold for food. One day, when following her customary avocation, she and the children, finding wood scarce, wandered further into the forest than usual, and, when it was time to return, they could not find their way out. They walked hither and thither looking for the path, but in vain, and at last, tired out and tormented with thirst, they lay down to rest under a large tree. This rested their limbs, but their thirst increased, and the two children filled the forest with their lamentations, crying to their mother for water. The poor woman, half distracted, sprang to her feet, and again searched in every direction for the path and for water, but fruitlessly, and when at last she returned to her children she found them almost at the last gasp. Then, prostrating herself upon the earth, she called upon the gods to come to her assistance and save her children. The gods listened to her prayer, and Iyewa was at once changed into a lagoon, at which the children drank and so recovered; while next day they were found by neighbours who had come in search of them, and taken back to the town. When the children grew up they built a house by the side of the lagoon, which, in memory of their mother, they called Odo Iyewa, "The Lagoon of Iyewa."

[1] See "The Tshi-Speaking Peoples of the Gold Coast," p. 227.
[2] "Custom and Myth," Art. "The Bull-Roarer."
[3] Tshi-Speaking reopies of the Gold Coast," chap. xi.
[4] "The Cyclades," p. 27.
[5] "De Re Rustica," 139.
[6] "Ewe Speaking Peoples," pp. 95, 97, and 98.
[7] London, R. Bentley, 1864.
[8] Mansfield Parkyns, "Life in Abyssinia," vol. ii. p. 146.

Chapter Seven - The In-Dwelling Spirits and Souls of Men

IN the first volume of this series we found that the Tshi-speaking peoples believe that every man has dwelling in him a spirit termed a *kra*, which enters him at birth and quits him at death, and is entirely distinct from the soul, which, at the death of the body, proceeds to the Land of the Dead, and there continues the life formerly led by the man in the world. In the second volume, we found that the Ewe speaking peoples have a similar belief, the indwelling spirit being by them termed a *luwo*. The Gã-speaking tribes, situated geographically between the Tshi and Ewe tribes, have modified this belief, and they assign to each individual two indwelling spirits, called *kla*, one male and one female, the former being of a bad and the latter of a good disposition. Each *kla*, like the *kra* and the *luwo*, is a guardian-spirit, but-and this is a new departure-they give good or bad advice, and prompt good or bad actions, according to their respective dispositions. The Yorubas also have modified what appears to be the original theory of one in-dwelling and guardian-spirit, and they hold that each man has three spiritual inmates, the first of whom, *Olori*, dwells in the head, the second, *Ipin ijeun*, in the stomach, and the third, *Ipori*, in the great toe.

Olori (*Oni-ori*, owner, or lord, of the head) sometimes called *Ori* (head, faculty, talent), seems to be the spirit which answers to the *kra* or *luwo*. He is the protector, guardian, and guide. Offerings are made to him, chiefly fowls, as with the *kra* and *luwo*, and some of the blood, mixed with palm-oil, is rubbed upon the forehead. *Olori* brings good-fortune, whence the proverb, "*Olori* causes the owner of the head to prosper, and not the crab on the bank of the river." The symbol of *Olori* is half a calabash studded over with cowries.

Ipin ijeun, or *ipin ojehun* (*ipin*, share, portion; *ijeun*, act of eating, from *je ohun*, to eat; hence "he who shares in the food"), is perhaps considered the most important of the three indwelling spirits, but as he shares in all that the man eats, he has no special sacrifice offered to him. A proverb says, "There is no *orisha* like the stomach; it receives food every day." In some respects hunger (*ebi*) seems to be personified, and to be considered the agent of *Ipin ijeun*; for he is said to communicate to the man, by pinching his stomach, the desire of his principal for food. Curiously enough, *Ipin ijeun* is connected with fire-worship. There is among the Yorubas no god of fire, answering to the Ewe god *Dso*, but fire (*ina*) was probably once personified, for it is still spoken of as Abanigbele, "the Inmate." It is not clear by what process fire-worship came to be blended with that of the indwelling spirit of the stomach; but the natives explain the connection between the two by saying that fire is necessary for the preparation of food, and food is necessary to *Ipin ijeun*, therefore he takes fire under his protection, and takes care that it is not extinguished. A proverbial saying runs, "*Ipin ijeun* does not allow fire to depart from the earth." When fire could only be produced by the tedious process of rubbing together two sticks, it was no doubt important to keep one or two embers of a fire always smouldering.

Ipori, the great toe, is the least important of the three guardian spirits, and sacrifice is rarely offered to him, except when a man is about to set out on a journey; in which case he anoints the great toe with a mixture of fowl's blood and palm-oil. Waterfowl are apparently "unclean" for this purpose, for a proverb says, "A waterfowl is not fit for the worship of *Ipori*."

The ghost-man, or soul, the "vehicle of individual personal existence," is called *iwin*, or *olcan*, but the latter also means "heart." Another word is *ojiji*, or *oji*, which has the meanings of ghost, shade, or shadow. After the death of the body, the ghost-man goes to *Ipo-oku*, "the Land of the Dead" (*Ipo*, place; *oku*, dead), which is beneath the earth, and where each man does that which he has been accustomed to do, and holds the same social position as he did in the world. To enable the ghost to reach this land it is essential that he should have the prescribed funeral rites performed over him. Should they be omitted, the ghost wanders about the world, cold, hungry, and homeless, and he runs the risk of being seized by some of the evil spirits which roam about the earth in great numbers, and cast by them into *Orun-apadi*, "the unseen world of potsherds," an uncomfortable place like a pottery furnace, heaped up with charcoal and the *débris* of broken earthen pots. Funeral rites cannot, of course, be performed at the moment that breath leaves the body, but as an earnest of their intention to perform them, and to prevent the evil spirits from seizing the ghost, the relations at once offer a sacrifice to propitiate them; and when the corpse is buried, a fowl, called *Adire-iranna*, [1] "the fowl that buys the road," that is, "that opens a right of way," is sacrificed.

A comparison of the beliefs held by uncivilised peoples concerning the dead, seems to show that when in a very low state of culture, the ghost, no doubt from the association of ideas, is held to remain in the vicinity of the grave in which the body was interred; and that the notion of a distinct and separate place of abode for the dead, or Deadland, is only formed when a higher degree of culture is attained. The first belief often lingers on alongside the second, as in England, where the churchyard is considered to be the most likely place in which to see a ghost; and a similar survival among the Yorubas, or a trace of the former belief, is found in the word *iboji*, "a grave," which means, literally, "place of the ghost" (*ibi*, place; *oji*, ghost).

The dead often return to earth, and are born again in the families to which they belonged in their former life. In fact, one might say that they always return, since every mother sends for a *babalawo* to tell her what ancestral ghost has animated her new-born child, and the *babalawo* always tells her which it is. As the births at least equal in number the deaths, and the process of being re-born is supposed to have gone on "from the beginning," logically there ought to be few, if any, departed souls in Deadland; but the natives do not critically examine such questions as this, and they imagine Deadland to be thickly populated, and at the same time every now-born child, or almost every one, to be a re-born ghost. As was mentioned in the volume on the Ewe-speaking peoples, this belief in metempsychosis is probably a result of a confusion between the *ñoli*, or disembodied *luko* (in Tshi, the *sisa*), and the soul or ghostman, and we may here endeavour to sketch in the origin and probable development of these vaxious beliefs.

There can be little reasonable doubt but that the notion that man possesses a soul, an entity that continues his personality after death, arose from dreams, after the manner shown by Mr. Herbert Spencer in his "Principles of Sociology." [2] A man dreams that he is going through various adventures, but, as the evidence of his companions shows him that he has not really left their company, he comes to the conclusion that he has a second individuality, something that is himself and yet is detachable, something that can go out of him, and does so go out when he is asleep. Among the lower races all over the world, dreams are believed to be the adventures of the spiritual man while detached from the bodily man during sleep. Then, as he dreams of men whom he knows to be dead and buried, and naturally dreams of them as he was accustomed to see them, he concludes that this second individuality can and does exist, entirely independently of the body, after death, and preserves the appearance and characteristics of the bodily-man. At this stage of belief the spiritual-man, or life-phantom, and the soul, or ghost-man, are one and the same. Then, seemingly, in some cases, this second individuality becomes divided into two separate entities-one, a life-phantom, which enters the body at birth, goes out and indulges in adventures during the sleep of the body, and quits it at death; the other, a soul, or death-phantom, which, after death, continues the life. and personality of the former bodily-man.

It is possible that this conception of two different entities was brought about, partly at least, by the desire to explain the reproduction by heredity of physical characteristics. Children generally resemble their parents, and frequently reproduce their mannerisms most remarkably. As soon as the savage begins to speculate at all, he begins to think of this phenomenon, which cannot fail to arrest his attention. He can, and no doubt often does, come to the conclusion that the dead are reborn again in their descendants; he invents the doctrine of metempsychosis; but in some cases, and the negro tribes of the Gold and Slave Coasts seem to be examples, he appears to feel that this explanation is unsatisfactory. And for this reason. He still dreams of persons who are dead, whence he believes that they exist after death; and he must often dream of dead friends or relations whose characteristics have been reproduced in their children, or, since they had a common ancestor, in some collateral member of the same family. He cannot, then, in these cases, conclude that the dead have returned to earth in the persons of their descendants; for the evidence of his dreams proves to him that they still exist as ghost-men, and are in every respect as they were when alive in the world. On the other hand, the evidence of his eyes shows him that their physical peculiarities are reborn in children now living. He therefore divides the second individuality into two -from, so to say, the *kra-soul*, which was one entity, he makes two, the *kra* and the soul, the former of which inhabits the body during life, and after death enters a new human body in the same family; while the latter remains dormant, as it were, during life, but after death continues the existence of the man as an individual. The reproduction of features, mannerisms, &c., is thus accounted for by the *kra*, while the theory of the soul satisfactorily accounts for what the uncivilised man believes to be the incontestable evidence of his dreams. [3]

If this view be correct it will probably be found that several other races have divided the originally conceived entity into two. The *genius natalis* of the Romans resembled the *kra* in that it was a gnardian-spirit which entered man at birth, but, unlike the *kra*, it perished at his death. It was certainly quite separate and distinct from the soul, or ghost-man, which went to Hades. We say advisedly that the *genius natalis* dwelt in the man from birth, because to practise abstinence was "to defraud one's *genius*," and to eat, drink, and be merry was "to indulge one's *genius*," [4] thus showing that the *genius* was bound up with the man just as is the *kra*. As with the *kra*, the birthday was particularly set apart for the worship of the *genius*. Subsequently, the Romans, under the influence of dualism, just as the Gã-tribes have done, divided the *genius* into two-one of a good disposition and one of a bad.

Similar conceptions of two entities, the *kra*, or life-phantom, and the soul, or death-phantom, among the Navajo and Algonquin Indians of North America, the Karens of Burma, and the Fijians, were mentioned in the last volume, but whether these people believe in metempsychosis is uncertain; and to them we may now add the Greenlanders, [5] and the ancient Egyptians, whose *ka* appears to closely resemble the *kra*. [6] A correspondent informs me that the Irish peasants of County Mayo also believe in an entity like the *kra*. They call it the "spirit," consider it to be perfectly distinct from the soul, and liable to be stolen by the fairies during the sleep of its possessor, who, on awakening, is ignorant of his loss, but gradually fades away and dies. It is also liable to be seized by the fairies, at the moment of death of the person whose body it bas tenanted.

The Yorubas, it seems probable, have arrived at the doctrine of inetempsychosis after having passed through a phase of belief similar to that now held by the Tshi and Ewe tribes. The belief in one indwelling spirit has been changed into a belief in three indwelling spirits, and this multiplication has caused confusion. These indwelling spirits do not, at the death of the body, enter a new-born human child in the same family, so that the phenomena of heredity cannot be explained as being due to their agency; and the Yorubas have reverted to the theory of metempsychosis to account for them. The belief in the spirits called *abiku* is very probably a corruption of the former *kra*-a belief, for if a *sisa*, or disembodied *kra*, enters a human body it causes sickness and death, just as the *abiku* does.

The souls of the dead are sometimes reborn in animals, and occasionally, though but rarely, in plants. In the ideas of the natives, animals, though they differ in shape from a man, possess passions and moral qualities identical with those of the human being. Animals also possess souls which, like the souls of men, go to Deadland. Hence, as men and animals have so many characteristics in common, it does not require any great stretch of iniagination for the native to fancy that the soul may be re-born in an animal. When a plant is concerned the difference is greater; but if, as we hold, the Yoruba tribes passed through a phase of belief similar to that held by the Tshi tribes at the present day, they at one time believed that trees, shrubs, &c., and, in fact, all things not made by human hands, were animated by kras, which may account for the extension of the doctrine of metempsychosis to objects so unlike man.

The animal in which human souls are most commonly re-born is the hyena, whose half-human laugh may perhaps account for the belief. Human souls are also reborn in different kinds of monkeys, but chiefly in the solitary yellow monkey, called *oloyo*; and in these cases the human appearance and characteristics of monkeys no doubt furnishes the key to the belief.

As has been said, the re-birth of a human soul in a plant is rarely spoken of, and usually we can discover the reason for the supposed transmigration, as in the following tale:

"There were two boys, brothers, who knew and sang the popular songs of the country so well, that they were in great demand for festive occasions.

"One day they were asked to go to a festival at a neighbouring village, and their mother gave them permission.

"They went to the village, where the people were assembled to play, and they sang their songs and beat their drums so well that the people rewarded them highly. They gave to each boy a thousand cowries, and plenty to eat and drink. Then they dismissed them next morning to return home.

"On the way back the elder boy, covetous of the thousand cowries that had been given to the younger, led him off the path into the forest, and murdered him. Then he took the thousand cowries, added them to those which he already had, and returned home.

"When he came back alone, his mother asked him where was his brother. 'I left him behind on the road,' said the boy.

"The day passed, and night began to fall, and still the younger brother had not returned home. Then his mother and her neighbours went to look for the child, but they could not find him. They searched for him for many days, but found him not. They concluded that someone had carried him off to sell him.

"Some months afterwards the mother went into the forest to look for leaves for medicine, and she came to the place where the child had been murdered. The body of the boy had already decayed, and from his bones had sprung up an *olu*. [7] The *olu* was very fine and large, and when the mother saw it she cried, I Oh! what a fine *olu*.' She was stooping down to pick it, when the *olu* began singing~--

'Do not pluck me, mother,
Do not pluck me, mother,
Do not pluck me, mother,
I'm a lowly plant on the ground.
I went to the village frolic,
I went to the village frolic,
I'm a lowly plant on the ground.
I was given a thousand cowries,
I'm a lowly plant on the ground.
'Do not pluck me, mother,
Do not pluck me, mother,
Do not pluck me, mother,
I'm a lowly plant on the ground.
'My brother receivcd a thousand cowries,
My brother received a thousand cowries,
I'm a lowly plant on the ground.

71

But he slew me here for *my* cowries,
I'm a lowly plant on the ground.'

"When the mother heard the *olu* sing this she ran home, called her husband, and the two returned to the forest. When the man saw the fine *olu*, he stretched out his hand to gather it, and the *olu* sang again-
'Do not pluck me, father.'
(etc., etc., as before.)
The father went to the king of the country, and told him all that had happened. The king himself came to see the *olu*. He stooped to pick the *olu*, and the *olu*, sang-
'Do not pluck me, *oba*.' [8]
(etc., etc., as before.)
Then the king sent and ordered the elder brother to be brought before him. And when the boy beard what the *olu* had sung he confessed. The king said, 'As you took your brother and slew him, so will we now take you and slay you. Then shall the child come back to life.'

"So the elder brother was killed and the younger came back to life, as the king had said."

Here the connection between the *obu* and the dead child is obvious. It sprang from his bones, and was nourished by his decaying body, so that it might well be imagined that the soul of the child, which stayed with the remains instead of proceeding to Deadland, because no funeral rites had been performed, passed into the fungus.

As we have said, the soul, or ghost-man, after the death of the body, proceeds to Deadland, and food, drink, cowries, and property of various kinds are placed in the grave with the corpse, to equip the ghost for his new sphere; while, before the grave is filled up, a goat is sacrificed to the deceased, and wishes offered for his safe journey, such as "May you arrive in peace," "May you not stray from the right path," &c.

It would certainly appear as if the dead were cognizant of and able to influence the affairs of the living, for it is usual for offerings and prayers to be made to them from time to time; and sometimes the skull of the deceased is exhumed and placed in a small temple, where offerings are made to it. Before taking the field for war, too, offerings are made at the graves of warriors of renown, and their assistance in the coming campaign is supplicated. Yet a proverb says, "As grass cannot grow in the sky, so the dead cannot look out of the grave into the street," from which it might be inferred that the dead are not cognizant of what is taking place in the world, or at all events do not know what is occurring till it is made known to them through the medium of sacrifice, and several folk-lore tales point to this conclusion as well. The following is an example:

A woman, an inhabitant of an inland town, who was going to the sea-shore to make salt by boiling sea-water, a common industry, and who expected to be away from home for some time, gave, on the eve of her departure, and in the presence of witnesses, a necklace of valuable beads to a neighbour, to be kept for her during her absence. The neighbour, a woman with two boys, accepted the trust, and, for safe custody, made a hole in the mud wall of her house, into which she put the necklace, and then closed the aperture with fresh mud, which she smoothed down to conform with the wall. Unfortunately the woman died before the owner of the necklace returned, and the secret of its hiding-place died with her, so that when the owner at last came back and claimed her property, it could not be found.

The woman made a great commotion about the loss. She would not believe the two children when they declared that they had not seen or even heard of the necklace, and she took them before the chief, and charged them with theft. The chief heard the case. The fact of the necklace having been entrusted to the deceased woman was proved; the boys declared that they knew nothing of it, but the chief held that they were responsible. If they had not stolen it they knew where it was. They must restore it or pay the value. Such was the chief's decision, and in order to compel the elder boy to make restitution, he caused the younger to be "put in log," and threatened to sell him if the missing property were not recovered within a certain time.

In this dilemma the elder boy, knowing that human agency could avail him nought, souoght assistance from the gods. He went to the head priest of the *babalawos* at the town of Ife, unfolded his tale, and begged for aid. The priest consulted the god Ifa, and Ifa replied that in order to know what his mother had done with the necklace, the boy must go to Deadland and ask her. The child said he was ready to go, but how was he to get there? Then the oracle instructed him as follows:--

"Let the child in search of his mother
Offer an ebon sheep to the dead,
When night falls in the grove of Ifa.
Let the child in search of his mother
Sprinkle his eyes with lustral water,
Then shall the dead be visible to him.
Let the child in search of his mother
Follow the shadows' noiseless footsteps,
So shall he reach the land of the dead."

The *babalawo* instructed the boy that, upon making the necessary, payment, the door-keeper of Deadland would allow him to enter, and he warned him not to touch any of the dead, or else he would not be able to return to earth. Supposing all went well, and he returned again to the grove of Ifa, from which he would set forth, he must again sprinkle his eyes with the water of purification, to restore their natural properties to them, and then offer a living sacrifice to Ifa in gratitude for his assistance.

The boy followed out his instructions to the letter, and arrived safely in Deadland, where he saw his mother seated near a spring, around which many other dead people were walking slowly or sitting down. He approached his mother and called to her, whereupon she rose and came to him, saying, "What brings thee here my son? Why hast thou come to the land of the dead?" The boy replied, "The chief has put my brother in log, and will sell him as a slave if the necklace which was given thee to keep is not restored to our neighbour. Ifa the Great, the Unveiler of Futurity, the Governor of Lots, has permitted me to come here to ask thee where it is. Say, where is it?" His mother told him that it was hidden in the wall, explaining to him how to find the exact spot, and the boy was so overjoyed that, forgetting the warning of the priest, he tried to embrace her; but she stepped back hastily and avoided him, saying, "Touch me not my son, or the road to the world will be closed to thee for ever. Go home and effect thy brother's deliverance, and make frequent offerings to me, for I need them much." Then she turned away and went and sat down again by the spring.

The boy came back to the world, and found himself in the grove of Ifa, where he sprinkled his eyes as directed, and offered sacrifices. Then he went to the chief and told him what had occurred; so the necklace was found and his brother released. The two boys were not neglectful of their mother's last request. Everyfifth day they placed fresh offerings on her grave, and kept it always plentifully supplied with fresh water.

In this story the dead mother evidently did not know what was going on in the world above, for she had to ask her son why he came, yet she was able to reap the advantage of the offerings made on her grave.

Ordinarily, people do not have to undertake the dangerous journey to Deadland in order to consult the dead. When the members of a family wish to know how a departed relative is faring below, they apply to a priest, who takes a young child, bathes his face in water of purification, which, it may be remarked, is prepared with edible snails aud shea-butter, offers a sacrifice in a new earthen vessel, digs a hole in the earth in a sacred grove in the middle of the night, and bids the child look into it. Through the magical properties of the lustral water, the child, on looking down into the hole, is able to see into Deadland, and so can tell the priest all that is going on there. When the priest has obtained the information he requires, he again bathes the child's eyes with the water of purification, which causes him instantly to lose all recollection of what he has seen and heard. The priest thus remains the sole possessor of the information, and be is able to tell the family that employed him what he pleases.

[1] *Adire*, a fowl; *iranna*, the act of purchasing a right of way, from *ra*, to buy, and *ona*, road,
[2] Pp. 148 *et seq.*
[3] The Awunas, an Eastern Ewe tribe, say that the lower jaw is the only part of the body which a child derives from its mother, all the rest being derived from the. ancestral luwoo (the Tshi *kra*). The father furnishes nothing.
[4] See *Tibullus*, Bohn's Edition, note 1, p. 126.

[5] Cranz, *Grönland*, p. 251.
[6] S. Laing, *Human Origins*, p. 119.
[7] Olu, an edible fungus.
[8] *Oba*, king.

Chapter Eight - Measurements of Time

THE Yorubas reckon time by moons and weeks. A moon, or month, is the period of time between one new moon and the next, and, as is the case with all peoples who count by lunar months, the day commences at sunset, that is at the hour at which a new moon would ordinarily be first perceived.

The custom of measuring time by lunar months appears to be common to all uncivilised peoples, the regular recurrence of the moon at fixed intervals of time affording a natural and easy mode of computing its lapse. The measurement of time by weeks, that is, by sub-divisions of the lunar month, seems, in the present state of our knowledge of the modes of measuring time amongst the lower races, to be rather exceptional; but the subject is one that has been much neglected by travellers, and there is but little information from which a conclusion may be drawn.

The Tshi-tribes of the Gold Coast have (as was stated in the first volume of this series) a seven-day week, or, to be more correct, they have divided the lunar month, which is approximately twenty-nine and a-half days long, into four parts, each of seven days and about nine hours. Hence, as before said, [1] each week commences at a different hour of the day, the reason of this arrangement being that twenty-nine and a-half will not divide exactly into halves and quarters. The first day of the first week of the lunar month commences when the new moon is first seen; the first day of the second week commences some nine hours later, and so on.

The Gã-tribes have an exactly similar mode of measuring time, but their names for the days of the week are not the same as those used by the Tshi-tribes. They are-

1st.	*Dsu.*
2nd.	*Dsu-fo.*
3rd.	*Fso.*
4th.	*So.*
5th.	*So-ha.*
6th.	*Ho.*
7th.	*Ho-gba.*

which, it will be seen, seem to consist of three pairs and an odd one, the third day.

The Yoruba week consists of five days, and six of them are supposed to make a lunar month; bnt, as a matter of fact, since the first day of the first week always commences with the appearance of the now moon, the month really contains five weeks of five days' duration, and one of four day-, and a-half, approximately. The Benin-tribes to the cast are said to have a similar method, and the Yoruba-tribes have perhaps borrowed the five-day week from them.

The Tsbi and Gã-tribes thus add a few hours to each seven-day week in order to make four of these periods coincident with a lunar month, and the Yorubatribes deduct about twelve hours from the last five-day week in order to make six of these periods agree with a lunar month. The reason is obvious. Twenty-nine and a-half will not divide, and the nearest numbers that will are twenty-eight and thirty. The Tshi and Gã-tribes have adopted the former as the integer to be divided, and consequently have had to add some hours, while the Yorubas have adopted the latter and have had to deduct.

We have said that to divide the lunar month into weeks appears to be exceptional among the lower races, but we have some examples. The Ahantas, who inhabit the western portion of the Gold Coast, divide the lunar month into three periods, two of ten days' duration, and the third lasting till the next new moon appears, that is, for about nine days and a-half. The Sofalese of East Africa must have had the same system, for De Faria says that they divided the month into three weeks of ten days each, and that the first day of the first week was the festival of the new moon. [2]

When a people has progressed sufficiently far in astronomical knowledge to have adopted the solar year as a measurement of time, the month, for the reason that an exact number of lunar months will not make up a solar year, becomes a civil period or calendar month, and is arbitrarily fixed at a certain number of days, or some months are made of one length and some of another. When this occurs, and the month is disconnected from the moon and its phases, it seems that the week-which was properly a sub-division of the lunar month, and was no doubt designed to mark the chief phases of the moon-also becomes a civil period, and is a sub-division of the civil month. The ancient Greeks had a civil month of thirty days, divided into three weeks, each of ten days; and the Javanese, before the seven-day week was adopted from the Mohammedans, had a civil week of five days. [3] The former thus resembled the Ahantas, and the latter the Yorabas, and no doubt when the Greeks and Javanese reckoned time by lunar months instead of by civil, they, like the Ahantas and Yorubas, struck off the superfluous hours from the last sub-division of the month.

The names of the days of the Yoruba week are as follows:--

1. *Ako-ojo.* First day.
2. *Ojo-awo.* Day of the Secret (sacred to Ifa).
3. *Ojo-Ogun.* Ogun's Day.
4. *Ojo-Shango.* Shango's Day.
5. *Ojo-Obatala.* Obatala's Day.

Ako-ojo is a Sabbath, or day of general rest. It is considered unlucky, and no business of importance is ever undertaken on it. On this day all the temples are swept out, and water, for the use of the gods, is brought in procession. Each of the other days is a day of rest for the followers of the god to which it is dedicated, and for them only, *Ojo-Shango* being the Sabbath of the worshippers of the thunder-god, and *Ojo-Ogun* for those of the god of iron, but *Ako-Ojo* is a day of rest for all. A holy day is called *Ose* (*se*, to disallow), and because each holy day recurs weekly,

Ose has come also to mean the week of five days, or the period intervening between two holy days.

There appears to be good reason for supposing that the institution of a general day of rest, not only among the Yorubas, but in most, if not all, other cases, may be referred to moon-worship. The first day of the first week of the lunar month is reckoned from the appearance of the new moon, and was, we think, a moon-festival, or holy day sacred to the moon. This holy day, before the invention of weeks, recurred monthly, but after the lunar month was subdivided, it recurred weekly, and was held on the first day of the week. The Mendis of the *hinterland* of Sierra Leone, who reckon time bv lunar months, but have not divided the month into weeks, hold a new-moon festival, and abstain from all work on the day of the new moon, alleging that if they infringed this rule corn and rice would grow red, the new moon being a "day of blood." From this we may perhaps infer that it was at one time customary to offer human sacrifices to the new moon. The Bechuanas of South Africa keep the twenty-four hours, from the evening on which the new moon appears till the next evening, as a day of rest, and refrain from going to their gardens. [4] These are examples of monthly moon. Sabbaths observed by peoples who do not reckon by weeks.

The first day of the Tshi week, which in the first week of the lunar month is the day of the new moon, is called *Dyo-da* (*Adjwo-da*) "Day of Rest," and is a general day of rest. The other days of the week are, as with the Yorubas, days of rest also, but only for particular persons, and not for the whole community. The second day, *Bna-da*, is sacred to the sea-gods, and is the fisherman's Sabbath; while the fifth day, *Fi-da*, is the Sabbath of agriculturists. The first clay of the Gã week, which is also a general day of rest, is called *Dsu*, "Purification." *Dsu* seems also to have been used as a title of the moon, for we find silver called *dsu-etci*, "moon substance," or "moon stone," and in the cognate Ewe and Yoruba languages, the moon is called *Dsu-nu* and *Oshu* respectively. Owing to later and more anthropomorphic conceptions of gods moon-worship appears to have died out, though all these peoples salute the now moon respectfully when it is first seen, and a Tshi epithet of the moon is *bohsun*, "Sacred," or "God." When, however, moon-worship flourished, the moon would undoubtedly have been a general god, worshipped by the community as a whole; and hence the day dedicated to the moon is a general day of rest, and not, like the other days of the week, a day of rest for certain persons only. In the case of the Tshi and Gã tribes, we thus have examples of a weekly moon-Sabbath, observed by peoples who reckon by weeks.

It seems probable that the Jewish Sabbath was also connected primarily with moon-worship, and at first was a monthly festival like that of the Mendis and Bechuanas, but became a weekly festival after the Jews adopted the seven-day week from the Babylonians. In the historical books of the Old Testament, viz., Joshua, Judges, the books of Samuel, and the first book of Kings, there is not only no mention of a weekly Sabbath, which is first spoken of in II. Kings iv. 23, but there is evidence that such an institution was unknown; for the encompassing of Jericho, [5] the events described in I. Samuel xxix. and xxx., and Solomon's fourteen-day feast, [6] would all have violated the injunction, "Let no man go out of his place on the seventh day," [7] had there been a weekly Sabbath. But while the weekly Sabbath is not mentioned we find a new moon festival spoken of. [8] In all the later works, written after contact with the Babylonians, we find frequent mention of Sabbaths, but nearly always in connection with new moons, and the day of the new moon was itself observed as a day of rest, or Sabbath. [9] That the Jewish Sabbath should come to be called the seventh day, though originally the day of the new moon, and consequently the first day of the limar month, can be readily understood. When a holy day recurs every seventh day, the day on which it is held is naturally called the seventh day. Thus the day of the Yoruba Sabbath, which recurs every fifth day, is called the fifth day of the week, though the meaning of the name *ako-ojo* is first day.

That, on a day dedicated to a god, no manner of work should be done by the followers of that god, seems to be a custom of universal application. Abstention from work was doubtless considered a mode of showing respect for the god, and Since a want of respect for a god would be commonly believed to be followed by some punishment inflicted by him, the proposition that it is unlucky to do work on a holy day naturally becomes accepted. Thus the Yorubas consider it unlucky for anyone to work on the *alo-ojo*, or general Sabbath, and for the followers of the gods to whom the other days are dedicated to work on those days. For a follower of a god to violate the day sacred to that god is as serious offence among the Tshi, Gã, Ewe, and Yoruba tribes, as to break the Sabbath was among the Jews; and, as with the Jews, is punished with death, the notion being that if the honour of the god is not vindicated by his followers, they will stiffer for the neglect. The Sabbath-breaker is, in fact, killed by the other worshippers of the god from motives of self -protection. On the Gold Coast any fisherman who dared to put to sea on *Bua-da*, the fisherman's Sabbath, would inevitably, in the old days, have been put to death. Persons who were not fisherinen, and who consequently were not followers of the gods of the sea, might do as they pleased; for in that spirit of toleration which always accompanies polytheism, they were held to be only accountable to their own gods.

Among the Yoruba tribes markets are held weekly, that is, every fifth day. The day of the market varies in different townships, but it is never held on the *alo-oljo*. From this custom of holding markets every fifth day has arisen another mode of computing time, namely, by periods of seventeen days, called *eta-di-ogun* (three less than twenty). This is the outcome of the *Esu* societies, or subscription clubs, which are general amongst the Yoruba tribes, and still exist, under the same name, among the negroes of Yoruba descent in the Bahamas. The members of an *Elsu* society meet every fifth market-day and pay their subscriptions, each member in turn taking the whole sum contributed at a meeting. The first and fifth market-days are counted in, and thus the number seventeen is obtained. For instance, supposing the second day of a month to be -a market-day, the second market would fall on the 6th, the third on the 10th, the fourth on the 14th, and the fifth on the 18th. The fifth market-day, on which the members meet and pay their subscriptions, is counted again as the first of the next series. These clubs or societies are so common that the seventeen-day period has become a kind of auxiliary measure of time.

Osan is day, in contradistinction to *oru*, night. The division of the day and night into hours is not known, but the day is divided into the following periods, viz., *kutu-kutu*, early morning; *owuro*, morning, forenoon; *gangan*, or *osan gangan* (*gangan*, upright, perpendicular), noon; *iji-she kpale* (shadow-lengthening), afternoon; and *ashale*, or *ashewale*, evening, twilight. The night is divided into periods of cock-crowing, as *akuko-shiwaju* (the cock opening the way), first cock-crowing; *ada-ji*, or *ada-jiwa*, time of second cock-crowing; and *ofere*, or *ofe*, the time of cock-crowing just before sunrise.

Odun means "Year," and, like the word *ose*, "week," also an annual festival which is celebrated in October, and the period of time intervening between two such festivals. The year is divided into seasons *Ewo-erun*, dry season; *Ewo-oye*, season of the Harmattan wind; and *Ewo-ajo*, rainy season. The last is again divided into *ako-ro*, first rains, and *aro-kuro*, last rains, or little rainy season.

[1] "Tshi-speaking Peoples of the Gold Coast" pp. 215, 216.
[2] Astley's Collection, vol. iii., p. 397.
[3] Raffles' "History of Java," vol. i. p. 475.
[4] Livingstone, "Travels in Sonth Africa," p. 235.
[5] Joshua vi. 13-16. t
[6] I. Kings viii. 65.
[7] Exodus xvi. 29.
[8] Samuel xx. 5, 18, 24, 26.
[9] Ezekiel xlvi. 1; Amos viii. 5. See also Nehemiah x. 23; Isaiah i. 13; 1xvi, 23; Ezekiel x1v. 17; Hosea ii. 11.

Chapter Nine - Ceremonies at Birth, Marriage, and Death

I. AT BIRTH.

THE ceremonies at birth resemble in the main those observed by the Ewe-speaking peoples, and described in the last volume, but there are a few changes which may be attributed to increased priestly influence.

As soon as the pangs of labour seize a woman a priestess takes charge of her, and has the care of her and the child; while, soon after the child is born, a *babalawo* appears on the scene to ascertain what ancestral soul has been re-born in the infant. As soon as this important point is decided, the parents are informed that the child must conform in all respects to the manner of life of the ancestor who now animates it; and if, as often happens, they profess ignorance, the *babalawo* supplies the necessary knowledge.

Seven days after birth, if the child be a girl, nine days, if it be a boy, the *babalawo* comes again and offers a sacrifice of a cock and a hen to Ifa and the Olori, or indwelling spirit of the child's head; after which, in order to prevent Elegba from interfering with the mother and child, the entrails of the two sacrifices are sprinkled with palm-wine, taken outside the house, and placed before his image.

Then follows a ceremony which appears to be one of purification, for here, as among the Tshi and Ewe tribes, the mother and child are considered unclean, as are women during the *menses*. The water which is always in the earthen vessels placed before the images of the gods, is brought to the house and thrown up on the thatched roof, and as it drips down from the eaves the mother and child pass three times through the falling drops. The *babalawo* next makes a water of purification with which he bathes the child's head, he repeats three times the name by which the infant is to be known, and then holds him in his arms so that his feet touch the ground. After these ceremonies have been duly performed the fare is extinguished and the embers carried away; the house is then carefully swept out, live coals are brought, and a fresh fire lighted. We thus appear to have a combination of a purification by water and a purification by fire. After the new fire has been kindled, another sacrifice of fowls is made to Ifa, and the proceedings are at an end.

II. AT MARRIAGE.

When a man desires to marry a girl, his parents visit her parents and make proposals of marriage. If they are accepted, the suitor sends a present of native cloths and kola-nuts, and, after consulting a *babalawo*, a day is appointed for the wedding.

The marriage-feast is held at the house of the parents of the bridegroom, and the bride is conducted there by a procession of women, who sing an epithalamium. The bride is put to bed by a female of the bridegroom's family, who remains concealed in the apartment till the bridegroom has joined the bride; after which she secures the "tokens of virginity," and, coming out of the room, displays them to the assembled company. She then carries them to the house of the parents of the bride, who never attend a daughter's wedding-feast, and next morning they are hung on the fence for the edification of the public. In this abstention of the bride's parents from the feasting and merrymaking, we perhaps find a lingering survival from marriage by capture. The producer of the "tokens" is selected from the family of the bridegroom to ensure that there is no deception, because the husband's family has no interest in falsifying the facts, while the wife's family has; but virginity in a bride is only of paramount importance when the girl has been betrothed in childhood. The marriage-feast is continued on the next day.

It is not uncommon for newly-married couples to visit some celebrated shrine and offer sacrifice together, a practice which, together with the fixing of the wedding-day by a *babalawo*, shows an increasing disposition on the part of the priests to control or interfere with matters which are purely social and quite beyond the domain of religion.

III. AT DEATH.

The ceremonies observed by the Yoruba tribes at death chiefly differ from those of the Ewe tribes in the addition of various religious observances.

When the breath has departed from the body there is the usual outburst of exaggerated grief, with loud cries, lamentations, and frenzied gestures, and the eldest son of the deceased, or the brother, if there be no son, at once sends for a *babalawo*, to ascertain if the deceased died from natural causes, or through the machinations of witches. The *babalawo*, after sacrificing. a fowl, inquires at the oracle of Ifa, by means of the board and sixteen palm-nuts; and if it affirms that the death was caused by witchcraft, further inquiry is made to know if any other member of the family is threatened with a like fate, and also if the soul of the deceased is in danger of further molestation from the evil spirits who have been influenced by the malpractices of the sorcerers. Should the oracle declare that the soul of the deceased is in danger, a sheep or goat is sacrificed, and the carcass, sprinkled with palm-oil, is carried outside the town, and deposited at a spot where two or more paths meet, which has the effect of causing the evil spirits to disperse in as many directions as there are paths. The *babalawo* then prepares the usual water of purification with shea-butter and edible snails, and dipping into the vessel a palm-branch, sacred to Ifa, sprinkles the corpse, the room, and the spectators with the fluid. At the same time he invokes the soul of the deceased to leave the house as soon as the funeral rites have been performed, and proceed peacefully to its destination, wishing it a safe journey. He says, "May the road be open to you. May nothing evil meet you on the way. May you find the road good when you go in peace."

After these preliminaries, the corpse is washedwith rum, or a decoction of aromatic herbs, and attired in its best clothes. The thumbs and the great toes are then tied tocether. If the deceased be a man the head is shaved, and the hair, carefully wrapped up in a piece of -white cotton, is buried in the earth behind the house. If a woman, the exposed parts of the body are stained with a decoction of the bark of a tree, which gives a reddish hue to the skin. Finally, the corpse is wrapped up in many native cloths, and placed on a mat at the door of the room.

In the meantime a death-feast has been prepared, and now commences, while outside the house a continual beating of drunis is kept up, together with frequent discharges of musketry, fired in honour of the deceased. The feast, at which intoxicants are used lavishly, soon becomes a veritable orgie, in which, however, the chief mourners, that is, the widows and daughters of the deceased, take no part; for as soon as they have performed the last offices for the dead, and have placed the corpse at the door, they are shut up in an adjacent apartment, where they are compelled by custom to remain during, the three days that a corpse invariably lies in state. While thus immured they are forbidden to wash, and usage requires them to refuse all food, at least for the first twenty-four hours, after which they usually allow themselves to be persuaded to take some nourishment.

The conventional mourning is the business of the women of the household, who, while the men are feasting utter loud lamentations in the room in which they are confined; and, in consequence of this, the epithet *isokun*, "a mourner," is often applied to a female child; a male, on the other hand, being sometimes called *iwale*, "a digger," i.e., of a grave. A father might thus say that he had begotten two mourners and a digger, meanin, two daughters and a son. Female friends usually come to join in the lamentations, the conventional character of which is referred to in the proverb "A mourner mourns and goes on her way (without afterthought), but one who ponders over sad memories mourns without ceasing." There are also professional mourners, chosen for their poetical turn of expression, whose services are engaged in well-to-do households, and who often contrive to work up the real mourners to a condition of frenzied grief. A professional mourner sings in a sad tone, which rises and falls in -a modulated wail; "He is gone, the lion of a man. He was not a sapling, or a bush, to be torn out of the earth, but a tree-a tree to brave the hurricane; a, spreading tree, under which the hearts of his family could rest in peace," &c. &c. while the widows and daughters lament their lonely and unprotected state, somewhat as follows:--

"I go to the market; it is crowded. There are many people there, but he is not among them. I wait, but he comes not. Ah me! I am alone.

"Never more shall I see him. It is over; he is gone. I shall see him no more. Ah me! I am alone. "I go into the street. The people pass, but he is not there. Night falls, but he comes not. Ah me! I am alone.

"Alas! I am alone. Alone in the day-alone in the darkness of the night. Alas! my father (or husband) is dead. Who will take care of me?"

On the afternoon of the third day of the wake the body is placed on some boards, or on a door taken off its hinges, covered with a rich native cloth, and borne at a trot through the streets by the men. Male friends and relations accompany the bier, singing the praises of the deceased, and throwing handfuls of cowries among the spectators. This procession returns to the house towards evening, and the corpse is then interred in a grave that has been dug in the earthen floor, and which is so contrived that the head of the deceased may project beyond the line of the outer wall of the house. Most of the cloths in which the corpse is wrapped are taken off, and the body, covered with grass mats so that no earth may soil it, is carefully lowered into the grave. A coffin is sometimes used, but not often. Food, rum, and cowries are placed in the grave, the body is sprinkled with the blood of a he-goat, sacrificed to propitiate Elegba, a few more cowries are thrown in, and then the grave is filled up amid the wishes for a safe and pleasant journey to which we have already referred. [1]

When the grave is full the earth is smoothed down, and sometimes, when many articles of value have been entombed, the surface is moistened with water to make the earth settle down, and slaves and dependents are made to sleep on it night after night, for the double purpose of protecting it and of obliterating all trace of its exact position. After the interment, the feast, which had been suspended since the afternoon, recom;inences; and drinking and shouting. amid the firing of muskets, the jangle of native gongs, and the dull thud of the drums, continues all night.

Next day, about noon, the male relations walk out in a body, and wander about the town, as if looking for the deceased, and chanting "We look for our father, and cannot find him"; to which the bystanders reply, "He has gone to his house." Returning from this, the mourners carry on the feast till the evening of the next day, when the bones of the victims that have been sacrificed, and those of the fowls and sheep that have been eaten by the guests, are collected and placed over the grave. All the articles which the deceased had in daily use, such as his pipe, the mat on which he slept, the plate or vessel froin which he ate, his calabashes, and other things of sinall value, are carried out into the bush and burned.

Up to this point the soul of the deceased is supposed to have been lingering near his old home, and this destruction of his property is intended to signify to the soul that he must now depart, since there is no longer anything belonging to him. In former tinics the destruction of property was carried much further than at present. Usually the apartment in which the deceased is buried is closed, and never used again, and sometimes the roof is removed. Rich families even abandon the house altogether, and it is said to have been usual in days bygone to burn it. The deceased is called three times by name, and adjured to depart, and no longer haunt the dwellings of the living. After this invitation to be gone, the fowl, called *adire-iranna*, is sacrificed, which, besides securing a right-of-way for the soul, is supposed also to guide it. The feathers. of the fowl are scattered around the house, and the bird itself carried out to a bush-road, where it is cooked and eaten. The road on which the adire-iranna is eaten must be outside the town and lead away from it, for though the natives believe that Deadland is under the earth, they think that it is necessary to eat the fowl on a road leading into the bush, in order to place it in a proper position for commencing its office of guide to the soul.

The relations may not wash themselves or comb their hair during the funeral ceremonies, in consequence of which the rites themselves are sometimes styled *Ofo*, "Unwashed." On the last day they shave their heads, and then pay visits of thanks to those who assisted at the funeral. The time of mourning after the conclusion of these ceremonies varies with the rank and influence of the deceased, and with the locality. Three months is usually considered long enough, but a commemoration-feast is often held a year after the death. During the period of mourning the hair must be left unkempt as it grows, and women must cover the head with a cloth of a dark blue colour. A widow remains shut up for forty days, and may not wash her cloths during that time.

It is considered the greatest disgrace to a family not to be able to hold the proper ceremonies at the death of one of their number, a notion which is comprehensible when we remember how much the welfare of the soul of the deceased is supposed to depend upon their performance. Hence families not unfrequently reduce themselves almost to beggary in order to carry them out, or pawn or sell their children to raise the money necessary. Sometimes, too, they conceal the death and bide the body until they have secured the requisite means, and such concealments have been known to last for three or four months. The body is treated with resinous herbs so that it becomes desiccated, and while it remains in the house, the soul is believed to abide in its old home, where food and drink are provided for it, till such time as the proper ceremonies can be held, and it be legitimately ushered on its new career.

A common imprecation is *Oku igbe*, "Bush death," meaning "May you die in the bush, alone and uncared for, and so receive no funeral-rites." A proverb contrasts a man's duties to his relations with those towards the members of any secret society to which he may belong, such as the *Ogboni*, and insists upon the importance of the former, because of the obligation upon his relations to bury him.

It runs, "A man must honestly perform all the duties incumbent on relationship, even though he may belong to a secret society. When he has attended to the society he must attend to his relations, because it is they who must bury him when he dies."

This desire for a very ceremonial funeral, which owes its origin to the native beliefs concerning the soul, lasts long after the negro has been transplanted across the Atlantic, and has lost all notion of its motive. In most of the West India Islands, but particularly in the Bahamas, where the bulk of the negro population is of Yoruba descent, a grand funeral is considered the greatest desideratum. To attain this end, burial-societies are formed, the members of which pay subscriptions all their lives in order to be buried with pomp. Every member of such a society is bound to attend the funeral of another member, and the result is a procession of men in uniforms, more or less grotesque, with banners and various insignia. Often a band heads the *cortége*, and many a man occupies his last moments in giving directions as to the manner in which the funeral is to take place."

When a man dies abroad his family make the greatest exertions to obtain something belonging to him, over which the usual rites may be held. Hair or nailparings are most sought for this purpose, but, if these cannot be obtained, a portion of the clothing worn by the deceased suffices. Such remains are called *eta*, a word which seems to mean something brought from one place to another. Through a confusion between objective and subjective connection, these relics, which bring the deceased to mind, are suppposed to bring the soul to the place where the funeral ceremonies are held.

[1] Chapter Seven.
[2] See the following, which appeared in the *Nassau Guardian*, New Providence, Bahamas, 10th January, 1891:--
    NOTICE.
    All to whom it may concern.
    Dear Friends,
    Mr. A- B- had been a member of the Grant's Town Friendly Society for many years, and was financial up to July, 1891. During his illness he requested that the Band of the said Society play the Dead March in Saul wben be died. The message came to the President from Mr. J- C. S-, ex-President of the Society. The Band, in conjunction with the members, was summoned to meet at the Society's Hall, in uniform, at 3 o'clock sharp. The members were present waiting on the Band, but only the Bandmaster and three other members came, and they had to leave the Hall, proceeding to the house of the deceased without the Band.
    I am sorry to say that if the Band cannot attend on members (deceased) of the Society to which they belong, it will be best for the Society to do away with the Band. If members are paying, their monies towards Band Funds, they should have the use of the Band when required.
    (Signed) Z. C-.
    Pres. G. T. F. Society.

Chapter Ten - Systems of Government

THE monarchical system of government prevails in most of the Yoruba tribes, but the king is merely the nominal head of the state, and has little real power, which remains in the hands of the chiefs and elders, without whom the king can do nothing. In each state there is a council of elders, without whose concurrence the king can issue no edict, and a two-thirds' majority of which is required for any new law. The sovereignty of a state is hereditary in one family, but the individual who is to succeed to the office is selected by the council. The monarchy is thus elective, though only men of a certain blood-descent are qualified for election. The council of elders, besides electing a king, controls his actions, and, should he show any disposition to make himself independent of it, invites him to "go to sleep," by sending him a present of parrots' eggs. The king is never allowed to see foreigners without some members of the council being present, and all his actions are closely watched. The king and the council make laws and decide all ordinary affairs, but, should any question of vital importance to the nation arise, the whole people is assembled for its discussion and settlement; and every individual, regardless of position, is allowed to express his opinion. The emblem of royalty is a conical head-dress of beads, from which hang long strings of beads, so arranged as to conceal the face of the wearer. An epithet applied to kings is *alaiye,* "Owner of the World."

The election of a king is preceded by a curious ceremony. When the council has selected the individual who is to succeed to the throne, the chiefs and elders proceed to his house on the day fixed for the coronation, seize him suddenly, and forcibly convey him to the palace, where they flog him vigorously with light whips. If he should cry out during the punishment, or show any signs of pain, he is at once rejected as unworthy, and the council makes a new choice; but if he bear himself bravely, without flinching, he is forthwith crowned. This ordeal appears to be designed to test the candidate's capacity for endurance, and his powers of self-restraint and concealment of thought. An exactly similar practice is found among the Timnis of Sierra Leone, who, on the day of election, scoff at and beat the new king while dragging him from his own house to the residence of his predecessor; where, if he has withstood the ordeal, the royal ornaments are put on him.

The chief officers of state are the *Bashorun,* or prime minister, the chief adviser of the king, who has the title of *Emewa (Eni-mo-ewa),* "He who knows the mind;" and the *Balogun (Oba-ni-ogun),* or "Chief of the Army." The military officer second in command, is styled the *Seriki.* Next to these high officials come the civil governors of towns (*Bale*), [1] each of whom exercises rule in his own domain. The *Bales* of towns correspond to the chiefs of districts among the Tshi tribes, and, as in their case, the king of the nation is the Bale of his own capital. Under the *Bales* of towns are the *Bales* of town-quarters and villages, and under these again are the *Bales* of households.

The *Bale* of a household is responsible for the preservation of order in the group of dwellings occupied by his family and dependents. He settles all minor disputes between those under his control, but if the matter involves the subordinates of another household-*Bale*, it is taken before the Bale of the town-quarter, who is responsible for peace and order within that area. If it be an ordinary "palaver," this functionary settles it, but if it be serious he must refer it to the Bale of the town. Unless the affair concerns another district also, or is of national importance, it need go no further, for in his own domain the town-*Bale* is almost independent. Persons subject to a *Bale* address him as Baha, "Father," or "Master," and he in turn calls them "my children."

In every town there is, besides the *Bale,* an *Iyalode* (*Iya-ni-ode*), "Mistress of the street," to whom all disputes between women are brought in the first instance, only those which she is unable to deal with being referred to the *Bale.* The *Iyalode* has as coadjutors an *Oton-Iyalode* (right-hand *Iyalode*) and an *Osin-Iyalode* (left-hand *lyalode*).

Members of council and town-*Bales* are *Oloris,* "chiefs," and form the aristocracy. Every *Olori* has in his service certain men termed *Onses,* who act as messengers, heralds, bailiffs, and police, and, at a pinch, as executioners. A king's *Onse* is called an *Ilari,* whence the proverb, "As no subject, however rich, may have an *Ilari,* so it is not every man who may own a palace."

Respect to kings and chiefs is shown by prostration, followed by rising and clapping the hands. Before entering the presence of a king or chief, the cloth is removed from the shoulder, over which it is usually worn, and wrapped round the waist. When a new title is conferred on a man a leaf of the akoko-tvee is given to the recipient as a sign of honour. All officers of state, members of council, and tovrn-Bales have *Ekejis,* "seconds," who assist in the management of affairs and rule in the absence of their principals. The king also has an *Ekeji,* and it is he who is usually selected to succeed him.

The foregoing applies generally to all the Yoruba tribes, but there are a few customs special to certain kingdoms, which it may be as well to note.

In Yoruba proper the king is styled the *Alafin,* and his eldest son, called the *Aremo* (*Are-ommo,* eldest child), governs conjointly with him. Under an old custom, the *Aremo* was obliged to commit suicide when the *Alafin* died; and the new king, who must be the descendant of one who had worn the crown, was chosen from another branch of the royal family. This custom was set at defiance by Adelu, who was the *Aremo* when his father died in 1860, and it was in consequence of this that the people of Ijaye rebelled. The custom has not since been observed. The tail of a white-bellied rat, called *Afe-imojo* (Rat of knowledge), is used by the *Alafin* as the symbol of royalty, and when he walks abroad he holds it to his lips.

In Yoruba the office of *Bashorun* is hereditary in one family, but the *Alafin,* in council, selects the member to fill it. He is obliged by law to reside in Oyo, the capital. Next in rank to the *Bashorun* is the *Are-Onakakanfo,* "First of the War-Captains," who can be selected from any family and live where he pleases. The council consists of twenty-two members, and is called *Isokan* (agreement, concord, or unanimity); the leader of the council is styled the *Onasokan,* "Channel to the Concord."

The *Ilaris* are the confidential advisers of the *Alafin*, and are of either sex, the females being chosen from among his wives. *Ilaris,* whether male or female, shave the head, leaving a small tuft, or tail, on the crown. In addition to these, the *Alafin* has a number of court-officials termed *Bafin,* or *Ibafin,* a word which seems to mean "Inmates of the Palace." Six of them, called the *Iwefa* (*Iwe-efa*) "the six papers," are chamberlains, the remainder are spies, or intelligence-officers, who keep the *Alafin* informed of everything that takes place. The chief chamberlain is styled the *Ona-iwefa,* and the two next in rank, the right-hand, and the left-hand. The *Tetu* is a kind of sheriff's officer, who arrests for debt. When making an arrest it is essential that he should pronounce the word ogiisa, "a shield." The *Ologbo* is the keeper of the ancient traditions, which he teaches to his pupils, and on certain occasions recites in public.

According to court etiquette, no word having more than one distinct meaning — and such words are very numerous in the Yoruba language — may be used when addressing the *Alafin,* if one of its meanings, no matter how inapplicable to the subject in hand, be unbecoming. At audiences the speaker addresses a eunuch, who repeats the words to the chief female *Ilari*, and she conveys what is said to the *Alafin.* No native may appear before the *Alufin* in any costume other than an ordinary native cloth, and the *Alafin* always speaks of his subjects as his "slaves."

Among the Egbas the *Alake* of Abeokuta is nominally the ruler of the whole collection of villages within the walls; but each village or township has its own *Bale,* who is virtually independent, and except in times of national danger or emergency the *Alake* is really only the *Bale* of his own township. The *Bales* of all the townships, except Ake, are elected by their own subjects, but the Bale of Ake, who becomes the *Alake,* is elected by the council, and the election must be confirmed by all the other Bales of townships. The *Bashorun* is here the chief of the council, and there is an official called the *Akpena,* whose duty it is to summon the council together. In Abeokuta the Ogbonis are the real rulers.

Ibadan. The *Bale* of the town of Ibadan exercises the kingly office, but next to him, and almost equal in rank and power, is the *Balogun,* who sits with the *Bale* to judge important cases. Two members of council, called the right-hand and the left-hand *Bale,* are the *Bale*'s chief advisers.

Jebu. The Council of the *Awujale* is called the *eketa-odi* (? third rampart), and his confidential adviser the *Agunri* ("One who brings to light"). The *Awujale* is surrounded by a great deal of mystery. Until recently his face might not be seen, even by his own subjects, and if circumstances obliged him to communicate with them, he did so through a screen which concealed him from view. Now, though his face may be seen, it is usual to conceal his body; and at audiences a cloth is held before him so as to hide him from the neck downwards, and is raised so as to cover him altogether whenever he coughs, sneezes, expectorates, or takes snuff. The face is partially concealed by the conical cap with hanging strings of beads. It is death for anyone, except members of the court, to sit or stand behind the *Awujale.* The umbrella is the symbol of sovereignty in Jebu, and it is a capital offence for a subject to use one.

88

Among all the tribes the revenues of the kings, chiefs, and *bales* of towns are derived from tribute paid by the dependent villages, and from duties levied upon goods and native productions brought into the towns. These duties are collected by officers called *Oni-bodes,* and are levied at custom-houses (*bode*) at the gates of towns, and also on the roads at the frontiers. The names of two frontier towns of the ancient kingdom of Yoruba, where duties used to be paid, but which have long since been destroyed, are still preserved in the proverbial saying, "Let the marvel stop at Ibese and not proceed to Ijanna." There is no fixed tariff and traders are largely at the mercy of the *Oni-bodes,* whose cupidity is only kept within reasonable limits through fear of complaint being made to the *Bale* of the town. A considerable proportion of the duties levied, nearly always in kind, sticks to their fingers.

Every *Bale* who adjudicates upon a case receives a hearing-fee, and both plaintiff and defendant usually see him in private before the case comes on, and seek to influence his decision by presents. These bribes, however, do not really produce much effect, for every case is tried in public, and no manifest injustice, or verdict given against the weight of evidence, would be allowed to pass unobjected to by the people, who would resent it in their own future interests. In cases in which the evidence for and against is nicely balanced, the decision is no doubt affected by the longest purse.

Sticks of office are used by all men in authority, and are received with the same ceremony and respect as among the Ewe tribes. [2] A royal stick-bearer is called an *Olokpaja-oba,* "Bearer of the king's stick." The Ogbonis have their own staff, or stick, ox a special pattern, called *edan.*

Public notices are proclaimed by a public crier, or herald, styled an *Akede* (*ke ode,* to exclaim in the street), who prefaces his announcement by cries of *"Atoto-o! Atoto-o!"* "Noise! noise!"

In time of war, all the men capable of bearing arms take the field under the military chiefs. They are accompanied by a number of women, who cook the food and carry the baggage, so that the size of a war-camp affords no fair indication of the number of combatants it contains. As tlie Yoruba tribes did not come into commimication with Europeans till about 1815, when the export slave-trade from Lagos and Badagry commenced, they have not been supplied with muskets for so long a period as the Tshi, Ga, and Ewe tribes, who have been accustomed to use firearms for such a length of time that all other kinds of weapons, except knives and swords, have long disappeared. Muskets do not seem to have come into common use among the Yoruba tribes until after 1860, and their old weapons are not quite displaced even yet. They used bows, with strings of raw hide, and cross-bows (*akatanpo*); and besides the arrows carried by each man in a quiver, there was a reserve of these missiles contained in a large receptacle called an *ada-gun-ile-apo,* and which was placed on the ground to supply the archers during a battle. Bowmen used an iron guard for the fingers, styled *ifarun* (*fa-orun:* "pull bow"), and a leather guard (*ijasan*) was worn on the left arm to protect it from the bowstring. Poisoned arrows seem to have been commonly used.

One of the ingredients of the poison was the leaf of a shrub called *ewe-ina* (*ewe,* leaf, *ina,* fire), "fire-plant," and so named because the hairs with which the leaf is covered raise blisters on the skin. Another poison is said to have been obtained by pounding up the large red ants.

Before the introduction of firearms an army was ordinarily divided into cavalry (*elesin*), archers (*olofa,* or *tafatafa*), and foot-soldiers (*elese*). Notwithstanding the enormous numbers of cavalry mentioned by Dalzel, the Yorubas do not seem ever to have had any considerable force of horsemen, and horses, which are not very common, are usually monopolised by men of rank. The bulk of the army was composed of foot-soldiers, who carried spears, swords, or axes, and shields. Another infantry weapon was called *gamu-gamu,* and was something like an old-fashioned halberd. Shirts of mail and breast-plates were sometimes seen, and appear to have been obtained from the natives of the Western Soudan. Each contingent fought under its own *Kakanfo* (captain), and the *Balogun* was the *Are-kakanfo,* or generalissimo. Under each *Kakanfo,* or leader of a local contingent, were three inferior officers, styled *Are alasa, Otin alasa,* and *Osin alasa,* the chief, right-hand, and left-hand *alasa.*

In battle the main bodies oppose each other at a distance of half-a-mile or a mile, and are covered by detachments from the various contingents. These detachments skirmish, keeping at the extreme range of their muskets, and hold their ground without advancing, till their ammunition is exhausted, when they retire for more. The skirmishers are never reinforced from the main body, and ordinarily the day passes without any decisive result. Sometimes, however, when the skirmishers of one army retire to replenish their ammunition, the opposing army advances, in which case the other endeavours to draw it into an ambuscade, which manoeuvre, if successful, is supposed to be decisive. There is no general plan of action; each contingent acts more or less independently, and the nominal commander of the army rarely knows bow many men he has under his command.

[1] Bale = Oba ile, literally, "chief of the house, or town."
[2] "Ewe-Speaking Peoples." pp. 178 to 181.

Chapter Eleven - Laws and Customs

(1) Laws relating to Kinship and Inheritance.

WE find a great change from the customs of the other tribal groups of this family of nations, in the Yoruba manner of tracing descent and blood-relationship; descent and consanguinity being no longer reckoned exclusively in the female line, with succession to chiefdom, office, and property from brother to brother, and then to sister's son; but in the male line, as far as succession to dignities is concerned, and on both sides of the house for blood-descent. The Yoruba family — using the word family as meaning a group of persons who are united by ties of blood — is thus quite a different organisation to that which we found existing among the Tshi and Ewe tribes, where a family consists solely of persons who are connected by uterine ties, and in which, as two persons of the same blood may not marry, the father is never related by blood to his children, and is not considered as belonging to the family. In the Tshi and Ewe tribes the clan-name is the test of blood-relationship, and as property follows the laws of blood-descent, it ensues that property never goes out of the clan; for, with descent in the female line, a family is only a small circle of persons, all of whom bear the same clan name, within the larger circle of the clan itself.

Among the Yoruba tribes the blood-tie between father and child has been recognised, and the result of this recognition has been the inevitable downfall of the clan-system, which is only possible so long as descent is traced solely on one side of the house, as may be readily shown. Since two persons of the same clan-name may, under the clan-system, never marry, it follows that husband and wife must be of different clans. Let us say that one is a Dog and the other a Leopard. The clan-name is extended to all who are of the same blood; therefore, directly the blood-relationship between father and child comes to be acknowledged, the children of such a pair as we have supposed, instead of being, as heretofore, simply Leopards, would be Dog-Leopards, and would belong to two clans. They in their turn might marry with persons similarly belonging to two clans, say Cat-Snakes, and the off-springs of these unions would belong to four clans. The clan-system thus becomes altogether unworkable, because, as the number of clans is limited and cannot be added to, if the clan name still remained the test of blood-relationship and a bar to marriage, the result in a few generations would be that no marriages would be possible. Consequently the clan-name ceases to be the test of consanguinity, kinship is traced in some other way, and the clan-system disappears; or, as appears to have been occasionally the case, descent is boldly transferred into the male line, and marriage in the father's clan is prohibited, that of the mother being ignored. The Yorubas have adopted what appears to have been the usual course, and blood-relationship is now traced both on the father's and on the mother's side, as far as it can be remembered, and marriage within the known circle of consanguinity is forbidden.

When we consider the extraordinary vitality the system of descents through mothers possesses, so long as it is undisturbed by foreign influence, it seems probable that the acknowledgment of a father's blood-relationship to his children was brought about by the intercourse of the northern Yorubas with the Mohammedan tribes of the interior. That the Yorubas formerly had the system of female descents is shown by an ancient proverb, which says, "The *esuo* (gazelle), claiming relationship with the *ekulu* (a large antelope), says his mother was the daughter of an *ekulu*." If the male system of descents had been in vogue when this proverb was invented, the esuo would have been made to say that his father was the son of an *ekulu.* Moreover, in spite of the legal succession from father to sons, children by different mothers, but the same father, are by many natives still scarcely considered true blood-relations.

It is no doubt in consequence of the change from kinship in the female line to kinship on both sides of the house that the family has become, to a certain extent, disintegrated. On the Gold Coast, where the uterine family is the only one known, the family is collectively responsible for the crimes or injuries to person or property committed by any of its members, and each member is liable for a proportion of the compensation to be paid. Similarly, each member of the family is entitled to a share of the compensation received for injury to the person or property of one of the members. The head of the family can, if the necessity should arise, pawn, and in some cases sell, a junior member; while, on the other hand, the junior members have a right to be fed and clothed by the head of the family. Among the Yoruba tribes there is no collective responsibility in a family, except that parents are responsible for crimes committed by their children; the head of the family cannot pawn the younger members, and the latter cannot claim, as a matter of right, to be supported by him.

When a man dies his sons divide all his property between them. The daughters have no inheritance in their father's house, but they divide between them the property of their mother, for here, as with the Tshi, Ga, and Ewe tribes, the property of a wife is always separate and distinct from that of her husband. If a man have no sons his property falls to his br6thers, or, if he have no brothers, to his sisters. From these laws of inheritance there is no departure, and a man cannot disinherit a legal heir. A man can, within certain limits, give away property during his lifetime, provided it is purely personal, and not family property; but he cannot make a will, or any arrangement for its disposal after his death. Succession to property entails the obligation of defraying the debts of the deceased.

The terms used to express relationship are very indefinite, and can be, and are, used not only to relations, but even to strangers, as terms of address.

Baba, father, is used not only to the actual father, but to uncles on both sides of the house, and to men to whom it is desired to show respect, provided that they are of an age which would admit of their being fathers to the speaker. *Iya,* mother, is also used to women of the generation next above the speaker, when it is desired to show respect. *Ara* is a term used to relations of the same age as the speaker, and is applied to brothers, sisters, and male and female cousins. It is of no gender, and to express brother and male cousin, or sister and female cousin, it is necessary to add *okonri,* man or male, or, *obiri,* woman, or female. Usually the relative age of the speaker to the person addressed is expressed by the word *egbon,* elder, senior, or *aburo,* younger. Thus, *egbon ara okonri* would mean an elder brother or male cousin, properly, an elder male relative of the same generation as the speaker. *Omo,* child, which also has no gender, and requires the qualifying words *okonri* or *obiri* to be placed after it when exactitude is necessary, is used to relations of the generation next below the speaker, that is to say, to sons, daughters, nephews, nieces, and children of cousins. It is also used as a term of address to domestic slaves. Grandfather, *baba-la* (*baba-nla*, great-father) is used to grandfathers and great-uncles, and *iya-la* (*iya-nla*, great-mother) to mothers and great-aunts. Grandchild is *omo-omo* (child-child), or *omo-loju* (front-child).

The foregoing are the terms commonly used. Of course it is quite possible to construct compound terms to express exactly the degree of relationship, just as we can, if required, say, "father's sister," instead of "aunt," or "father's brother's son," instead of "cousin"; but the Yorubas do not make use of such terms any more than we do. Thus "aunt" could be expressed by *ara-biri ti baba, or ara-biri ti iya,* "relative of same age, female, of the father," or "relative of same age, female, of the mother," but *iya* is always used instead.

It will thus be seen that the terms used to express relationships are applied to five groups or classes: —

(1) The grade of the speaker's grand-parents.
(2) The grade of the speaker's parents.
(3) The grade of the speaker.
(4) The grade of the speaker's children.
(5) The grade of the speaker's grand-children.

This system is what the late Mr. Morgan termed the classificatory system of relationships, and, on the assumption that the terms used were from their very inception devised to express actual degrees of blood-relationship, he endeavoured to show that the human family had passed through regular stages of peculiar types of marriage. [1] But it appears certain that these terms were originally terms of address to persons of different grades, being probably designed to show the relative positions of the individuals composing the group or community, and had nothing whatever to do with consanguinity. As the Yorubas trace descent on both sides of the house, they might, assuming that the terms did imply blood-relationship, very properly use the term for a male of the generation next above the speaker, either to the father's brother or to the mother's brother, just as we ourselves say "uncle"; but the Tshi and Ga tribes, who trace descent solely through the mother, equally have this classificatory system, and also use one and the same term to relations on the father's side or on the mother's. That is to say, these tribes use these terms indifferently to blood-relations and to persons who, according to their system of consanguinity, are not relations at all; and the conclusion is that the terms of the classificatory system do not primarily imply consanguinity, whatever they may come to mean afterwards.

The lack of precision in the terms used by the Yorubas to express relationships would at first sight seem to show that they, and other races who follow the classificatory system, do not lay much stress upon blood-relationship, the more especially as they use the same terms both to *consanguinei* and to per-

93

sons who are not akin; but the fact appears to be that the classificatory system is at first always combined with the clan-system, and as the clan-name is the test of consanguinity, precision in terms of address is not really of much moment. After the clan-system breaks down, and the clan-name ceases to be the test, some other mode of denoting blood-relationship becomes necessary; and it seems probable that it is under the stress of these new circumstances that the terms formerly applied to whole grades are narrowed in their application to the household circle, and new descriptive terms, such as uncle, nephew, and cousin, are invented to define the remoter degrees of con-sanguinity. In this connection we may note that among the younger generations of the Yorubas the word *egbon,* which really only means "elder," is rapidly coming into use as a term of address to the father's brother and the mother's brother, and so is acquiring the meaning of "uncle"; but the old people still cling to the classificatory term *baba.*

Investigation shows that the Yoruba terms used to express "father" and "mother" have no reference to fatherhood or motherhood. *Baba* now means lord, master, great personage, or father. It appears to be derived from a root having the meanings of violence, strength, and power, and so, in the classificatory system, might well be applied to the grade of men who would be the hunters and warriors of the community. *Oba,* king, lord, or master, is from the same root. In Ewe we found that the word *fofo* (father) meant "maintainor," a designation which also might well be applied to the men who defended the group from foes and provided the food.

Iya means mistress, lady, or mother, or any vessel used to contain food, such as as an earthen pot, basin, or calabash. It is derived from a root meaning primarily to feed, whence to nourish, cherish, and be glad. *Iya* would thus mean "the feeder," and, in a community, would equally apply to young women, who were mothers suckling their children, and to those who were not, since it is the business of the young women to prepare the food. Similarly we found in Ewe that *da,* or *dada,* mother, was derived from *da,* to cook. Ara appears to mean "one of the same kind," hence "companion, co-habitant," &c. *Omo,* child, is literally "suckling," and comes from *mo,* or *mu,* to drink, suck, as does *omo,* or *omu,* breast, udder.

(2) Marriage Laws and Customs

Wives are married by purchase, the amount paid for a bride varying with the rank of the father and also with that of the husband, for a man of wealth and position is expected to give more for a wife than one lower in the social scale. The poorest always pay a small sum for their wives, so as to give the union the title of a marriage, and distinguish it from concubinage. The amount paid for a wife is regarded as a compensation to her parents for the loss of her services in the household, and the transaction is not in any sense the purchase of a chattel.

By marriage a man acquires the services of his wife in domestic affairs and an exclusive right to her embraces. That is, she may not have intercourse with other men without his knowledge and consent, but there is no objection to his waiving his right in favour of some other person, and men sometimes lend their wives to their guests or friends, though more frequently their concubines, for in a household there are both wives and concubines, the latter usually being slaves. Bach wife has her own house, situated in the "compound" of the husband, and her own slaves and dependants. The wife first married is the head wife, and is charged with the preservation of order among the women. She is styled *Iyale* (*Iya ile*), "Mistress of the house." The junior wives are called Iyawo (*Iya owo*), "Trade-wives," or "Wives of commerce," probably because they sell in the markets.

Girls of the better classes are almost always betrothed when mere chjldren, frequently when infants, the husband *in futuro* being sometimes a grown man and sometimes a boy. Betrothal confers upon the male all the rights of marriage except consummation, which takes place shortly after the girl arrives at puberty. Since the early age of betrothal makes ante-betrothal unchastity a physical impossibility, the absence of the primitix when the marriage is consummated proves that the girl has been unchaste after betrothal, that is, after the husband in futuro had acquired an exclusive right to her person, and consequently he has a right to repudiate her. In such a case he may dismiss her, sending a few broken cowries to her mother, and the girl's family must return the amount paid for her, and the value of all presents made; but it is more usual to effect some compromise.

In this custom of infant or child-betrothals we probably find the key to that curious regard for ante-nuptial chastity found not only among the tribes of the Gold and Slave Coasts, but also among many other uncivilised peoples in different parts of the world; and which certainly cannot be attributed to any feeling of delicacy, since husbands lend their wives without the least compunction, and often merely as a sign of friendliness. In West Africa virginity in a bride is not valued *per se*, but because it is a proof that the betrothed has not infringed the exclusive marital privileges of the husband *in futuro;* and non-virginity in a bride is only a valid ground for repudiation when the girl has been betrothed af a tender age, for unbetrothed girls can bestow their favours upon whom they please. Thus, no man who marries a girl without early betrothal feels aggrieved if she should prove not to be a virgin, for until she is married or betrothed she is perfectly free, and mistress of her own actions.

Girls of the lower classes, who are seldom betrothed, can lead any life they choose without incurring reproach, and without affecting their future prospects of marriage; but girls of the upper classes, who are almost always betrothed, must be chaste. If, then, the great majority of girls were betrothed in childhood, it may readily be conceived that a notion might be formed that a bride ought to be a virgin, and be made of general application quite independent of betrothals. At present, the feeling of annoyance, which a Yoruba bridegroom experiences when he finds that his bride has been unchaste, is not due to jealousy or sentiment, but to a sense of injury, because his rights acquired by betrothal have been trespassed upon; but no doubt, in course of time, the sentimental grievance would be produced. Whether this feeling ever extends to the lowest classes is uncertain, but at all events it has scarcely yet done so in Europe.

A great deal of evidence might be adduced to show that the custom of child-betrothal leads to virginity being expected in a bride, and its absence being regarded as a just ground for repudiation. In New Zealand, girls were occasionally betrothed in infancy, and in that case had to be chaste; but girls not betrothed in childhood were allowed, on growing up, to bestow their favours on whom they pleased. [2] In Fiji and Samoa it appears that only the daughters of chiefs were expected to be virgins when married, and it was only the daughters of chiefs who were betrothed early in life. [3] The Mosquito Indians betroth children, and if, when the marriage takes place, the girl is not a virgin, the match is broken off. Similar evidence is forthcoming in regard to the Bagas, Fulas, Timnis, and Fans, in Africa, the Kirghese and Ouzbeks, in Asia, and many others.

Parents cannot force a daughter to marry a suitor who is distasteful to her, but they can prevent a girl from marrying a man of whom they do not approve, and if she should misbehave with him they can shut her up and chastise her. If, however, she runs off with him, they usually take no further trouble. Most girls have lovers in secret.

Children are usually suckled for three years, and during the period of lactation the wife must not cohabit with her husband.

When a man dies his wives and concubines are divided among his sons, whose wives and concubines they then become; but no son is allowed to take his own mother. Formerly the Levirate was in force, and when an elder brother died the brother next in order of age married the *iyale,* or head wife, and so in succession from brother to brother. There was no obligation to marry the subordinate wives of a deceased elder brother, and they usually devolved upon the legal heirs. If the deceased were childless, the son first born of the new union of the younger brother with the widow was named after the deceased, and was considered to fill the place of the son; he did not, however, as among the Jews, succeed to the property to the exclusion of the Levir — his inheritance jay solely in the house of his actual father. At the present time a widow-*iyale* is not obliged to jnarry her deceased husband's brother, but she does not, on the other hand, become the wife of one of the husband's sons, as do the subordinate wives. She usually goes to live with the relatives of her late husband; and, should she contract a second marriage with some man other than her brother-in-law, the second husband has to repay to the relatives of the first the amount that the latter paid for his wife.

Adultery can only be committed with a married woman. Adultery in a wife is punishable by death or divorce, but as a rule the injured husband beats his erring wife, and recovers damages (*oji*) from the adulterer. In extreme cases, where the husband is a man of rank, and discovers the couple in the fact, they are sometimes both put to death.

If a husband should divorce his wife for adultery he can claim the restitution of the money he paid for her, but not if he sends her away for any other cause. When a wife is divorced or put away, no matter for what cause, the husband retains any children she may have borne him; but if a child be too young to leave the mother, it does not come to the father till ten or twelve years of age. We see here a great change from the customs of the Tshi tribes, among whom, under every circumstance of divorce or separation, the mother retains her children, though she is liable to her husband for a certain sum to compensate him for what he has paid for their maintenance. There, children belonged exclusively to the mother, but here they belong to the father, and the innovation is undoubtedly due to the alteration in the system of descents.

When a husband systematically neglects his wife and refuses to perform his marital duties, she can call upon her family to assemble and hold a palaver; when, if the husband promises to amend his ways, he is given an opportunity of retrieving his character. If, after all, there is no improvement, or if he refuses to treat his wife properly, she is then at liberty to leave him, and sometimes, if he be of inferior rank, the indignant family tie him up and flog him.

The daughters of kings or chiefs can live with or marry whom they please, and change their partners as often as they please. Women of the royal blood of Ashanti and Dahomi have or had the same liberty, which is perhaps a survival from a former sexual freedom once enjoyed by all women, dating, if McLennan's theory be correct, from the time when the position and influence of women was enhanced by the scarcity of the individual, but now only lingering in the case of women in the highest rank, who would be just those most likely to retain the privilege longest.

Marriage is forbidden in the same blood; and, as descent is traced on both sides of the house, it is consequently forbidden both in the father's and mother's families, as far as relationship can be traced. This, however, is not far, as there is no longer the clan-name, which, as long as descent was traced on only one side of the house, remained the test of kinship to perpetuity, and a people who do not write have no means of recording genealogies. As a rule relationship does not seem to be traced further than second-cousins, and the prohibitive degrees of marriage are for a man, mother, aunt, sister, daughter, niece, cousin, and second-cousin. In consequence of descent being traced on both sides, half-brother cannot marry half-sister; but on the Gold Coast such marriages are permitted, provided the pair have not the aaine mother. Relationship by aflfinity has not yet been invented, and a man may marry two or more sisters, aunt, and niece, and even mother and daughter, but the last unions do not often occur.

(3) Land Laws

Land belongs to the community collectively, and is vested in the chief, who distributes it amongst households and families as required. No man can be dispossessed of land once allotted to him, and the usufruct descends to his children, but the land cannot be sold. The land being more than sufficient for all requirements, this commimal system presents no difficulties, as practically everybody can have as much as he wishes to cultivate. When land goes out of cultivation, and is allowed to be overgrown with bush or forest, it reverts to the community.

On the Gold Coast private property in land is not recognised, and the sale or purchase of land is unknown, except when Europeans or Anglicised natives desire to acquire landed property, in which case the consent of the community as a whole to the transaction has to be obtained. Among the Yoruba tribes, however, the notion that land, and not merely its usufruct, may be the property of the individual, instead of the community, is beginning to appear, for a chief can sell or give away land. No one but a chief can sell land; it is one of the prerogatives of chieftainship; but the land sold or given away must be unoccupied wasteland, the usufruct of which has not been yielded to any member of the community.

When, under this custom, land is given, the ownership is not complete, for though the individual or family which receives it can retain it and use it for ever, it cannot be disposed of to any third party. Land acquired by purchase becomes the absolute property of the purchaser. The purchase of land does not, however, carry with it the ownership of anything on the land, such as trees, crops, or houses, which still remain the property of the vendor, unless sold separately. Houses can only be sold by permission of the king or chief, and, as they are family property, the consent of the whole family has to be obtained to the transaction.

(4) Laws on Debt.

A man can be imprisoned for debt, and in every town of importance there is a debtor's prison (*lle-emu,* house of seizure), in which the *Bale* confines a debtor till the debt is discharged. There is also a custom similar to our putting a man in possession, a bailiff's officer, called *ogo,* being placed in the debtor's house to enforce payment.

A man who causes the ordinary funeral-rites to be performed over another, thereby becomes responsible for all the debts of the deceased, unless he first obtains permission from the creditors. The creditors nearly always consent upon the relations becoming collectively responsible for the discharge of the debt; but if they refuse permission, and no one is willing to accept the responsibility, the corpse is placed on a raised platform of wattles outside the town, and remains there till the debt is paid. This seldom occurs, except in the case of a stranger, as the omission to bury reflects the greatest disgrace upon the family concerned.

A man is responsible for any debts his wives may contract, but not for those contracted by his children.

(5) Criminal Laws.

When there is not sufficient evidence to establish the guilt of an accused, he has to prove his innocence by "drinking *orisha*," that is, he is subjected to an ordeal, or, in other words, human means having failed, the burden of a decision is thrown upon the gods. The draught, which is nearly always a decoction of *odum*-bark, is prepared by a priest, who thus has it in his power to make it harmless or effective. It is a powerful poison, and if not at once rejected by the stomach, as often happens, causes death, in which case the *orisha* is considered to have declared his guilt by slaying him. A guilty man does not dare to "drink *orisha*," but the innocent will submit to the ordeal without fear, and, indeed, frequently demand it in order to prove their innocence, whence it follows that it is the guiltless who ordinarily perish.

As a rule, murder, arson, and treason are punished with death. A first offence of theft is punished by flogging and a fine, a second by mutilation, and a third by death. When, however, cattle or sheep-stealing, becomes prevalent, a detected thief is put to death, as a warning to others. In such a case, the criminal, instead of being executed by the Ogboni in secret, is decapitated on Ogun's stool, by the sword-bearers of the chiefs, in some public place. Criminals who cannot pay their fines are flogged with the *kpashan*, a formidable whip made of hippopotamus hide, which draws blood at each stroke.

The relatives of a person who has been executed for crime are not entitled to bury him without paying ransom for the body, which, as in the case of a man dying in debt, is placed on a platform of sticks outside the town, until the ransom is paid.

[1] "The Systems of Consanguinity and Affinity of the Human Family" (Washington, U.S. of America, 1871).
[2] Surgeon-Major Thompson, "Story of New Zealand," pp. 176, 177.
[3] Wilkes, "U.S. Exploring Expedition," pp. 92 and 210.

Chapter Twelve - Language

(1) *Verbs.*

(1) IN Yoruba, as in Tshi, Ga, and Ewe, all simple roots are monosyllabic verbs, consisting of a consonant followed by a vowel. These, which are the primitive verbs, we will call verbs of Class I. Examples: —

Ba, to meet.   *Je,* to eat.   *Wa,* to come.
Bi, to beget.   *Mo,* to drink.   *Mi,* to breathe.
Da, to make.   *Lo,* to go.   *Wo,* to see.

(2) Verbs of Class II. are formed from Class I., by adding a liquid *n.*

Yan, to gape, yawn; from *ya,* to open, part.

(3) Verbs of Class III. are formed by using together two verbs of Class I., which are, however, separated by the objective noun. They are what we styled, in Ewe, "Separable Compound Verbs." Examples: —

Ba-ja, to fight with; from *ba,* to meet, and *ja,* to fight.
Ba-ro, to advise; from *ba,* to meet, and *ro,* to consider,
Di-mo, to enclose; from *di,* to shut, and *mo,* to stop.
Gba-la, to rescue; from *gba,* to take, and *la,* to save.
Du-ro, to desist, cease; from *du,* to strive, and *ro,* to ease.

(4) Verbs, of Class IV. are formed by joining a verb of Class I. and a noun, as:

Bila, to give way, give place; from *bi,* to shove, and *ila,* opening.
Laja, to reconcile; from *la,* to savo, and *ija,* strife.
Kpeja, to fish; from *kpe,* to kill, and *eja,* fish.
Da-meji, to divide; from *da,* to make, and *meji,* two.

(5) Further compound verbs are made by using verbs of Classes II. and III. with verbs of Class I., as: —

(a) *Da duro,* to prevent; from *da,* to make, and *duro,* to cease.
Da koja, to neglect; from *da,* to make, and *koja,* to omit.
Kpe kpada, to recall; from *kpe,* to call, and *kpada,* to come back.
(b) *Te balle,* to bend down; from *te,* to bend, and *balle,* to touch the ground.
Ba wijo, to judge from ba, to meet, and *wijo,* to complain.

(6) Verbs of another class, and which may be called "verbs of possession," are formed by placing the verb *ni,* to have, before a noun. Before the vowels a, e, o, and u, *ni* is changed euphonically to *li,* or *l'.* Thus:—

Ni'dagiri, to be alarmed; from *ni,* and *idagiri,* alarm.
Ni'beru, to fear; from *ni,* and *iberu,* fear.
Ni-kpekun, to terminate; from *ni,* and *ikpekun,* end.
Laba (*ni-aba*), to be hopeful; from *ni,* and *aba,* hope.
Laga (*ni-aga*), to be weary; from *ni,* and *aga,* weariness.
Lebi (*ni-ebi*), to be hungry; from *ni,* and *ebi,* hunger.
Lete (*ni-ete*), to intend; from *ni,* and *ete,* intention.
Lowo (*ni-owo*), to be rich; from *ni,* and *owo,* wealth.
Loyun (*ni-oyun*), to be pregnant; from *ni,* and *oyun,* pregnancy.

Conjugation of Verbs

The Infinitive is expressed by the verb in its simple form, as: —

Fe, to love.

Indicative Mood

The ordinary rules for forming tenses in the Indicative appear to be: —
(1) Present Indefinite, or Past Indefinite; the verb in its simple form.
(2) Future; by the prefix *yio,* which is commonly abbreviated to *o.*

(3) Perfect, Pluperfect, and Second Future; by placing *ti* before the verb. *Ti* is probably a contraction of *tan,* to be at an end, be done.

Present Indefinite, or Past Indefinite

Emi ofe, I love, or loved.   *Awa ofe,* We love, or loved.
Iwo fe, Thou lovest, or lovedst.   *Enyin fe,* You love, or loved.
On fe, He loves, or loved,   *Awon fe,* They love, or loved.

Future

Emi ofe, I shall love.   *Awa ofe,* We shall love.
Iwo ofe, Thou shalt love.   *Enyin ofe.* You shall love.
On ofe, He shall love.   *Awon ofe,* They shall love.

Perfect, or Pluperfect

Emi ti fe, I have, or had, loved.   *Awa ti fe,* We have, or had, loved.
Iwo ti fe, Thou hast, or hadst, loved.   *Enyin ti fe.* You have, or had, loved.
On ti fe, He has, or had, loved.   *Awon ti fe.* They have, or had loved.

Second Future

Emi oti fe, I shall have loved.   *Awa oti fe,* We shall have loved.
Iwo oti fe, Thou shalt have loved.   *Enyin oti fe.* You shall have loved.
On oti fe, He shall have loved.   *Awon oti fe,* They shall have loved.

Each of these tenses can be made more definite by prefixing *n* to the verb. This prefix is no doubt the verb niy to be. It conveys an allusion to the present time, and the notion of an action not yet completed. Thus:—

Present

Emi nfe, I am loving.   *Awa nfe,* We are loving.
&c. &c.

Future

Emi n ofe, I shall be loving.   *Awa n ofe,* We shall be loving.
&c. &c.

Perfect, or Pluperfect.

Emi ti nfe, I have, or had, been loving.   *Awa ti nfe,* We have, or had, been loving.
&c. &c.

Imperative Mood

The Imperative Mood is formed by using the verb *jeki* with the verb. *Jeki* appears to be a compound verb, having the meaning "to permit, let," and to be compounded of *je,* to be willing, and *ki,* to fulfil. The Imperative Mood is thus really expressed by a compound verb of Class V., and the objective noun, or pronoun, is, according to the rule which governs compound verbs, placed between the two verbs. Thus:—

Jeki emi fe, Let me love. *Jeki awa fe,* Let us love.
Jeki o fe Let him love. *Jeki awon fe,* Let them love.

In the second person the verb ^e is not used, as: —

Ki iwo fe, Love thou. *Ki enyin fe,* Love ye.

This is sufficiently comprehensible when we consider the meaning of *jeki. Je,* conveying the meaning of permission, is not here required, and *ki,* conveying the sense of fulfilling, remains. In the same way the "let" of the English Imperative disappears in the second person.

It should be mentioned that the letter *o* is frequently prefixed to the verb in the Imperative, and is no doubt the sign of the Future.

Subjunctive Mood

The Subjunctive Mood is expressed by means of a verb meaning to be able, can, may, which, with the verb proper, forms a compound verb of Class III.

Present

Emi le fe, I may love.   *Awa le fe,* We may love.
Iwo le fe, Thou mayest love.   *Enyin le fe,* You may love.
On le fe, He may love.   *Awon le fe,* They may love.

Past

Emi le life, I may have loved.   *Awa le ti fe,* We may have loved.

In the Ewe language we found this plan much further elaborated, Consecutive, Iterative, Intentative, and Continuative Moods being formed by using with the verb verbs conveying the notion of action in the immediate future, repeated action, intended action, and continued action respectively. [1]

Passive Voice

There are no passive verbs in Yoruba, but there is a mode of expressing the idea conveyed by a passive verb, viz.: by prefixing *a* to the active verb and placing the pronoun after the verb. A appears to be a contraction of the personal pronoun *awon,* they, here used in the sense of "one," "some one." Thus:—

Afe, to be loved.

Indicative Mood

Present Tense

Afe 'mi, I am loved (lit. one loves me).   *Afe 'wa,* We are loved.
Afe 'wo, Thou art loved.   *Afe 'nyin.* You are loved.
Afe o, He is loved.   *Afe 'won,* They are loved.

Future

A ofe mi, I shall be loved (one   *A ofe 'wa,* We shall be loved, will love me).
&c. &c.

Perfect, or Pluperfect

Ati fe 'mi, I have, or had, been loved.
Ati fe 'wa, We have, or had, been loved.

Second Future

A oti fe 'mi, I shall have been loved.
A oti fe 'wa, We shall have been loved.

Imperative Mood

Jeki afe 'mi, Let me be loved.
&c. &c.

Subjunctive Mood

Present

Ale fe 'mi, I may be loved.
Ale fe 'wa, We may be loved.

Past

Ale ti fe 'mi, I may have been loved.
Ale ti fe 'wa, We may hare been loved.

Negative Voice

As in Tshi, Ga, and Ewe, verbs are also conjugated negatively. In Yoruba this is effected by placing the negative particle ai before the verb. Thus: —

Fe, to love.   *Aife,* not to love.

Ai is compounded of *a*, not, and the substantive formative prefix i, signifying a state of being.

The negative particle of a verb of possession is *lai*, which is simply *ai*, with the verb *ni*, to be, euphonically changed to *l*, placed before it. Example: —

Lowo (*ni-owo*), to be rich, have wealth.
Lai-lowo, not to be rich (literally, "not to be to have wealth").

Many verbs denote a quality, as: —

Le, to be hard, or strong.
Du, to be black.
Mo, to be clean.

Articles

The indefinite article is expressed by *okan* (one) being placed after the noun. It is almost invariably abbreviated to *kan*.

The definite article is expressed by the demonstrative pronoun *na* (that), which is placed after the noun. Thus: —

Okonri kan, a man; literally, "one man."
Okonri na, the man; literally, "that man."

Pronouns

(1) Personal pronouns.
When used in conjunction with a verb, the personal pronouns are: —

Emi, mo, or ng, I.   *Awa*, We.
Iwo, or *o*, Thou.   *Enyin*, You.
On, or *no*, He, she, or it.   *Awon*, or *nwon*, They.

Mo, I, cannot be used with the future tenses. *Ng* is more commonly used in the future than *emi*, and is often used whenever the *n*, signifying action not yet completed, is prefixed to the verb. The independent forms of the personal pronouns are the same as those given first above. The personal pronouns are made possessive by placing *ti* before them. *Ti* is an obsolete verb, now only used in the sense of "of" or "belonging to." Thus: —

Ti emi, or *t'emi*, Mine.   *Ti awa*, or *t'awa*, Ours.
Ti iwo, or *t'iwo*, Thine.   *Ti enyin*, or *t'enyin*, Yours.
Ti on, or *t'on*, His.   *Ti awon*, or *ti'won*, Theirs.

The objective personal pronouns are: —

Mi, Me.   *Wa*, Us.
Wo, or *o*, Thee.   *Nyin*, You.

A, e, i, o, or *u.* Him, her, it.   *Won,* Them.

As will be seen, they are, with the exception of the third person singular, the nominative personal pronouns with the initial vowel omitted. The particular form to be used to express him, her, or it, is determined by the vowel-sound of the verb, a being used with a verb in which the sound of a occurs, and so on. Thus: —

a would be used with the verb *ba,* or with *kan.*
e would be used with the verb *ge.*
i would be used with the verb *si,* or with *rin.*
&c. &c.

The personal pronouns are made reflexive by adding *ti-kara* (*ti,* of, or belonging to; *ara,* body, form): —

Tikara 'mi, Myself.   *Tikara 'wa.* Ourselves.

By placing na (the same that) after a personal pronoun the particularising power is increased. It denotes the exclusion of any other person, and answers to "myself," "himself," &c.:—

Emi na, I myself.   *Awa na,* We ourselves.

(2) Relative pronouns.
There is only one, viz.: *ti,* which means who, whom, which, that.
In the nominative case the personal pronoun to which it relates is always placed after it, as *Iya ti o fe 'mi,* "the mother who loves me," literally, "the mother who she loves me." In the objective case the relative pronoun is governed by the verb, and the personal pronoun is not required. Thus *Iya ti emi fe,* "the mother whom I love."
(3) Demonstrative pronouns.
These are: —

Eyiyi, eyi, or *yi* This.   *Wonyi,* These.
Eyini, eni, ni or *na,* That.   *Wonni,* Those.

Eyiyi, eyi, or *yi,* seems to mean literally "the thing taken," and *Eyini* to be composed of *eyi,* and *eni,* one. *Won,* is an abbreviation of *awon,* they.
The adverbial demonstrative pronouns of time, place, and manner are expressed by: —

Nigbana, then, at that time (*ni,* to be; *igba,* time; *na,* that).
Nihin-yi, here, in this place (*niha,* locality, place; *eyi,* this).
Nibe-na, there, in that place (*nibe,* in or at a place; *na,* that).
Bai, thus, in this manner (is perhaps a contraction of *ba-eyi,* to meet this).

(4) Interrogative pronouns.
105

Tani, Who.
Ewo, Which.

The possessive cases are made by prefixing *ti,* "belonging to": —

Ti-tani, Ti-ewo.

Nouns.

Nouns are formed in the following ways: —
(1) From the verb, with the prefix i. This prefix seems to convey the notion of things regarded collectively, or in the abstract.

Ife, love, willingness, from *fe* to love.
Iga, height, loftiness, from *ga,* to be high, or tall.
Ika, computation, reckoning, from *ka,* to count.
Iri, a seeing, sight, from *ri,* to see.
Ilo, the act of going, from *lo,* to go.
Ita, pain, smart, from *ta,* to sting.
Idu, blackness, from *du,* to be black.
Ise, cookery, from *se,* to prepare food.
Ikpamo, the act of hiding, from *kpamo,* to hide.
Ikpare, erasure, *kpare,* to rub out.

(2) From the verb, with the prefix a. This prefix seems to limit the abstract notion of the verb and make it more concrete. Properly speaking, it seems to carry with it a suggestion of passiveness, or of individuality of things rather than of beings, but nouns expressing personality are nevertheless sometimes formed with this prefix. *A* is occasionally changed to *e.*

Afe, pleasure, a state of loving, from *fe,* to love.
Aga, a chair, elevated seat, from *ga,* to be high.
Aka, a storehouse, from *ka,* to count.
Alo, departure, from *lo,* to go.
Ata, pepper, capsicum, from *ta,* to sting.
Elo, utensil, from *lo,* to use.
Edu, cinder, from *du,* to be black.
Ela, splinter, chip, from *la,* to split, cleave.
Akpeja, fisherman, from *kpeja,* to fish.
Afonnu, boaster, from *fonnu,* to boast.

(3) From the verb, with the prefix o. This prefix is the personal pronoun *o,* he, she, or it, and conveys the idea of distinct or active personality. It gives the meaning of "one who," or "that which."

Obi, parent (one who has borne), from *bi,* to bear, beget.
Obo, nurse, from bo, to feed, maintain.

Oku, corpse, from ku, to die.
Olu, borer, gimlet (that which bores), from *lu,* to perforate.
Omi, water (that which is swallowed), from *mi,* to swallow.
Oka, ring (that which is coiled) from *ka,* to coil.
Oyun, pregnancy, from *yun,* to be pregnant.

Obiri; woman; *okonri,* man; *ofe,* parrot; *oforo,* squirrel; *ogbo,* wild cat; *okete,* bandicoot; *oloyo,* monkey; *owiwi,* owl; *omo,* child; *oba,* king.

(4) By joining a verb and a noun.

Arin-ko, chance, from *arin,* middle, midst, and *ko,* to meet.
Ajin-ta, kidnapper, from *ajin,* darkness, depth of night, and *ta,* to pass from one place to another.
Atiko, teaching, from *ati,* purpose, intention, and *ko,* to teach.
Ati-lo, departure, from *ati,* and *lo,* to go.

(5) From the verb, by reduplication. This mode is common to the other cognate languages, and is probably primitive.

(a) Regular reduplication: —

Fofo, foam, from *fo,* to float,
Nani, owner, from *ni,* to possess.
Riri, sight, from *ri,* to see.
Konrinkonrin, singer from *konrin,* to sing.
Gbenagbena, carpenter, from *gbena,* to carve, work in wood.

(b) Irregular reduplication: —

Mimu, something to be drunk, from *mu,* to drink.
Tito, sufficiency, from *to,* to be enough.
Giga, height, from *ga,* to be tall.
Jija, fight, battle, from *ja,* to fight.
Jijin, depth, from *ji,* to be deep.

(6) By prefixing the personal pronoun o (he, she, or it) to a verb of possession, as: —

Onija, antagonist, fighter, from *nija* (*ni ija*), to have strife.
Onijo, dancer, from *nijo* (*ni ijo*), to have a dance.
Onidajo, judge from *nidajo* (*ni idajo*), to have judgment.

Where the *ni* of the verb of possession has been euphonically changed to *li,* or *l,* the initial vowel of the original noun becomes the prefix of the noun of possession. Thus: —

Alafose, diviner, from *lafose* (*ni-afose*) to have divination.
Aladugbo, neighbour, from *ladugbo* (*ni-adugbo*), to have vicinity.

Elekun, mourner, from *lekwn* (*ni-ekun*), to have grief.

Elegan, slanderer, from *legan* (*ni-egan*), to have slander,

Olowo, rich man, from *lowo* (*ni-owo*), to have riches.

Olofo, loser, from *lofo* (*ni-ofo*), to have loss.

We may here show the successive changes by which the noun of possession is formed from the primitive monosyllabic verb: —

Monosyllabic Verb.	Noun.
Ru, to carry.	*Eru,* burden.
Fo, to be empty.	*Ofo,* emptiness, loss.
Da, to make.	*Ida,* act of making.

Verb of Possession.	Noun of Possession.
Leru (*ni-eru*), to have a burden.	*Eleru,* carrier.
Lofo (*ni-ofo*), to have loss.	*Olofo,* loser.
Nida, to have the making.	*Onida,* maker.

(7) By joining two nouns, as: —

Ebado, river-side, from *eba,* brink, edge, and *odo,* river, brook.

Eyinju, oye-ball, from *eyin,* egg, and *oju,* eye.

Iboji, grave, from *ibi,* place, and *oji,* shade, ghost.

Innajo, travel, from *irin,* a walk, and *ajo,* journey.

(8) By prefixing a, "not," to nouns commencing with *i.* This gives the notion of a negative quality in the abstract. Thus: —

Aife, unwillingness.   *Ailo,* inutility.

From the foregoing it will be seen that all nouns begin with a vowel, except those formed by reduplication from a verb. A few nouns may be found which appear to be exceptions to this rule, but on investigation they are found to be either: —

(a) Nouns of foreign importation, such as *gabas,* east, a Hausa word, or

(b) Nouns whose vowel-prefix has been dropped.

Of the latter, we find *boji,* a grave; *balogun,* war-chief; *baluwe,* bath-room; *bode,* custom-house; and, as we as often hear *iboji* as *boji,* and *ibalogun* as *balogun,* we conclude that *bode,* and a few other similar words, originally had the vowel-prefix.

Conversely, all words beginning with a vowel are nouns. A few words used as adjectives, adverbs, or conjunctions, appear at first sight to be exceptions, but they are all really nouns. Thus: —

Abiye, used as an adjective, "winged," really means "something possessing wings." (*Abi,* something possessing).

Abila, used to express "striped," similarly means "something possessing stripes."

Igbana, used to express "then," is really *igba* (time) and *na* (that).

Okpo lokpo, used as an adverb, "plentifully," is a reduplication of the noun *okpo,* plenty, and means literally "plenty-plenty."

Nouns are not declined. The noun in the nominative, or subjective, case is placed before the verb, and, in the objective, after it. The genitive is either expressed, as in Ewe, by position, as *ile okonri,* house (of the) man, or by means of *ti,* belonging to, as *ile ti okonri,* house of the man.

The plural is formed by placing the demonstrative pronoun *wonyi* (these), or *wonni* (those), after the noun, except when a number is used, in which case the number itself, placed after the noun, sufficiently indicates the plural.

There is, properly speaking, no gender in Yoruba, as is shown by the same word serving for he, she, or it. In the case of human beings, infants excepted, sex is indicated by the nouns *okonri* (man) and *obiri* (woman). Thus: —

Omo-konri, son.   *Omo-biri,* daughter.

In the case of all other living creatures, human infants included, it is indicated by the words *ako* (a male) and *abo* (a female), as: —

Ako-malu, bull.   *Ako-elede,* boar.
Abo-malu, cow.   *Abo-elede,* sow.

Ako and *abo,* when applied to infants, stand alone, without being joined to a noim meaning child or infant.

Adjectives

Adjectives are expressed in various ways.

(1.) By verbs, as: —

Ga, to be tall.   *Wo,* to be bent.
Mo, to be clean.   *Ro,* to be soft.
Yi, to be tough.   *Te,* to be flat.

These adjectival verbs admit of comparison, and are the only words qualifying nouns that can be compared. The comparative is formed by adding the verb ju (to surpass, be more than); and the superlative by adding the verb lo (to leave, depart), to the comparative. The comparative is thus expressed by a compound verb of Class III., and the superlative by one of Class V. Example:

Ga, to be tall.
Ga-ju, to be taller (to be tall, to surpass).
Ga-ju lo, to be tallest (to be tall, to surpass, to leave).

(2) By verbs of possession, as: —

Nikpara (*ni-ikpara*), to have harm, expresses harmful.
Nibo (*ni-ibo*), to have breadth, expresses wide.
Nikpa (*ni-ikpa*), to have strength, expresses powerful.
Laiya (*ni-aiya*), to have courage, expresses brave.

These can also be used in the negative. Thus: —

Lai-nikpara, not to have harm, expresses harmless.
Lai-nibo, not to have breadth, expresses narrow.
Lai-nikpa, not to have strength, expresses powerless.

(3) By nouns with the negative particle ai (no, not), or lai (not being), prefixed. Thus: —

Aidaba (*ai idaba*, no hope) can be used to express hopeless,
Aigbona (*at igbona*, no warmth) can be used to express cold.
Lai daju (*lai idaju*, not being certainty) can be used to express uncertain.
Laidon (*lai idon*, not being sweetness) can be used to express unpleasant.

The only adjectives proper are those formed by reduplication from a verb, ordinarily an adjectival verb. Examples: —

Wiwo, bent, crooked, from *wo,* to be bent.
Tito, straight, from *to,* to be straight.
Lile, hard, from *le,* to be hard.
Lele, pliant, from *le,* to be pliant.
Giga, high, tall, from *ga,* to be high or tall.
Dudu, black, from *du,* to be black.
Kukuru, short, from *kuru,* to be short.
Ruru, disordered, from *ru,* to stir up, mingle.
Juju, confused, from *ju,* to surpass, differ.

Adverbs

Adverbs are usually expressed by verbs, nouns, adjectives, or compounds of these, used adverbially. The word used as an adverb is always placed after the verb or objective noun. Examples: —

Awhile, for a time, by *osa,* time, interval of time.
Before (sooner), by *sin,* to lead the way.
Afterwards, by *dehin* (*de,* to reach, ehin, the back).
Late, by *pe,* to be long.
There, by *ibe,* place.
Far, by ji, to be far
Aside, apart, by *soto,* (*so,* to turn, and *to,* to go to)

110

Down, beneath, by *sale,* base, bottom.
Quite, by pe, by *pe,* to be complete.
Foremost, in front, by *tiwaju* (*ti,* to push, and *iwaju,* face, front).
Freely, by *fati,* to draw aside.
Coolly, calmly, by *shon,* to take a little at a time.
Closely, by *mo-ara,* to adhere to the body.

Verbs of possession are very commonly used adverbially. Thus: —

Across, may be expressed by *nibu* (*ni ibu*), to haye breadth.
Now may be expressed by *nigbayi* (*ni-igba-yi*), to haye this time.
Afterwards may be expressed by *nigbehin* (*ni-igba-ehin*), to have the time back.
Proudly may be expressed by *nirera* (*ni-irera*), to have pride.

There are, however, a number of words which appear to be true adverbs, but may only be adjectives used adverbially, since they are all formed by re-dupli- cation from verbs. Examples:—

Yara-yara, quickly, from *yara,* to be quick.
Tutu, entirely, from *tu,* to loosen, untie.
Jale-jale thoroughly, from *jale,* to go through.
Fule-fule, softly, from *fule,* to be soft.
Rege-rege evenly, equally, from *re,* to agree *and ge,* to be equal.
Sege-sege, unevenly, unequally, from *se,* to miss the mark, and *ge,* to be equal.
Jeje, gently, softly, from *je,* to comply.

A peculiarity is that many adverbs can only be used with a special verb or adjective. There is, of course, some connection between the adverb and the word it qualifies, which connection we can in a few cases discover by refer-ring to Tshi, Ga, or Ewe, but in others it remains obscure.

For example, take the following adverbs, each of which can only be ren-dered in English by "very," or "exceedingly."

1. *Biri'hiri,* very, can only be used with the verb *shu,* to be dark, or gloomy, as *oju-orun shu biri-biri,* "the sky is very gloomy." Here the connection is discovera-ble, as there is in Tshi a verb, *biri,* to be dark, gloomy, or black, so that *biri- biri* itself would properly mean "gloomy."

2. *Fio-fio,* very, can only be used with the verb *ga,* to be tall, or with the adjec-tive *giga,* tall. This is explained by the verbs *fro,* to ascend, climb (Tshi); *fu,* to shoot up (Gã); *fo,* to rise, raise (Ewe); and *fo,* to jump, leap (Yomba), which showthat *fio-fio,* properly means raised.

3. *Rin-rin,* very, can only be used with the verb *wuwo,* to be heavy. As it is a re-duplication of *rin,* to be saturated, to press down to the ground, the connection can be seen.

4. *Janjan,* very, can only be used of the heat of the sun. *Je,* is the sun in Ewe.

5. *Gara,* very, can only be used with reference to transparency, clearness; as *omi mimo gara,* "very clear water." The hard "g" is only a softened "k," and we find *ko,* to be clear, pure (Ewe), and *kron,* pure, clear (Ga).

6. *Ram-ram,* very, can only be used with the verb *ke,* to roar, utter a cry or sound. *Ra-ra,* loudly, can only be used with the same verb.

7. *Nini,* very, can only be used with *tutu,* to be cold.

8. *Dodo,* very, can only be used with *ro,* to slacken, to cool ardour. This is perhaps explained by the verbs *de,* to slacken (Yoruba); *do,* to let go, *do,* to be grieved, troubled (Ewe); and *do,* to grant (Gã).

9. *Jojo,* very, can only be used with a verb of abundance, as, for instance, with *po,* to be many. *Eniu po jojo,* "the people are very many."

10. *Koro,* very, can only be used with *jale,* to go through. It is perhaps from *ko,* to meet, and *ro,* to give way.

11. *Kpere-kpere,* very, can only be used with *du,* to be black. It is probably from *kpe,* to endure, last, and *re,* to dye.

Similarly each colour seems to have an adverb proper to it, to convey the meaning "beautifully." Thus, *beleje* can only be used of yellow, and *fo* of a

bright yellow. The latter is explained by the fact that fu means yellow in Ga. Roki-roki and roro can only be used with the verb pon, to be red, and holojo only of a jet-black.

In the same way, *jigbini* (abundantly) can only be used of fruits; *papa* (violently) only with *wa,* to tremble; *lulu* (entirely) only with *son,* to burn; and so on.

Conjunctions

There are no conjunctions properly speaking, their place being supplied by verbs, nouns, or compounds of the two. Examples: —

And, also,   by *sin,* to accompany.
If, or whether,   by *bi,* to ask.
Since,   by *ti,* to support.
Notwithstanding, by *adi,* the act of shutting, closing, or blocking.
Or, nor, either, neither, by *tabi* (*ta,* to pass from one place to another, and *ibi,* place).
Because, by *nitori* (*ni,* to have; *itori,* share, lot).
Although, by *tile* (*ti,* to have; *le,* to replenish).
Unless, by *bike* (*bi,* to bear, beget; *ikose,* hindrance).

Prepositions

Prepositions are also expressed by verbs, nouns, or compounds of the two. Examples: —

Under, beneath, below,   by *nisale,* to have the lower part.
Over, upon, above,   by *loke* (*ni-oke*), to have the top, or by *lori* (*ni-ori*), to have the head.
In, within,   by *nino* (*ni-ino*), to have the interior.
To, against,   by *si,* to go to.

At, in,   by *ni,* to occupy, get.
Between,   by *larin* (*ni-arin*), to have the centre.

Numerals

The primary numerals are: —

One, *Eni.*   Nine, *Esan.*
Two, *Eji.*   Ten, *Ewa.*
Three, *Eta.*   Twenty, *Ogun.*
Four, *Erin,* or *Merin.*   Thirty, *Ogbon.*
Five, *Arun.*   Two Hundred, *Igba.*
Six, *Efa.*
Seven, *Eje.*
Eight, *Ejo.*

As the vowel-prefix shows, these are all nouns.
The numbers from eleven to fourteen are formed by suffixing *la,* a euphonic change from *'wa,* ten, to the units. Thus: —

Eleven, *Okan-la.*   Fourteen, *Erin-la,*
Twelve, *Eji-la.*
Thirteen, *Eta-la,*

It will be observed that the word *okan,* which stands for "one" in the compound "one-ten," is different from "one" as above. The word *okan* is evidently
the same as the Tshi numeral *eko,* or *akon,* "one"; and the existence in the
Yoruba language of such words as *ako-bi* (first-born), *ako-ro* (the first rains),
ako-so (first fruits), shows that *ako,* or *akon,* formerly stood for "one," instead
of the present word *eni.*
The numbers from fifteen to nineteen are formed by deducting from twenty. Thus: —

Fifteen, *Edogun* (*arun-di-ogun,* five less than twenty).
Sixteen, *Erin-di-logun* (four less than twenty).
Seventeen, *Eta-di-logun* (three less than twenty).
Eighteen, *Eji-di-logun* (two less than twenty).
Nineteen, *Okan-di-logun* (one less than twenty),

Di is a verb, to be short of, or less than. The letter I is inserted between *di*
and *ogun,* for the sake of euphony.
The tens from forty to two hundred which contain a complete number of
scores, are formed by placing *ogun,* twenty, before the imits. Thus: —

Forty, *Oji* (*ogun-eji,* twenties-two).
Sixty, *Ogota* (*ogun-eta,* twenties-three). It is commonly abbreviated to *Ota.*

113

Eighty, *Ogorin* (*ogun-erin*, twenties-four). Abbreviated to *Orin.*
One hundred, *Ogorun* (*ogun-arun*, twenties-five). Abbreviated to *Orun.*
One hundred and twenty, *Ogofa* (*ogun-efa*, twenties-six).
One hundred and forty, *Ogoje* (*ogun-eje*, twenties-seven.)
One hundred and sixty, *Ogojo* (*ogun-ejo*, twenties-eight).
One hundred and eighty, *Ogosan* (*ogun-esan*, twenties- nine).

The tens from forty fco two hundred which will not divide by twenty are formed by deducting ten from the ten next above. Thus: —

Fifty, *Adota* (*ewa-di-ota*, ten less than sixty).
Seventy, *Adorin* (*ewa'di-orin* , ten less than eighty).
Ninety, *Adorun* (*ewa-di-orun*, ten less than one hundred).
One hundred and ten, *Adofa* (*ewa-di-ogofa*, ten less than one hundred and twenty).
One hundred and thirty, *Adoje* (*ewa-di-ogoje*, ten less than one hundred and forty).
One hundred and fifty, *Adojo* (*ewa-di-ogojo*, ten less than one hundred and six-ty).
One hundred and seventy, *Adosan* (*ewa-di-ogosan*, ten less than one hundred and eighty).
One hundred and ninety, *Ewa-di-nigba* (ten less than two hundred).

The numbers between the tens are expressed on the same principle as those from eleven to nineteen, viz.: from one to four by joining the lower to the higher (in this case by means of the verb *le*, to add), and from five to nine by deducting from the ten next above by means of the verb di. Thus: —

Twenty-one, *Okan-le-ogun* (one added to twenty).
Twenty- two, *Eji-le-ogun* (two added to twenty).
Twenty-three, *Eta-le-ogun* (three added to twenty).
Twenty-four, *Erin-le-ogun* (four added to twenty).
Twenty-five, *Edogbon* (*arun-di-ogbon*, five less than thirty).
Twenty-six, *Erin-di-logbon* (four less than thirty).
Twenty- seven, *Eta-di-logbon* (three less than thirty).
Twenty-eight, *Eji-di-logbon* (two less than thirty).
Twenty-nine, *Okan-di-logbon* (one less than thirty).

From two hundred upwards the Yoruba peoples reckon by two hundreds. When the number is odd they say "So many two hundreds, less one hun-dred," and to facilitate this process they have a word *ede*, which means "mi-nus one hundred," or "minus one thousand," according to whether it is used in connection with hundreds or thousands. Two hundred is ten score, and computation by two-hundreds is as natural to people who reckon by scores as that by hundreds, *i.e.*, ten tens, is to people who reckon by tens.

The numbers from two hundred upwards are, however, ordinarily ex-pressed in cowry nomenclature. These shells are pierced and strung on strings to the number of forty or fifty, and five of the former or four of the latter make up two hundred cowries, or a small bundle, called *igbawo* (*owo,* cowries), which word is frequently abbreviated to *igbio.* Ten small bundles, or two thousand cowries, make a large bundle, *egbawa,* or *egba,* and ten large bundles, or twenty thousand cowries, make a bag, *oke kan* (*oke,* bag, *okan,* one). Thus: —

Six hundred is *egbeta* (*igbio-eta*), three small bundles.
Five hundred is *edegbeta* (*ede-egbeta*), three small bundles minus one hundred.
Twelve hundred is *egbefa* (*igbio efa*), six small bundles.
Six thousand is *egbata* (*egba-eta*), three large bundles.
Five thousand is *edegbata* (*ede-egbata*), three large bundles minus one thousand.

When twenty thousand — one bag — is arrived at, the computation is continued by bags: —

Eighty thousand, *oke-merin* (bags-four).
One hundred thousand, *Oke-marun* (bags-five).

This system of numeration is clumsy, and compares unfavorably with those evolved by the Tshi, Gã, and Ewe-speaking peoples, which are very regular. It exhibits rather stronger traces of the primitive practice of counting by fives, tens, and twenties — that is, by one hand, two hands, and hands and feet — than do the other systems. *Okan,* one, means "something alone," and no doubt refers to the thumb. [2] *Eji,* two, is probably from *ji,* to pick, and means "the picker," that is, the index-finger. This verb appears again in *eje,* seven, which would be counted on the index-finger of the other hand. *Eta,* three, is from the verb *to,* to shoot out lengthwise, and the third, or middle finger, is the longest. *Erin,* four, is seemingly from the verb *rin,* to go, progress, and would mean "the progressing." *Arun,* five, is from *run,* to bring to an end, finish. It means "the ending," and five brings to an end the counting of the fingers of one hand. *Efa,* six, which would be counted on the thumb of the other hand, seems to mean "that which leads or attracts," and to be from *fa,* to lead, attract, draw; and *ewa,* ten, is probably from the verb *wa,* to come together, and refers to the closing of the two hands when the counting is finished. The derivation of *ejo,* eight, and *eran,* nine, is not clear. Then eleven, twelve, thirteen, and fourteen are respectively ten-one, ten-two, ten-three, and ten-four; but fifteen, which completes the counting on one hand, is five less than twenty. The computation is then carried to the other hand, and we get four less than twenty, three less than twenty, and so on, till twenty is reached. From twenty to two hundred the computation is by scores, that is, by hands and feet.

The ordinal numbers are formed by prefixing *ekon* — completion, fulness, generally contracted to *ek'* — before the cardinal numbers, but complete tens above ten, that is, twenty, thirty, &c., do not take this prefix. Thus:—

First. *Ek-eni.*
Second. *Ek-eji.*
Third. *Ek-eta.*
Tenth. *Ek-ewa.*
Eleventh. *Ek-okanla.*

Twentieth. *Ogun.*
Twenty-first. *Ek-okan-le-ogun.*
Twenty-fifth. *Ek-edogbon.*

When answering the question "How many?" it is necessary to prefix *m* to the cardinal number, except in the case of one, ten, twenty, thirty, &c. Thus, *mefa*, six, instead of *efa; meji*, two, instead of *eji*, and so on.

The numeral adverbs of time are formed by prefixing *ara*, usually contracted to *e*, before the cardinal numbers, as used in answer to a question. Thus:—

Once, *ekan* (*ara-kan*).
Twice, *emeji* (*ara-meji*).
Thrice, *emeta* (*ara-meta*).
Four times, *emerin* (*ara-merin*),

Ara is a noun which has the primary meaning of custom, fashion, but also means a repetition.

The numeral adverbs of order are formed by prefixing the verb lelce, to be prominent, or uppermost, abbreviated to leW before the cardinal numbers. Thus:—

Firstly, *lek-eni.*   Secondly, *lek-eji.*   Thirdly, *lek-eta.*

From the preceding it will have been seen that, as in Tshi, Gã, and Ewe, all the words in the language are derived from the simple monosyllabic verbs. The list of Yoruba simple monosyllabic verbs will be found in the Appendix, where the four languages are compared.

There is the usual want of definiteness in expressing colours. *Fufu* means white, or any light colour; *dudu*, black, dark blue, dark green, purple, or any dark colour; and *pupa*, red, scarlet, or yellow. Colours are thus grouped into three classes, light, dark, and reddish. To express different shades of colour with exactness recourse is had to natural objects. Thus, grey is expressed by *eru*, "ashes"; blue, by *awo-aro*, "colour of the aro," a small bird of blue plumage; light blue by *awo-oju-orun*, "sky-colour"; green by *obedo*, "duck- weed"; purple by *awo-aluko*, "colour of the aluko," a bird of a purplish hue; and yellow by *iyeye*, the name of a yellow plum, or by *shafa-pupa*, literally "faded, scraped, red."

That, in speaking, the words should follow one another in the natural order in which they would occur to the mind, is what is to be expected from a people who have not invented an elaborate syntax. Thus the adjective always follows the noun, and a native would say "Handkerchief red," instead of putting the attribute before the subject, as we do, and saying "Red handkerchief." Similarly they say "Water bring," instead of "Bring water," and "Cold blows the wind," or, literally, "Coldness owns the wind," instead of "The wind blows cold." In short, the notion which comes first to the mind is that which is first expressed.

[1] "The Ewe-Speaking Peoples of the Slave Coast," p. 235.
[2] Thumb is *atampako.*

Chapter Thirteen - Proverbs

THE Yorubas have an extraordinary number of proverbial sayings, and regard a knowledge of them as a proof of great wisdom, whence the saying, "A counsellor who understands proverbs soon sets matters right." They are in constant use, and another saying runs, "A proverb is the horse of conversation. When the conversation droops a proverb revives it. Proverbs and conversation follow each other." Several of the proverbs given in the volume on the Ewe-speaking peoples are known to and used by the Yoruba-speaking peoples; but they have hundreds of others which appear to be peculiar to themselves, and from these the following are taken as examples:--
    1. Secrets should never be told to a tattler.
    2. What is not wished to be known is done in secret.
    3. He who has done something in secret, and sees people talking together, thinks they are talking of his action.
    4. A whisperer looks suspiciously at the forest when he hears a noise, but the forest does not tell tales.
    5. Rags make up a pad.
    6. Continual sweepings make a dust-heap.
    7. One here: two there: a great crowd.
    8. One here: two there: the market is filled up.
    (Nos. 5 to 8 are equivalent to our "Many a mickle makes a muckle.")
    9. Boasting is not courage.
    10. He who boasts much cannot do much.
    11. Much gesticulation does not prove courage.
    12. It is easy to cut to pieces a dead elephant.
    (Nos. 9 to 12 resemble our "Deeds, not words.")
    13. "I nearly killed the bird." No one can cat nearly in a stew.
    (Answers to "Catch your hare before you cook him.")

14. A hog that has wallowed in the mud seeks a clean person to rub against.

15. A man in a white cloth is never looked for in the palm-oil market.

(Is something akin to "You cannot touch pitch without behig defiled.")

16. The cross-roads do not fear sacrifices.

17. The sieve never sifts meal by itself.

18. Disobedience will drink water with his hands tied up.

19. Disobedience is the father of insolence.

20. Calamity has no voice; suffering cannot speak to tell who is really in distress.

21. He who owns the inner square of the house is the master of the outer.

22. Peace is the father of friendship.

23. Strife never begets a gentle child.

24. He who forgives ends the quarrel.

25. A sharp word is as tough as a bow-string. A sharp word cannot be cured, but a wound may.

26. A peacemaker often receives blows.

27. There is no medicine against old age.

28. The *afomo* (a parasitical plant) has no roots; it claims relationship with every tree.

29. A man with a cough can never conceal himself.

30. Full-belly child says to hungry-belly child, "Keep good heart."

31. A jealous woman has no flesh upon her breast, for however much she may feed upon jealousy, she will never be satisfied.

32. Houses that are not adjacent do not readily catch fire.

33. Do not attempt what you cannot bring to a good end.

31. Each coloured cloth has its name.

35. He who marries a beauty marries trouble.

36. A man of the town knows nothing about farming, or the seasons for planting, yet the yam he buys must always be large.

37. A witch kills but never inherits.

38. Unless the tree falls you will never be able to reach the branches.

39. Another's eye is not like one's own.

40. The bite of the sand-fly is not so bad as poverty.

41. Poverty destroys a man's reputation.

42. A poor man has no relations.

43. Poverty never visits a poor man without visiting his children also.

44. The white man is the father of merchants, and want of money is the father of disgrace.

45. A man may be born to a fortune, but wisdom only comes with length of days.

46. People think that the poor are not so wise as the rich, for if a man be wise, why is he poor?

47. The appearance of the wise differs from that of the fool.

48. The labourer is always in the sun, the plantation-owner always in the shade.

(Answers to "One sows, another reaps.")

49. A lazy man looks for light employment.

50. Laziness lends assistance to fatigue.

51. The potsherd goes in front of the man who has taken embers on it from the fire.

(Means that every enterprise requires a leader.)

52. The partridge says: "What business has the farmer to bring his cloth here?" (fearing it may be a bird-trap). The farmer says: "How could I go to my farm without my cloth?"

(This means that there are two sides to every question.)

53. Ear, hear the other before you decide.

54. He who annoys another only teaches him to streno, then himself.

55. He who waits for a chance will have to wait for a year.

56. When the jackal dies the fowls do not mourn, for the jackal never brings up a chicken.

57. When fire burns in the bush, smuts fly into the town.

(Answers to "Evil communication corrupts good manners.")

58. Tale-bearing is the older brother, vexation the younger.

59. He who knows a matter beforehand confuses the liar.

60. Time may be very long but a lie will not go to forgetfulness.

61. A lie costs nothing to a liar.

62. A man walks calmly in the presence of his defamer; -a man walks proudly in the presence of his slanderer, when he knows that the slanderer has only twenty cowries in his house.

63. To be trodden upon here, to be trodden upon there, is the fate of the palm-kernel lying in the, road.

64. The sole of the foot is exposed to all the dirt of the road.

65. He who eats *akashu* does not know that a famine prevails.

(*Akashu* is a large ball of *agidi*, and hence emblematic of plenty.)

66. Consideration is the senior, calculation the junior, and wisdom the third-born.

67. Want of consideration and forethought made six brothers pawn themselves for six dollars.

(Instead of one brother pawning himself for the whole amount, in which case the others would be free to work and earn money with which to redeem him.)

68. An obstinate man soon falls into disgrace.

69. Inquiry saves a man from making mistakes. He who makes no inquiry gets himself into trouble.

70. Though a man may miss other things, he never misses his mouth.

71. Not to aid one in distress is to kill him in your heart.

72. Charity is the father of sacrifice.

73. Covetousness is the father of disease.

74. Never did our fathers honour an *orisha* of this kind.

(Is used to discountenance innovations.)

75. A white cloth and a stain never agree.

76. Thorns do not agree with the foot.

77. The stream may dry up, but the watercourse still keeps its name.

78. When water is poured on the head it finds its way down to the feet.

79. A gift is a gift, and a purchase is a purchase; so no one will thank you for saying "I sold it You very cheap."

80. Hawks go away for the nesting-season, and fools think they have gone away for ever.

81. Ashes fly back in the face of him who throws them.

(Is equivalent to our "Curses come home to roost.")

82. It is the path of the needle that the thread is accustomed to follow.

83. If a matter be dark, dive to the bottom.

84. He who is pierced with a thorn must limp off to him who has a knife.

85. Every man's character is good in his own eyes.

(This resembles "Self-praise is no recommendation.")

86. Wherever a man goes to dwell, his character goes with him.

87. Frogs' spawn does not attract the attention of the robber.

(Frogs' spawn is supposed to resemble a mass of beads.)

88. The white ant may well admire the bird, for it loses its wings only after only one day.

89. Gently! gently! still hurts the snail.

90. A bribe blinds the judge's eyes, for bribes never speak the truth.

91. A witness speaks the truth; a witness is not a partisan.

92. Iwo is the home of the grey parrot, Ibara the home of the hawk, but where is the home of the green parrot?

(Is used to persons making false pretences.)

93. Bank rises after bank, and ditch follows after ditch. When the rain falls into the ditch the banks are envious.

(Is said of those who are dissatisfied with their station in life.)

94. The strength of a mortar (made of wood) is not like the strength of a pot (made of clay). Place a mortar on the fire and it will burn; pound a yam in a pot and it will break.

(Means that there is a proper use for everything.)

95. When the monkey jumps from the tree he jumps into the house.

(Inculcates the danger of leaving one's proper station.)

96. A tick having fixed itself on the mouth of a jackal, a fowl was asked to take it off; but the fowl knew that she was food for the jackal just as the tick was for her.

97. Gossip is unbecoming in an elder.

98. Three elders cannot all fail to pronounce the word *ekulu*; one may say *ekúlu*, another *ekulú*, but tho third will say *ekulu*.

(Ekulu is the name of antelope. The saying means that there is safety in a number of counsellors.)

99. The younger should not thrust himself into the seat of the elders.

100. The young cannot teach the elders traditions.

101. As a calabash receives the sediment of the water, so inust in elder exercise forbearance.

102. A man does not run among thorns for nothing. Either he is pursuing a snake or a snake is pursuing him.

103. As no subject may keep a herald, so it is not every man who may own a palace.

104. Everyone in the assembly has a name, but when you are summoned "in the name of the assembly" (instead of in the name of some individual in it) evil awaits you.

105. A near neighbour need not say good-bye till to-morrow.

106. A thing thrown forward will surely be overtaken, and a thing put in the ground will be there to be dug up; but if nothing has been thrown forward, what shall be overtaken? and if nothing has been buried, what shall be dug up?

(Is used to inculcate provident habits.)

107. The name given to a child becomes natural to it.

108. Gold should be sold to him who knows its value.

109. Time is longer than a rope.

110. The dawn does not come twice to wake a man.

111. If clothes remain long in the bag they rot.

112. The *agbi* (a bird with blue plumage) is the dyer in blue; the *aluko* (a bird with purple plumage) is the painter of purple; but the *lekileki* (the white crane) is the owner of the white cloth.

(Means each to his own pursuits.)

113. When the rain fell upon the parrot the *aluko* rejoiced, thinking that the red tail of the parrot would be spoiled, but the rain only increased its brilliancy.

114. The *akala* (vulture) smells the carrion, no matter how high in the air he may be.

115. The bat hangs with his head down, watching the actions of the birds.

(Is used to inculcate silent observation.)

116. He that has copper ornaments looks after the lime; he that has brass ornaments looks after the *awedi*.

(The lime is used for cleaning copper and the *awedi* for cleaning brass.)

117. Though the *dengi* is cold on the top, yet the inside is very hot.

(Dengi is a kind of gruel made of pounded maize. The proverb means "Do not judge by appearances.")

118. A small bed will not hold two persons.

119. The elephant makes a dust and the buffalo makes a dust, but the dust of the buffalo is lost in that of the elephant.

120. Though you appear very sharp you cannot tell nine times nine.

121. A large morsel chokes a child.

122. He who cannot lift an ant, and yet tries to lift an elephant, will find out his folly.

123. He who tries to shake the trunk of a tree only shakes himself.

124. The world is the ocean and mankind is the lagoon. However well a man can swim he cannot cross the world.

(Nos. 119 to 124 are used to check presumption and over-confidence.)

125. When the *eya* (a wild cat) has reached to the ferocity of the leopard he will kill animals to feed on.

126. Though the fire is burning the walls do not shrink from it, and yet the fire is trying to burn the water.

(Is said of persons who aim at the greater when they cannot accomplish the less.)

127. The cry of the bird *kegio* does not reach the sky.

(Is used of one whose opinion or advice is not valued.)

128. Cocoa-nut is not good for a bird to eat.

(This is used in the same way as our "Sour grapes.")

129. The bill-hook cuts the bush, but receives no profit from the bush. It clears the road, but receives no profit from the road. The bill-hook is badly bent, the bill-hook is badly bent. The billhook is bent; it pays five cowries to bind its neck (handle) with a ring. When the bill-hook reaches its owner's farm with the ring on its neck, it is girded tightly for new works.

(This saying refers to the labour of slaves, which brings them no remuneration. In the original it forms a kind of verse. Thus:--

Ada shan igbo,
Ko ri ere igbo.
O ro ona,
Ko ri ere ona.
Ada da ida kuda,
Ada da ida kuda.
Ada da; o fi arun gbadi o di oko olowo.
Ada li eka oron gbadsa giri-giri.)

130. The pot-lid is always badly off, for the pot gets all the sweet and the lid nothing but the steam.

("Pot-lid" is here used to mean "slave.")

131. Job-work is not the slave's first care; the master's work has the first claim on his time.

132. A slave is not the child of a tree (*i.e.*, made of wood). When a slave dies his mother hears nothing of it, but when a free man dies there is mourning; yet the slave, too, was once a child in his mother's house.

133. As the yam-flour was once a soft unripe yam, so was the slave once a child in his father's house.

134. Birth does not differ from birth; as the free man was born so was the slave.

135. You find a hen in the market and hasten to buy her. Had she been worth keeping the owner would not have sold her.

(This is said in warning to any man who is about to buy a female slave.)

136. He who gathers locust-fruit spends the money of death.

(Is used to check rashness. The wood of the locust-tree breaks easily, and this proverb contemplates a man perched on a lofty limb to pick the fruit.)

137. A hunchback is never asked to stand up straight.

(That is, no one expects the impossible.)

138. He who has only an eyebrow for a bow can never kill an animal.

139. You cannot kill game by looking at it.

140. When the hawk hovers the fowl-owner feels uneasy.

141. No one carrying elephant-beef on his head should look for crickets underground.

(Elephant-beef here means the food of the rich, and crickets that of the poor. The saying means tbat the rich should not stoop to petty gains.)

142. No one should draw water from the spring in order to supply the river.

(This means that no poor man should stint himself in order to make presents to the rich.)

143. The glutton, having eaten his fill, then calls his companions to come also.

144. If you are not able to build a house at once, you first build a shed.

145. If one has not an *adan* (a large kind of bat), one sacrifices an *ode* (small bat).

(Nos. 144 and 145 mean "Do your best.")

146. If one is carrying water, and it gets spilt, so long as the calabash is not broken one can still get more.

(Is used to encourage those who think a disaster irreparable.)

147. No snuff-seller likes to own that she sells bad tobacco, but all profess to sell tobacco as sweet as honey.

("No one cries stinking fish.")

148. The *esuo* (gazelle), claiming relationship with the *ekulu* (a large antelope), says his mother was the daughter of an *ekulu*.

149. If you abuse the *etu*, you make the head of the *awo* ache.

(The *etu* and the *awo* are two varieties of guinea-fowl. The proverb means that people do not like to hear their relations badly spoken of.)

150. He runs away from the sword and hides himself in the scabbard.

This answers to our "Out of the frying-pan into the fire," as the sword will return to the scabbard.)

151. The sword shows no respect for its maker.

152. The spoon, seeing death, ventures his head into it.

(That is, into the boiling fluid. The proverb is used to check rashness.)

153. After the *agbeji* has saved men from starving, it is thought only fit to be cut into a common calabash.

(The agbeji is a kind of calabash-gourd, which ripens early in the season, when vegetables are scarce. When over-ripe it is bitter to the taste. The saying is used to reprove ingratitude.)

154. The *agbeji* is never bitter in a large family.

(This resembles "Hunger is the best sauce.")

155. Leprosy, desiring to disfigure a man, attacks the tip of his nose.

(Said of one who tells the faults of another in public.)

156. The first-born is due to the sheep-owner.

(This answers to "Give to each one his due." It refers to a custom by which, when ewes are put in charge of a shepherd, he receives in payment a certain proportion of the young, after the first-born.)

157. Contraction of words conceals the sense.

(The Yorabas talk habitually with great rapidity, contracting words, and often not giving themselves time to think of the proper word to use. Hence, the meaning of what they say is very often obscure, and their convenation is in consequence continually interrupted by the question"*Ogbo*?" "Do you understand?" literally,"Do you hear?")

158. When the face is washed you finish at the chin.

(This is a saying used when a dispute is ended. It means, "Well, that's settled.")

159. No one should ask the fish what takes place on the land, nor should the rat be asked what takes place in the water.

160. A large cook does not allow a small one to crow.

161. A rock is the father of stones.

162. Two rams cannot drink out of the same calabash.

163. No one will throw away antelope-venison to pick up squirrel-meat.

164. When the spider intends to attack you it encircles you with its web.

165. The deaf look with surprise at a speaker's mouth.

166. Although you are about to die, need you split up the mortar for firewood?

(Means, have some consideration for others.)

167. "To-day I am going; to-morrow I am going," gives the stranger no encouragement to plant the *ahusa* (a plant which bears fruit very rapidly).

168. What good have the gods done to the hunchback that he should name his child Orishagbemi (the gods have blessed me)?

(This means, why should one return thanks when unkindness only has been experienced?)

169. He who does not understand the cry of the palm-bird (*ega*) complains of the noise it makes.

(Means that people are prone to contemn [*sic*] what they do not understand.)

170. A large cock, crowing in the middle of the night, settles the dispute (as to what the time is).

171. A lame man said the load on his head was not properly balanced, and was told "Its unevenness began from the ground" (*i.e.*, from his lame leg).

(This is used to reprove those who find fault when the fault really lies with them.)

172. When the bush is on fire the pigeon leaves the grass; when the fire is extinguished everyone returns home.

173. The *akpena* says to the cotton, "Do not hang your trouble round my neck.",

(The *akpena* is a kind of spindle, on which spun cotton is wound for sale. The proverb is used to one who is involving another in a difficulty.)

174. The *aro* does not bear its load for ever; sooner or later it will put it down.

(The *aro* is the hearth, or fire-place, consisting of three rounded cones of clay, between which the fire is lighted, and on which the cooking-pot rests. The proverb means, "Sooner or later matters must mend.")

175. Self-conceit deprives the wasp of honey.

176. He who begs with importunity will obtain what he wants.

177. The pond stands aside, as if it were not related to the river.

(Is used to reprove pride.)

178. The *ago* (a striped rat noted for its cunning) is caught in a trap, how much more then the *malaju* (a water-rat remarkable for its stupidity).

179. The *ajao* (flying-fox) is neither rat nor bird.

(Is used of a person who remains neutral during a quarrel.)

180. When a Mohammedan is not pinched with hunger he says, "I never eat monkey."

181. The rat has no voice to call the eat to account.

182. When the man on the stilts falls, another hand gets possession of the sticks.

183. One man makes bill-hooks and others use them.

181. If you send no one to the market the market will send no one to you.

185. There is no tallness among pigeons; they are all dwarfs.

186. No one would expose fowls on the top of a rock in sight of a hawk.

187. The rat does not show his companion the hole in the roof.

(Each one for himself.)

188. You cannot shave a man's head in his absence.

(This means that a matter cannot be settled in the absence of the people concerned.)

189. A bald-headed man does not care for a razor.

190. A mouth not keeping shut, and lips not keeping close, bring trouble to the jaws.

(Answers to our "Speech is silver, bat silence is gold.")

191. With the forefinger one takes up the sauce.

192. A chicken having been delivered from death (*i.e.*, from the hawk) by being shut up, complained because it was not allowed to feed openly on the dust-heap.

193. The dog that is known to be very swift is the one chosen to catch the hare.

194. If the dog has his master behind him he will not be afraid of the baboon.

195. An old dog cannot be taught.

196. The butcher pays no regard to any particular breed of animals.

(That is, "All it; fish that comes to his net.")

197. A rogue never closes the mouth of his wallet.

198. The birdlime is the death of the bird.

199. When the shin-bone is not hurt, it says it has no flesh to protect it.

(This means, "You do not know what you can do till you try.")

200. Working in competition quickens the hands.

201. The coloured calico deceives the country-cloth, but it is not really what the country-cloth takes it to be, for the thread is fine.

(Country-cloth, that is, native-made cotton-cloth, is only dyed to disguise its coarseness, and it is here represented as imagining that coloured calico is coloured for the same reason. The proverb means that first impressions are often erroneous.)

202. He who goes into a river, may fear, but the river does not fear.

203. No one confesses that he has eaten yam with a knife that is missing.

204. A fool of Ika and an idiot of Iluka meet together to make friends.

("Birds of a feather flock together.")

205. The palm of the hand deceives no one.

(This answers to our "A bird in the hand is worth two in the bush.")

206. No matter how well an idol is made, it must have something to stand on.

(Is used like our "There is no smoke without fire.")

207. Though the host may be obliged to eat *gbingbindo*, the guest expects at least to be given a handful of corn.

(The fruit of the *gbingbindo* is only eaten in time of famine. The proverb is used to check unreasonable demands.)

208. When a fish is killed its tail is put in its mouth.

(Is said of those who reap, the fruit of their own misdeeds.)

209. Thanks are due to the shoulders which keep the shirt from slipping off.

210. As one is walking, so is he met.

211. The monkey is sure to tear the cloth of anyone who resembles himself.

212. An accident is not like a result that is foreseen.

213. One lock does not know the wards of another.

214. If the stomach is not strong, do not eat cockroaches.

215. The pangolin dwelt in a forest, not in a plain.

(This is a mode of saying that a person is bashful.)

216. If a man powerful in authority should ill-treat you, smile at him.

217. He who claps hands for a fool to dance is no better than the fool.

218. When the *agbali* is overpowered, there remains only the strength of the *arabi* to be overcome.

(The *agbali* and *arabi* are two insects which, it is popularly believed, are always found in company.)

219. The thumb cannot point straight forward.

(Is used when a person has been detected in some deceit.)

220. To prostrate oneself and keep the elbows close (to the side) does something for you.

(This resembles our saying about holding a candle to the devil.)

221. The trader never acknowledges that he has sold all his goods. When asked, he will only say, "Trade is a little better."

222. Everything has a price, but who can put a price on blood?

223. Famine compels one to eat the fruit of all kinds of trees.

("Necessity knows no law.")

224. A fugitive does not stop to pick the thorns from his foot, neither does he make choice of his sauce.

225. The ground-pig (bandicoot) said: "I do not feel so angry with the man who killed, me, as with the one who dashed me on the ground afterwards."

("Insult adds to injury.")

226. Never take hold of a man who has a drawn knife in his hand.

227. By labour comes wealth.

228. A thief is more merciful than a fire.

229. Odofin tells a bigger lie than Aro.
Aro says he dropped his needle in the water;
Odofin says he heard the splash of it.

230. A knife cannot be so sharp as to sharpen its own handle.

231. Joy has a small body.

232. Number one always precedes number two.

233. The horse never refuses a homeward gallop.

234. The wife saying, "I am going to see my mother," deceives the husband.

235. He who waits to see a crab wink will tarry long upon the shore.

236. The butterfly that brushes against thorns will tear its wings.

237. If an *orisha* would kill a man for cooking an unpalatable soup, what would become of those who cook nothing at all?

238. A rat that has a navel is a witch.

239. That which a child likes never injures its stomach.

240. Quick loving a woman means quick not loving a woman.

("Marry in haste and repent at leisure.")

241. One cannot show darkness by, pointing it out.

242. The greater covers the less.

243. Ropes are entangled when goats are tied to the same post.

244. Hilts are unconscious of the strain to which the blades are subjected.

245. We say, "Know it who can." The knower will know.

("The cap fits.')

246. Without bad news there is no sadness of heart.

247. The dove would not eat the ground-nuts, or the crow the white beans.

("One man's food is another man's poison,")

248. Health is the stepping-stone to wealth.

219. Dada cannot fight, but he has a brave brother.

250. As a girl is, so is her "head-money."

Many of the proverbial sayings run in couplets, and resemble in construction some of those found in the Hebrew Book of Proverbs, the object being to establish an antithesis between two consecutive lines, in which noun is made to answer to noun, and verb to verb. For instance, compare:--

The simple inherit folly,
But the prudent are crowned with knowledge.

(Proverbs xiv. 18).

A gracious woman retaineth honour,
And strong men retain riches.

(Proverbs xi. 16.)

with the following Yoruba aphorisms:--

1. Ordinary people are as common as grass,
But good people are dearer than the eye.

2. A matter dealt with gently is sure to prosper,
But a matter dealt with violently causes vexation.

3. Familiairity induces contempt,
But distance secures respect.

4. The public assembly belongs to the town,
But a select council belongs to the king.

5. Anger does nobody good,
But patience is the father of kindness.
Anger draws arrows from the quiver,
But good words draw kola-nuts from the bag.

6. A fruitful woman is the enemy of the barren,
And an industrious man is the foe of the lazy.

7. Beg for help, and you will meet with refusers;
Ask for alms, and you will meet with misers.

8. A wild boar in the place of a hog would ravage the town,
And a slave, made king, would spare nobody.

9. When there are no elders the town is ruined,
And when the master dies the house is desolate.

10. The absence of powder converts a gun into a stick,
And the death of a father causes the dispersion of his children.

11. The sharpness of an arrow is not like that of a razor,
And the wickedness of a horse is not like that of a man.

12. A pistol has not a bore like a cannon,
And a poor man has not money like a rich.

13. Sorrow is after weeping,
And mortification is after trouble.

14. To-day is the elder brother of to-morrow,
And a heavy dew is the elder brother of rain.

15. A ram's mane gives him a noble appearance,

And a father's honour makes a son proud.

16. No one can separate the *agbali* from the *arabi*, [1]

And no one can deprive a man of his inheritance,

The Yoruba-speaking peoples are fond of composing punning sentences, made up of words having similar sounds but different meanings. Thus:--

(1) *Abebi ni ibe iku.*

Abebi ni ibe orun.

Bi oru ba inu abebi ni ibe e.

Abebi means a fan, an advocate, or an intercessor, and the above is

An intercessor (with the gods) wards off death.

An advocate (with the judge) wards off punishment.

A fan wards off the heat when it is hot.

(2) *Igun ti ogun mi ko jo i egun.* Stabbing is not like pricking me with a thorn." The play here is in the resemblance between the words *igun*, *ogun*, and *egun*.

(3) *Bi alapata ba pa eran, awon alagbata abu u li ajan.* When the butcher kills the animal the retailers cut it into pieces." Here the play is upon the words *alalgata* (butcher) and *alagbata* (pedlar, retailer, petty trader).

(4) The following is on the words *bata* (shoes), *bata-bata* (an ono-matopœic word like our "patter patter "), *apata* (rock), *ajulabata* (chief drummer), and *bata* (a long drum):--

Ojo pa bata, bata-bata-bata, li ori apata; li ode ajulabata, bata ni igi, bata li awo.

"The rain on the *bata* (shoes), goes patter, patter, patter, as on the *apata* (rock); in the street of *ajulabata*, the *bata* (drum) is wood, the *bata* (shoes) are of hide."

(5) *Igba dodo li agbado, igba ni?* "What supports the people if it is not maize?" Here the play is on *igba dodo* and *agbado*.

It is a favourite game to repeat as fast as possible sentences difficult to pronounce, like the following:--

Iyan mu ire yo; iyan ro ire ru. "When there is famine the cricket is fat" (that is, is considered good enough to eat); "when the famine is over the cricket is lean" (i.e., is rejected).

Kanakana ba kanakana ja, kanakana da kanakana. "The crow met the crow and fought, the crow beat the crow."

The two following are examples of a play of a different sort:--

(1) The cry of the squirrel sounds like the word *korokoro*, whence "It was the squirrel's own mouth that betrayed her, for when she had brought forth two young ones she carried them to the roadside and said, My children are very sound, very sound, very sound (*Omo mi ije korokoro, korokoro, koroko-ro.*)

(2) The cry of the bush-fowl (partridge) resembles the words *kiki ora*, "nothing but fat"; hence the saying, "With its mouth the bush-fowl declares its fatness, crying, 'Nothing but fat! Nothing but fat.'" (*Kiki-ora! Kiki-ora.*)

Riddles are sufficiently common, but few of them are good. The following are examples:--

Q. A small confined room, with hardly anything in it but pegs.
A. The mouth, with the teeth.

Q. An associate who cannot be tamed.
A. Fire.

Q. There is no market in which the dove with the prominent breast has not traded.
A. The cowry.

Q. A hen that has many chickens.
A. The Milky Way.

Q. I am long and slim, I am engaged in commerce, and yet I never reach the market.
A. The canoe (which carries the goods but stops at the landing-place).

[1] See Proverb 218.

Chapter Fourteen - Folk-Lore Tales

THE Yoruba folk-lore tales are very numerous. The word now commonly used to mean one of these popular fables is *alo*, which more properly means a riddle, or something invented, literally something twisted, or inverted. A reciter of tales, called an *akpalo* (*kpa-alo*) "maker of *alo*," is a personage highly esteemed, and in great demand for social gatherings. Some men, indeed, make a profession of story-telling, and wander from place to place reciting tales. Such a man is termed an *akpalo kpatita*, "one who makes a trade of telling fables." As among the Ewe tribes, the professional story-teller very often uses a drum, with the rhythm of which the pauses in the narrative are filled up. When he has gathered an audience around him, he cries out, "My *alo* is about so-and-so," mentioning the name of the hero or heroine of the tale; or "My *alo* is about a man (or woman) who did so-and-so," and, after this preface, proceeds with the recital. The professional story teller must not be confounded with the *arokin*, or narrator of the national traditions, several of whom are attached to each king or paramount chief, and who may be regarded as the depositaries of the ancient Chronicles. The chief of the *arokin* is a councillor, bearing the title of *Ologbo* "one who possesses the old times," and a proverb says *"Ologbo baba arokin"* "Ologbo is the father of chroniclers."

I.

My alo is about a woman whose little girl made palm-oil.
One day when she had made palm-oil she took it to the market to sell.

She stayed in the market selling her palm-oil until it was quite dark. And when it was dark, a goblin [1] came to her to buy palm-oil, and paid her with some cowries.

When the little girl counted the cowries she found that there was one short, and she asked the goblin for the cowry that was wanting.

The goblin said that he had no more cowries, and the little girl began crying, "My mother will beat me if I go home with a cowry short."

The goblin walked away, and the little girl walked after him.

"Go away," said the goblin; turn back, for no one can enter the country where I live."

"No," said the little girl; "wherever you go I will follow, until you pay me my cowry."

So the little girl followed, followed a long, long way, till they came to the country where the people stand on their heads in their mortars and pound yams with their heads.

Then they went on again a long way, and they came to a river of filth. And the goblin sang:--

"Oh! young palm-oil seller,
You must now turn back."

And the girl sang:

"Save I get my cowry,
I'll not leave your track."

Then the goblin sang again:--

"Oh! young palm-oil seller,
Soon will lead this track,
To the bloody river,
Then you must turn back."

And she:--

"I will not turn back."

And he:--

"See yon gloomy forest?"

And she:--

"I will not turn back."

And he:--

"See yon craggy mountain?"

And she:--

"I will not turn back.
Save I get my cowry
I'll not leave your track."

Then they walked on again, a long, long way; and at last they arrived at the land of dead people.

The goblin gave the little girl some palm-nuts, with which to make palm-oil, and said to her: "Eat the palm-oil and give me the *ha-ha*. [2]

But when the palm-oil was made the little girl gave it to the goblin, and eat the *ha-ha* herself, and the goblin said, "Very well."

131

By-and-by the goblin gave a banana to the little girl, and said: "Eat this banana, and give me the skin." But the little girl peeled the banana and gave it to the goblin, and eat the skin herself.

Then the goblin said to the little girl: "Go and pick three *ados*. [3] Do not pick the *ados* which cry 'Pick me, pick me, pick me,' but pick those which say nothing, and then return to your home. When you are half-way back break one *ado*, break another when you are at the house-door, and the third when you are inside the house." And the little girl said, "Very well."

She picked the *ados* as she was told, and returned home.

When she was half-way she broke one *ado*, and behold, many slaves and horses appeared, and followed her.

When she was at the house-door, the little girl broke the second *ado*, and behold, many creatures appeared, sheep, and goats, and fowls, more than two hundred, and followed her.

Then, when she had entered the house, the little girl broke the last *ado*, and at once the house was filled to overflowing with cowries, which poured out of the doors and windows.

The mother of the little girl took twenty countrycloths, twenty strings of valuable beads, twenty sheep and goats, and twenty fowls, and went to make a present to the head wife. [4]

The head wife asked whence all these things came, and when she had been told, she refused to accept them. She said she would send her own child to do the same, and that she could easily get as much. [5]

Then the head wife made palm-oil, and gave it to her own little girl, and told her to go and sell it in the market.

The little girl -went to the market. The goblin came, bought palin-oil of her, and paid her with cowries. He gave the proper number of cowries, but the little girl hid one and pretended that he had not given her enough.

"What am I to do?" said the goblin. "I have no more cowries."

"Oh," said the little girl, "I will follow you to your house, and then you can pay me."

And the goblin said: "Very well."

Then the two walked together, and presently the goblin began singing, as he had done the first time. He sang:--

"Oh young palm-oil seller,
You must now turn back."

And the little girl sang:--

"I will not turn back."

And the goblin:--

You must leave the track."

And the girl:--

"I will not turn back."

Then the goblin said: "Very well. Come along." And they walked on till they reached the land of dead people.

The goblin gave the little girl some palm-nuts, and told her to make palm-oil. He said: "When the palm-oil is made, eat it yourself, and bring me the *ha-ha*." And the little girl eat the palm-oil and brought the *ha-ha* to the goblin. And the goblin said: "Very well."

Then the goblin gave a banana to the little girl, and told her to peel it. He said: "Eat the banana yourself and bring me the skin." And the little girl eat the banana and carried the skin to the goblin.

Then the goblin said: "Go and pick three *ados*. Do not pick those which cry 'Pick me, pick me, pick me,' but pick those which say nothing."

The little girl went. She found *ados* which said nothing and she left them alone. She found others which cried, "Pick me, pick me, pick me," and she picked three of them.

Then the goblin said to her, "When you are halfway home break one *ado*; when you are at the door break another; and break the third when you are inside the house."

Half-way home the little girl broke one *ado*, and behold, numbers of lions, and leopards, and hyenas, and snakes, appeared. They ran after her, and harassed her, and bit her till she reached the door of the house.

Then she broke the seeond *ado*, and behold, more ferocious animals came upon her and bit her and tore her at the door. The door was shut, and there was only a deaf person in the house. The little girl called to the deaf person to open the door, but he heard her not. And there, upon the threshold, the wild beasts killed the little girl.

[1] *Iwin*, goblin, spirit, ghost.
[2] *Ha-ha*, the stringy remains of the pulp of the nut after the oil has been expressed.
[3] The *ado* is a very small calabash, commonly used for keeping medicinal powders in.
[4] Head wife, *Iyale* (*Iya-ile*, Mistress of the House). As already explained, the subordinate wives, of which the mother of the girl in the story was one, are called *Iya-wo*.
[5] From the European point of view this would appear to be a good trait on the part of the *iyale*, for the inference would be that she did not wish to deprive the sub-wife of so much property, but that is not the native view. To the native mind a person only refuses a present when he is nurturing rancour against the donor, and to refuse a gift is regarded is a sign of enmity.

II.

My *alo* is about a poor young woman. [1]

There was a poor young woman who had a child. She was so poor that she could not even buy a cloth to wear, and her child was held on her back with a plantain-leaf.

The poor young woman used to go into the forest to cut fire-wood to sell. One day she went there as usual. There was a tall tree, and under it she put down her child to sleep in the shade.

Now in this tree there was an *aranran*, [2] and while the young woman was cutting fire-wood, the *aranran* seized the child, and carried it up into the tree.

When the young woman had made up her bundle of wood, she came back to the place where she had left her child, and could not find it.

She looked everywhere, but still could not find it, and she ran to-and-fro, crying bitterly.

At last she looked up, and then she saw her child in the claws of the *aranran*, high up in the tree-top. And she began to sing:--

"*Aranran, eiye igbo, igbo*, [3]
 Give me back my child, oh, *igbo*.
 Here is a rope of tie-tie, [4] *igbo*;
 Quickly let my child down, *igbo*."

When the young woman had sung this, the *aranran* threw down to her a bag of coral beads.

The young woman ran to the bag and opened it, but her child was not in it, so she threw the bag down and sang again:--

"*Aranran, eiye igbo, igbo*,
 Give me back my child, oh, *igbo*.
 Here is a rope of tie-tie, *igbo*;
 Quickly let my child down, *igbo*."

Then the *aranran* took all kinds of valuable property, and threw them down to her. And the mother looked here and looked there as the things fell, but her child was still not there, so she sang again, the same song, a third time.

Then the *aranran* took the child and flew down with it and placed it gently on the ground.

The young woman ran to her child, took him up, and put him on her back. She picked up also all the things that the *aranran* had thrown down to her. And from being poor, she now became rich.

After returning home the young woman took twenty strings of coral beads, and went to offer them to the *iyale*; but the *iyale*, when she learned how the young woman had come by the beads, refused them.

The *iyale* took a child belonging to one of the other wives and carried it into the bush. She put it under the tree of the *aranran*, and went away to cut wood.

But while she was away cutting wood the *aranran* carried off the child, and killed and ate it.

When the *iyale*, returned to the foot of the tree, and could not find the child, she began to sing, as the young woman had done:--

Aranran, eiye igbo, igbo,
Give me back my child, oh, *igbo*.
Here is a rope of tie-tie, *igbo*;
Quickly let my child down, *igbo*."

Then the *aranran* voided copiously into a bag, tied up the neck of the bag, and throw it down.

The *iyale* ran to the bag, picked it up, and untied it. She found it full of filth, and she threw it away. Then she sang again, as before.

This time the *aranran* made water in a large calabash, and let it fall, so that it broke upon the woman's head. And the *iyale* sang a third time:--

Aranran, eiye igbo, igbo,
Give me back my child, oh, *igbo*.
Here is a rope of tie-tie, *igbo*;
Quickly let my child down, *igbo*."

Then the *aranran* took up the bones of the child and throw thein down -at her.

The *iyale* ran and looked at the bones of the child, and she cried out, "This is not my child. It is the child of another woman that this bird has killed, believing it to be mine." And she went away.

When she reached home, the mother of the child came to the *iyale* for her little one. And the *iyale* said that the child was quite well, but was not with her.

Many times the mother came to ask for her child, and when three months had passed and the child had not been restored to her, she carried the case before the king.

She told the king all that had taken place, that the *iyale* had taken the child from her hands, and, though three months had passed, had not yet brought it back.

The king summoned the *iyale* to his court, and asked her, "What have you done with the child? Where is it?" And the *iyale* answered, "What do you suppose I should do with it?"

Then the king said to the people who were assembled, "If this woman belonged to you, what would you do with her?" And all the people replied, "If she belonged to us we would put her to death."

And the king said, "Let her then be put to death." And so the *iylale* was killed.

[1] This story is also about the discomfiture of an *iyale*, which is a favourite theme. The plot resemblcs the foregoing.

[2] *Aranran*, a bird of prey; probably from *ra*, to hover.
[3] *Eiye*, bird; *igbo*, forest, bush. Hence *eiye igbo* answers to our "wild bird." The native words are here retained in order to preserve the rhythm.
[4] Tie-tie is an Anglo-African term for the various kinds of parasitical vines which are used as substitutes for cord. They are sometimes called "bush-rope."

III. Why the ajao remained unburied.

My *alo* is of the *ajao*. [1]

The *ajao* lay in his house very sick, and there was no one to tend him. The *ajao* died.

The neighbours said, "The *ajao* is dead; we must call his relatives to come, and perform the funeral ceremonies, and bury him." And they went and called the birds, saying "Your relation is dead."

The birds came, and when they saw that the deceased was an *ajao*, they said, "This is not one of our family. All our family wear feathers, and you see the *ajao* has none. He does not belong to us." And they went away.

The neighbours consulted together. They said, "The birds are right. The *ajao* has no feathers, and is not of the family of birds. He must be of the family of rats." And they went and called the rats, saying, "Your relation is dead."

The rats came, but when they saw that the deceased was an *ajao* they also denied him. They said, "This is not one of our family. Everyone who is of our family has a tail, and you see the *ajao* has none." And they went away.

Thus the *ajao*, having no relations, remained unburied. [2]

[1] *Ajao,* a kind of flying-fox, or large bat.
[2] *See* Proverb 179.

IV.

My *alo* is something about a certain king.

One day the king called all the birds to come and clear a piece of ground. But be forgot to call *kini-kini*. [1]

All the birds came. They set to work, and they cleared a large piece of ground.

In the middle of the piece of ground was an *odan*-tree. [2] At mid-day, when the sun was hot, and all the birds had left their work for the day, *kini-kini* came and perched on the *odan*-tree, and began to sing:--

The king sent to invite my companions,
Kini-kini.
He assembled all the children of the folk with wings,
Kini-kini.
Grow grass, sprout bush,
Kini-kini,

Come, let us go to the house,
Kini-kini.
And there we can dance the *bata*,
Kini-kini.
If the *bata* will not sound we will dance the *dandun*,
Kini-kini.
If the *dundun* will not sound we will dance the *gangan*, [3]
Kini-kini."

Next morning, when the birds came to work, they found the ground they had cleared all grown over with grass and bush. They went and told the king. The king said, "That is nothing; clear it again."

The birds went to work and cleared it again, and at mid-day went away. The *kini-kini* came back and sang his song again, and again the grass and bush sprang up.

Next day the birds, when they saw what had happened, went and informed the king. "No matter," said the king, "clear the ground again."

A third time the birds cleared the ground and went away, and a third time the *kini-kini* came and sang so that the grass and bush sprang up.

The next day, when. the birds found the ground covered with bush, they went to the king. They asked the king to give them authority to seize the person who had played this trick. The king said, "Very well."

Then all the birds went back to the piece of ground; they put a great quantity of birdlime on the *odan*-tree; then they went home.

Next morning they came and cleared the ground again, and at mid-day went and hid in the bush close by.

The *kini-kini* came and perched on the *odan*. He sang his song, and the grass and bush grew up. Then he wanted to fly away, but he found himself held by the birdlime.

Then all the birds flocked to the tree and saw the *kini-kini*. They seized him and brought him to the king. They said to the king, "Behold the one who has caused us so much trouble."

The king made the *kini-kini* come near. "What have I done to you," he asked, "that you should act thus?" The *kini-kini* said, "When you called all my companions to clear the ground you left me out, therefore I have revenged myself."

When the king heard this, he raised his hand to give the *kini-kini* a slap.

"Pardon, pardon," said the *kini-kini*." If I find any cowries I will give them to you. When I get any kola-nuts I will bring them to you."

The king gave the bird a slap, and the *kini-kini* voided out cowries till the room was filled.

"What is this?" said the king, much astonished, and he raised his hand again to give the *kini-kini* a slap.

"I beg pardon," said the bird. "If I find any cowries I will give them to you. When I get any kola-nuts I will bring them to you."

The king gave him a slap, and the *kini-kini* voided from his body still more cowries than the first time.

Tile king sent messengers through all the country, and summoned all his people to assemble on the fifth day, to see a marvel. All the people promised to come.

Then.the king put the *kini-kini* in a basket. He covered the top of the basket and went out. His little son, who wanted to give the *kini-kini* a slap himself, uncovered the basket, and the bird flew away.

When the king came home he went to the basket. He found no bird in it, and he called his son.

"Where is the *kini-kini*?" he asked.

The little boy answered that he had gone to play with it, and that the bird had flown away. The king took the little boy and beat him. He beat him-he beat him, and, in his anger, he cut off one of his ears. "Go quick," he said. "Go quick, and find the bird." He pushed him out of the house.

The boy made a little drum, and went on the road to the bush. He sat down in a place in the bush where the birds were accustomed to come. He began to beat on his drum, and the drum said:--

"Tinliki, thiliki, tinli-puru. Tinli-puru."

All the birds flocked round, and each danced in turn. When it came to the turn of the *kini-kini* to dance, the *kini-kini* did not want to dance. All the birds begged him to dance, but he refused.

Then the boy played quicker on the drum. He beat, and beat, and beat, while all the birds begged the *kini-kini*.

At last the *kini-kini* began to yield. He twisted here and he twisted there. He flew three times round the head of the little boy. The boy continued beating as if he had not noticed anything, and the *kini-kini* began to dance.

He turned here and twisted there. He turned, and twisted, and turned, till he came quite close up to the drum. Then the little boy thrust out his hand and seized the *kini-kini* by the leg. All the other birds flew away.

The boy brought the *kini-kini* to his father. "I have caught him," he said. "Here he is. Won't you do something now to restore my ear?"

Then the king got up. He took a dead leaf and put it in the place of the ear. And the dead leaf softened and changed into an ear.

We now come to those tales which may be called "Tortoise Stories," since the tortoise (*awon*) always plays a leading part in them. The tortoise has, in these tales, various superhuman powers attributed to him, and, in most, is described as acting craftily or mischievously. He, in fact, fills in the folk-lore tales of the Slave Coast the place of the spider (*anansi*) in the tales of the Gold Coast, and which are in consequence known as *Anansi 'sem* (*Anansi asem*), "Spider Stories." In these the spider is always depicted as showing great skill and craft, and, like the minor gods, is represented as speaking through the nose.

The names Tortoise and Spider are in these stories used as the proper names of anthropomorphic personages, and among the Tshi tribes the latter is called *Ajya Anansi*, "Father Spider," or "Father Anansi." Thus, the Yoruba proverbial saying, *Eji Awon ko kon ni li owo*, used to convey the meaning that a matter which at first sight appears insignificant may really be one of great importance, should not be translated

"The blood of the tortoise is not a handful" (literally, does not fill a hand "), but "the blood of *Awon*" (the mythical personage, or anthropomorphic tortoise) "is not a handful." An epithet of the tortoise is *ajapa*, "bald-headed elf," or "hairless elf" (*aja*, elf; *pa*, to be bald or bare). The flickering appearance seen near the ground on sultry days is called "tortoise-fire," and is believed to be caused by a subterranean fire made by the tortoise to destroy the roots of trees. The tortoise appears in several proverbial sayings, as "The tortoise (or *Awon*) is always the subject of an *alo*" (tale), and "The house of the tortoise is not large enough for itself. The verandah" (that is, that part of the shell which projects over the tail) "of a tortoise will not accommodate a guest. The tortoise, having built its house, makes the verandah behind it;" while "As the tortoise meets with due regard, so also should the snail," seems to indicate that the tortoise is regarded with reverence or respect.

It is possible that totemism lies at the root of these phenomena. On the Gold Coast there is a tradition that all mankind are descended from *Anansi*, and on the Slave Coast the figure of the tortoise is frequently seen carved on the doors of temples, together with the leopard, serpent, and a fish. On the whole, however, it seems more probable that the peculiarities which make the spider and the tortoise each in its own way remarkable, have led to their selection for the chief role in the popular fables. The tales being largely about animals, those creatures which most excited wonder and speculation in the minds of the natives would be the ones to which the most wonderful attributes would be ascribed; and, in the case, of the spider, the ingenuity and patience displayed by it in the construction of its web would be attributed to the anthropomorphic spider of the stories. There is at the present time no spider-clan among the totem-clans of the Gold Coast, and, as the communities of the Gold Coast are heterogeneous, we cannot suppose that an entire clan has become extinct, unless the extinction took place in the remote past when cominunitics were hornogeneous; in which case there seems no sufficient reason for the memory of the totem-ancestor being preserved, after the disappearance of all those who were supposed to be descended from him.

[1] A small black and white bird, sometimes called the doctor-bird. It is named from its cry, which rescinbles the words *kini-kini*.

[2] *Odan*, a variety of *ficus*, which is planted in streets and open spaces as a shade-tree.

[3] *Bata*, *dundun*, and *yangan*, are the names of different kinds of drums. The *bata* is a tall drum, the *dundun* is hung with little bells, and the *yangan* is properly a war-drum. These names are onomatopœic. Each drum has its own measure and rhythm, and people say "to dance the *bata*, to dance the *dundun*, or to dance the *yangan*," just as we say, "to dance a waltz, to dance a polka, or to dance a quadrille."

Tortoise Stories. I.

My *alo* is something about a woman named Olu.

Olu had a son named Sigo, and Sigo determined to be a hunter.

His father gave him a horse, his mother gave him a sheep, and they told him to go and hunt. So Sigo took his bow and arrows, mounted the horse, and rode away into the bush.

He travelled a long way, and at last arrived at the haunt of animals.

Then the sky became overcast, and it grew so dark that Sigo could scarcely see. Soon the rain poured in torrents. It fell so heavily that Sigo was washed by the water into a deep gully. He tried to get out, but could not, and remained there weeping and lamenting.

The rain ceased, and Tortoise, always on the lookout for opportunities, came to the gully.

Sigo saw him, and stretched his neck up to the brink of the gully. "Hi! Tortoise! Oh! bald-headed elf! Hi!" he cried.

Tortoise came and leant over the edge of the gully to see who was calling him. "What are you doing there?" he said. "The flood of the rain washed me in here," said Sigo.

What will you give me if I pull you out?" asked Tortoise. "I will be your slave," replied Sigo. "Very well," said Tortoise, the bald-headed elf.

Tortoise climbed down into the gully and took Sigo out. He said to him, "I am going to make a large drum, and shall put you inside it. When we come to any house, and I begin playing on the drum, take care that you sing well." "I understand," said Sigo.

When he reached the town in which he lived, Tortoise, the bald-headed elf, went to the king and boasted of the fine sound of his drum. The king ordered Tortoise to bring the drum and beat it in his presence, so that he could hear the sound.

"Very well," said Tortoise, "send and call all the town to the dance." "Very good," said the king, and be sent all through the town to invite the people to come and dance. When all the people had assembled the king sent to call the bald-headed elf. The bald-headed elf took his drum, and came into the midst of the assembly. He beat the drum with the stick, and the drum sounded, saying:--

Sigo is the son of Olu; [1]
Ah! let me be rescued.
His mother gave him a sheep, and told him to go and hunt;
Ah! let me be rescued.
His father gave him a horse, and told him to go and hunt;
Ah! let me be rescued.
Listen to what I say. He went to the elephant's haunt;
Ah! let me be rescued.
Listen to what I say. He went to the buffalo's lair;

Ah! let me be rescued.
The flood of the rain wasbed him into the cleft;
Ah! let me be rescued.
And so he became the Tortoise's slave;
Ah! let me be rescued.

The people were much astonished, and clapped their hands to their mouths in wonder. The king told Tortoise to beat the drum again, and let him hear once more.

Tortoise beat his drum a second time, and the people cried out aloud at the marvel. Then Tortoise returned home.

Before long the mistresses of the house to which Sigo belonged came to Tortoise, and asked him to come and beat his drum at a dance they were about to have. The bald-headed elf said "Very good." He took his drum and he went there.

When he arrived the wives made ready some gruel of Indian corn, [2] and bought some rum. They asked Tortoise to beat his drum. Tortoise beat his drum, and the drum sang:--

"Sigo, is the son of Olu;
Ah! let me be rescued.
His mother gave him a sheep, and told him to go and hunt;
Ah! let me be rescued.
His father gave him a horse, and told him to go and hunt;
Ah! let me be rescued.
Listen to what I say. He went to the elephant's haunt;
Ah! let me be rescued.
Listen to what I say. He went to the buffalo's lair;
Ah! let me be rescued.
The flood of the rain washed him into the cleft;
Ah! let me be rescued.
And so he became the Tortoise's slave;
Ah! let me be rescued.

They gave Tortoise to eat. Tortoise ate. They gave him rum to drink. He drank, and, becoming drunk, fell asleep.

When Tortoise was asleep they took his drum. They took off the drum-head, and took Sigo out. Then they put the head back as it was before.

When he awoke, Tortoise took his drum and began beating on it. A crow croaked in the drum. Tortoise beat harder and quicker, and the crow croaked louder and louder. He cried, as loud as he could, "Why, when you were eating, did you not give something to eat to the drum? Why, when you were drinking, did not you give some of the rum to the drum?"

Tortoise went home. He took off the drum-head, and found a crow in the drum.

[1] There is perhaps some pun in this. *Olu* means a clapper, or anything to strike with, and *ilu* means a drum.

[2] Oka.

II.

My *alo* is something about a certain king.

The king had a daughter who was dumb. The girl's name was Bola.

The king did all he could to make his daughter speak. All that he did was of no avail, so he did not keep the girl in the town; he sent her into the country.

Tortoise, of the thousand cunning tricks, came to the king and said to him, "What will you give me if I make your child speak.?" "I will divide my house into two halves," said the king, "and I will give you one half."

The bald-headed elf went and bought a bottle of honey, and came to the bush, where the girl was living. He put the honey on the ground and went and hid himself.

The girl came and saw the bottle of honey and put out her hand to it.

Tortoise cameout of his hiding-place, came behind the girl, and gave her a slap, crying, "Thief! So it is you who steal my honey and eat it."

"I?" said the young girl. I have stolen your honey to eat? I?"

Then Tortoise, the crafty, tied her with a rope, and sang:--

"Bola stole honey to eat;
Kayin, Kayin. [1]
Bola is a cunning cheat;
Kayin, Kayin.
Bola is a shameless thief;
Kayin, Kayin."

When Tortoise sung this, the young girl sang:--

"Into the wood of the elephant I went with the elephant;
Kayin, Kayin.
Into the wood of the buffalo I went with the buffalo;
Kayin, Kayin.
And Tortoise has come to accuse me of stealing honey to eat
Kayin, Kayin."

Tortoise, the mischievous, led the young girl back to the town. He was singing his song, and she was answering with her song. In this manner they arrived before the king), who cried out with astonishment, "My daughter, who has never been heard to speak, speaks to-day!"

The king divided his palace in half, and gave one half to Tortoise, the bald-headed elf.

That is how Tortoise succeeds in everything.

[1] *Kayin* (*ka-iyin*), to celebrate, or sing the praises of.

142

III.

My *alo* is about Tortoise and the elephant.

The bald-headed elf one day told the other animals that he would ride the elephant, but all the animals said: "No, you can't ride the elephant."

The bald-headed elf said: "Well, I will make a wager that I will ride the elephant into town." And the other animals agreed to the wager.

Tortoise went into the forest and met the elephant. He said to him: "My father, all the animals say you are too stout and big to come to town."

The elephant was vexed. Ile said: "The animals are fools. If I do not come to town it is because I prefer the forest. Besides, I do not know the way to town."

"Oh!" said the bald-headed elf, "then come with me. I will show you the way to the town, and you can put all the animals to shame."

So the elephant followed him.

When they were near the town the bald-headed elf said: "My father, I am tired. Will you kindly allow me to get, on your back."

"All right," said the elephant. He knelt down, and Tortoise climbed -up on his back. Then they went on along the road.

The bald-headed elf said: "My father, when I scratch your back you must run, and when I knock my head against your back you must run faster; then you will make a fine display in the town." The elephant said: "Very well."

When they came near the town, the bald-headed elf scratched the elephant's back, and he began to run. He knocked his back with his head, and the elephant ran faster.

The animals, when they saw this, were frightened. They went into their houses, but they looked out of their windows. And Tortoise called out to them: "Did I not say I would ride my father's slave to town?"

"What do you mean by 'your father's slave'?" said the elephant, growing angry.

"I am only praising you," said Tortoise.

But the elephant saw the other animals laughing, and grew more angry. "I will throw you down on the hard stones here, and break you to pieces," he cried.

"Yes, yes, that is right," said the bald-headed elf.

"Throw me down here. That will be all right. 'Then I shall not die; then I shall not be hurt. If you really want to kill me, you ought to carry me to a swamp. There I shall die at once, for the mud and water will drown me."

The elephant believed the bald-headed elf. He ran to the swamp, and threw Tortoise into the mud.

Then he stretched out his foot to kick him, but the bald-headed elf dived in the mire, and came up in another place.

The other animals were there, looking on, and Tortoise called out to them, "Did I not say I would ride my father's slave to town?"

When the elephant found that he could not catch the bald-headed elf, he ran away at full speed back to the forest.

When he reached there he said to the other elephants, "Do you know what that broken-back [1] has done to me?" And he told them the story.

The other elephants said, "You were a fool to carry that broken-back to town."

Since then the elephant has not come to town any more.

[1] An epithet of the tortoise. It probably refers to the notched appearance of the back.

IV.

My *alo* is about a woman named Adun.

Adun was very beautiful, and all the men wanted her. They were always entreating her, but she always refused.

One market-day a person borrowed legs from one, arms from another, and a body from a third. He joined all together, and went to the market. He wanted Adun, and he would have her.

His appearance pleased Adun, and they talked together. Although he belonged to a distant country, she consented to go with him. She took him to the

house and showed him to her mothers. [1] Her mothers said, "Very well, go with him."

They went. On the road, the master of the legs took away the legs, the master of the arms took away the arms, and the master of the body took away the body. Nothing was left but the head. And the head went on, on, while Adun, nearly dead with fear, could not run away.

They arrived at the house of the head.

Next morning, before he went to work in his plantation, the head said to Tortoise, "If Adun tries to run away, sound the horn to warn me."

The head had scarcely gone out of sight when Adun took her bundle, and began to run away.

Then Tortoise sounded the horn. "Head, head," he cried, "Adun is going. She has tied up her calabaslies, she has gathered her dishes."

The head ran up and made big round eyes. "Where are you going?" he asked. "I am going to relieve nature," [2] said Adun. "You are running away," said the head.

Every day Adun tried to run away, but without success. Then she went to ask the *babalawo* what she should do.

The *babalawo* said, "Go and buy some *ekurus*. [3] Buy plenty of them. Soak them in palm-oil, and stuff them into Tortoise's horn." "Very good," said Adun.

She did as she was told. Then she took up her bundle and started off. Tortoise took the horn to blow it. The *ekurus* came into his mouth. He ate, ate, ate, and Adun ran away.

[1] The wives in the household.
[2] The ordinary excuse of a native who has no pretext ready.
[3] *Ekuru* is a cake made of the flour of a white bean called *ere*. It is very dry, and a proverbial saying, said of a tedious visitor, runs, "He chokes me like *ekuru*."

V.

My *alo* is about a maiden named Buje, the slender.

There was a young maiden named Buje, the slender, whom all the men wanted. The rich wanted her, but she refused. Chiefs wanted, and she refused. The king wanted her, and she still refused.

Tortoise came to the king, and said to him, "She whom you all want, and cannot get, I will get. I will have her, I." And the king said, "If you succeed in having her, I will divide my palace into two halves and will give you one half."

One day, Buje, the slender, took an earthen pot and went to fetch water. Tortoise, seeing this, took his hoe, and cleared the path that led to the spring. He found a snake in the grass, and killed it. Then he put the snake in the middle of the path.

When Buje, the slender, had filled her pot, she came back. She saw the snake in the path, and called out "Hi! hi! Come and kill this snake."

Tortoise ran up, with his cutlass in his hand. He struck at the snake, and wounded himself in the leg.

Then he cried out "Buje, the slender, has killed me. I was cutting the bush, I was clearing the path for her. She called to me to kill the snake, and I came quickly. Buje, the slender, Buje, the slender, I have killed the snake, but I have wounded myself in the leg. Oh, Buje, the slender, Buje, the slender, take me up on your back like a child. Take me up on your back and hold me close."

He cried this many times, and at last Buje, the slender, took Tortoise and put him up on her back. And then Tortoise slipped his legs down over her hips, and violated Buje, the slender, from behind.

Next day, as soon as it was light, Tortoise went to the king. He said, "Did I not tell you that I would have Buje, the slender? Call all the people of the town to assemble on the fifth day, and you will hear what I have to say."

When it was the fifth day, the king sent out his crier to call all the people together. The people came. Tortoise cried out, "Everybody wanted Buje, the slender, and Buje refused everybody, but I have had her."

The king sent a messenger, with his stick, to summon Bujo, the slender. When she came the king said, "We have heard that Tortoise is your husband; is it so?"

Buje, the slender, was ashamed, and could not answer. She covered her head with her cloth, and ran away into the bush.

And there she was changed into the plant called Buje. [1]

[1] There is a version of this story, current among the English and Americans, which makes Buje be ravished by a deformed man, instead of by the Tortoise. It is to be found, I believe, in "Central Africa," a work I have not seen, but which was written. by Mr. Bowen, an American Missionary, and published at Charleston, United States of America. in 1857. All natives are agreed that this version is incorrect, and that Tortise was the ravisher, and the only probable explanation of the mistake seems to be that Mr. Bowen learnt the story from a native who spoke French, and either confused *la tortue* with *le tortu*, or concluded that the narrator meant the latter when he said the former. If the hearer had never heard of the mythical personage, the antbropomorphic Tortoise, he, thinking it impossible that Buje could be violated by a tortoise, would very naturally suppose that the narrator meant to say *le tortu*, and erred through an insufficient knowledge of French.

The pulp of the fruit of the Buje-shrub turns black when exposed to the air, and is used by the natives to stain the skin in imitation of tattooing. It leaves marks like lamp-black.

VI.

My *alo* is about Tortoise.

There was a famine, and there was a great scarcity of food all through the country.

One day the lizard was in a plantation searching for something to eat, when he found a large rock full of yams.

The owner of the plantation was near the rock. He cried "Rock, open," and the rock opened. He went in and took yams, and came out again. Then he said, "Rock, shut," and the rock closed up.

The lizard saw all this. He heard also what the man said, and he went home.

Next morning, at cock-crow, he went to the rock. He said, "Rock, open," and the rock opened. He went in and carried out yams to take home and eat. Then he said, "Rock, shut," and the rock shut. Every day the lizard did this.

One day Tortoise, the bald-headed elf, met the lizard on the road carrying yams. He said to him, "Where did yoti get your food from, comrade?

The lizard said, "If I were to tell you that, and take you to the place, I should be killed." The baldheaded elf answered, "No, I will not say a word to anyone. Please take me." And the lizard said, "Very well, then; come and call me tomorrow morning at cock-crow, and we will go together."

Next morning, long before cock-crow, Tortoise came to the house of the lizard. He stood outside the house and cried "Cock-a-doodle-do." [1] Again he cried "Cock-a-doodle-do." Then he went in and woke the lizard. "The cock lias crowed," he said.

"Let me sleep," said the lizard; "it is not yet cock-crow." "Very well," said Tortoise. And they both went to sleep till cock-crow.

Then the lizard got up, and the two went together. As soon as they arrived at the. place the lizard said, "Rock, open," and the rock opened. The lizard went in, took yams, and came out again.

He said to Tortoise, "It is time to go. Take your yams and come." "Wait a mimite," said Tortoise.

"Very well," said the lizard. "Rock, shut." And he went away without waiting.

Tortoise, the bald-headed elf, helped himself to yams. He put yams on his back and yams on his head; he put yams on his arms and yams on his legs.

The lizard had already gone home. He lighted a fire. Then he lay on his back, with his feet in the air, as if he were dead; and he remained like that all day.

When Tortoise, the bald-headed elf, was ready to go, he wanted to make the rock open. But he could not remember what he ought to say. He said many many words, but not the right words; and the rock remained shut.

By-and-bye came the plantation-owner. He opened the rock, and found Tortoise inside. He took him and beat him. He beat him badly.

"Who brought you here?" asked the man. "It was the lizard who brought me," replied Tortoise. Then the man tied a string to Tortoise, and took him to the lizard.

When the man reached the house of the lizard, he found the lizard lying on his back, with his feet in the air, as if he were dead. He shook him. He said to him, "This bald-headed elf says it was you who took him to my plantation, and showed him my store of yams."

"I?" said the lizard. "You call see for yourself that it is impossible. I am not in a state to go out. I have been sick here for three months, lying on my back. I do not even know where your plantation is."

Then the man took Tortoise and smashed him. And Tortoise, groaning and moaning, said in a pitiful voice, "Cockroach, come and mend me. Ant, come and mend me."

And the cockroach and the ant mended him. And the places where they mended him are those parts of Tortoise which are rough. [2]

[1] In Yoruba, *kekere-ke*, an onomatopœic word supposed to resemble the crow of a cock. It is from keke, which, like our onomatopœic word "cackle," means the cry of the hen.]

[2] In this tale, Tortoise's usual cunning fails him. It is to be noted that, whenever be is shown as being over-reached or unsuccessful, the want of success is due to greediness-as in the first tale, where be eats and drinks till he falls asleep, so that Sigo is rescued from the drum; and in the fourth talc, where he is so busily engaged in eating the *ekuras* placed in the horn, that he forgets to sound it. Here his greediness wakes him stay behind, to get more yams.

Chapter Fifteen - Conclusions

IN the preface to the second volume of this series it was said that, in collecting information concerning the religions of the cognate tribes dealt with, my chief purpose was to endeavour to ascertain to what extent different conditions of culture led to the modifications of religious conceptions. Three groups of tribes have now been considered, the Tshi, the Ewe, and the Yoruba, who represent three stages of progress, the Tshi being in the lowest stage and the Yoruba in the highest. As these tribal groups undoubtedly had a common origin, it is reasonable to suppose that the Yoruba tribes were once in the social and mental condition in which the Tshi tribes are now, and that, in fact, in these groups we find the same race in different states of culture. Assuming then, as we legitimately may, that the religious beliefs of the Ewes are modifications of earlier belief resembling those now held by the Tshis, and that those of the Yorubas are similarly modifications of beliefs like those now held by the Ewes, we here have an opportunity of observing how the evolution of religion may proceed.

Among the Tshi-speaking tribes we found that everything in nature is believed to be animated-that is to say, everything not inade by human hands has an animating principle, spiritual second-self, or indwelling spirit, possessing powers which may be beneficial or prejudicial to man, according to whether it is propitiated or neglected. It seems probable that the belief in all nature being thus animated was an extension of the belief that man possesses a spiritual second-self, or indwelling spirit, which belief is beyond dispute the result of savage speculation concerning dreams. Man, having decided that he possessed an indwelling spirit, would extend the same possession to animals, then to vegetable life, and finally to inanimate nature, partly because he does not perceive any strict line of demarcation between these, and partly because he as frequently sees the phantoms of such things in his dreams as he does the phantoms of living men. He would be led to extend the indwelling-spirit theory to all nature, because it would account for many things that would otherwise be incomprehensible, since uncivilised man believes that every occurrence is the result of design, and that nothing ever happens by accident. The theory that a man who is drowned has been drawn down and strangled by the water-spirit, seems to him much more satisfactory than to suppose that the death was the result of chance circumstances.

All indwelling spirits are, however, not equally revered. Those of bushes, grasses, stones, &c., are not much regarded, and the most important are those of rivers, lagoons, the sea, mountains, rocks, and shoals. The reason of this, no doubt, is that no loss of life or injury to person or property can be directly connected with a bush, or grass, or a stone, without, at least, the intervention of human agency; while, in the nature of things, men must occasionally be drowned in rivers, canoes capsized in the sea, and property and life destroyed or injured by flood or landslip, or other natural causes. *Timor fecit deos*, and those natural features and objects which experience has shown to be more frequently the apparent cause of mishaps, have more regard paid to them, or rather to their animating principles, than those which have proved to be innocuous. Every man worships that from which he has most to fear or most to expect, and it is commonly something with which he is daily brought into contact. Thus, fishermen pay most attention to the indwelling spirits of the sea and of the shoals and reefs on which their canoes might be wrecked; while the agriculturist worships the spirit of the stream that flows near his dwelling, or that of the cliff or mass of rock which overhangs his plantation, and those of the gigantic silk-cotton trees, whose downfall so frequently crushes to death the inhabitant of the forest. Objects of worship are thus local, and are worshipped only by those in the neighbourhood. In most cases worship and sacrifice are made in the habitat of the spirit, or god, under the boulder of rock, or on the bank of the, stream or lagoon; and, as the nature of the god is well understood, as he is believed to be the indwelling spirit of the rock or the stream, there is no need for any myth explanatory of his origin, or for an image or tangible representation of him. This is the condition in which the great majority of the Tshi tribes are at the present day.

The first change appears to be caused by the making of an image, or *simulacrum*, of a god, which has the effect of weakening the tie between the indwelling spirit and the object it animates. If the image were kept in the habitat of the local god, the connection of the god with the particular rock, cliff, or stream would not be lost sight of; but it would serve no useful purpose to keep an image there, since the god himself is present, and the only object in making one is to bring the god to some place nearer at hand, which will be more convenient for the worshippers, and at the same time bring the protecting power more directly into contact with them. To effect this removal of a god it is a *sine qua non* that the *simulacrum* must be made from material obtained from the habitat of the god, or be a portion of that which he animates. A fragment of rock from a boulder inhabited by an indwelling spirit, or a figure carved from wood taken from a tree in a grove inhabited by a spirit, preserves in the minds of the worshippers the subjective connection between the fragment and the boulder, or the figure and the grove; and, by a confusion of ideas which is well known, he thinks that the objective connection is likewise unbroken, and that the god, or spirit, is by means of the simulacrum brought before him.

This removal, as it were, of a god from his proper dwelling-place, necessarily leads, first, to a weakening of the tie between the god and that which he animates, and, finally, to the nature of the god, as an indwelling spirit of a natural object, being completely lost sight of. Let us imagine, for example, that the inhabitants of a village who have been in the habit of worshipping the indwelling spirit of a precipitous cliff in the neighbourhood, come to the conclusion that it would be more convenient, and at the same time place them more effectually under the protection of the spirit, if they were to bring him into the village. They accordingly make a figure of clay taken from the cliff, and set it up in the village in a miniature hut erected for its protection. This hut then becomes the sacred place, and the sacrifices and sacred dances are performed before it, instead of, as heretofore, at the cliff. The god, however, is not supposed to have absolutely abandoned the cliff, and persons whose avocations took them to it would still think it necessary to propitiate him with small offering of food. Practically he is believed to be in the cliff and yet also in the image in the village, for although a man, if asked to explain the seeming impossibility of one and the same person being in two places at once, might say that the god only entered the image in order to receive the offerings and listen to the prayers of the faithful, or that the image merely served as an instrument through which the god could take cognizance of the wants of his followers, yet, as a matter of fact, they never seem to think about the matter at all, and it is taken for granted by the villagers that the god is in their midst. Generations are born and die, and are succeeded by others, all of which have been accustomed to perform religious ceremonies before the miniature hut, and the inevitable result is that, sooner or later, the connection of the god with the cliff, of which he was the aniniating principle, is completely lost sight of, and he is regarded as the tutelary deity of the village, pure and simple. In this way undoubtedly originated many of the tutelary deities of towns and villages on the Gold Coast, for the process can be seen going on at the present day. By carrying it a little further, tribal or national gods might be similarly produced, but, with two or three exceptions, the Tshi tribes have not progressed so far as that, and most of the gods worshipped by complete tribes are simply the indwelling spirits of very remarkable natural objects situated in the territories occupied by the tribes.

Besides the gods which are the animating principles or indwelling spirits of natural features and objects, and which we may call nature-gods, we have objects of worship of another class, which are the product of manes-worship, and which we may therefore term ghost-gods. The ghosts, or souls of deceased men of rank and power, are supplicated and propitiated in the same way and to the same extent as are the nature-gods, and it is often difficult to decide where the one worship begins and the other ends.

Manes-worship reaches its fullest development in the royal houses of Ashanti and Dahomi, that is to say, in those situations where the conditions are most favourable for preserving the memory of the wisdom and power of deceased men. In both these houses periodical human sacrifices are made on the tombs of the former kings, in addition to the daily minor offerings of food and drink. We find the same confusion between objective and subjective connection in the case of these ghost-gods as we do in that of the nature-gods; and the skulls of chiefs and others are often exhumed and placed in small temples adjoining the dwelling-houses, in the idea that the guardian-ghost is thereby brought to the spot. At the battle of Dodowah, near Accra, where the Ashantis were defeated in 1826, a head, wrapped in a silk handkerchief, and covered with a leopard-skin, the emblem of royalty, was captured. This was the head of the late king, Tutu Kwamina, and his successor had brought it with him, in the idea that he would thereby be able to obtain the support of the gliostly king against his enemies. Before the battle offerings were made to it, and the ghost was invoked to cause the heads of all the white men in the field to he beside his before night.

Many tutelary deities of towns, clans, and families doubtless owe their origin to manes-worship. The dead are ordinarily, one might almost say invariably, buried in or near to the habitations of the living, and it is certain that in many cases the habit of offering sacrifices at the place of sepulture has been continued, simply through habit, long after the fact that a man was buried there has been forgotten. In such a case, the guardian-ghost being lost sight of, the god is simply a tutelary god, whose origin is either unexplained, or which the priests explain in any way that may suit them best. We thus have two explanations of the origin of tutelary deities. They are either nature-gods who have been severed from their proper surroundings, or ghost-gods whose origin has been forgotten. Of couse the manes themselves are tuletar.

Nature-gods themselves are no doubt in several cases blended with ghost-gods. The reverence paid to certain rivers, cliffs, &c., must have often dated from some fatal accident that occurred in connection with them. It was this which first attracted attention, and primitive man would not be likely to discriminate between the ghost of the victim, which would haunt the spot where the latter lost its life, and the indwelling spirit of the natural feature. Nevertheless, that the nature-gods are, as a whole, the product of manes-worship, is, we think, a theory not warranted by the evidence, though apparently supported by the high authority of Mr. Herbert Spencer. It often occurs that a family settles near to some river, lake, or hill, and forthwith commences a cult of this indwelling spirit, without any catastrophe having taken place near it. In fact, it may be said to be the rule that whenever a Tshi group takes up its abode near any remarkable natural feature of object, it worships and seeks to propitiate its indwelling spirit, fearing that otherwise it may do some harm. Many of the nature-gods are non-terrestrial, and it is difficult to see by what process they could ever become confused with dead men. Nobody could be buried in the sky, sun, moon, rainbow, or wind; and if these could be conceived to be animate without the intervention of the souls of the dead, why could not terrestrial objects also? Manes-worship is the result of the belief that man has an indwelling spirit which survives after the death of the body, and nature worship is the result of the belief that all nature is animate. Which was first in order it would be difficult to determine with absolute certainty, but, from the analogy of the lower animals, it seems probable that the second was. Animals regard objects which move as alive, whout having come to the conclusion that they themselves have spiritual second selves, and primitive man, who would know litle more of naturea cuasation than an animal does, probably did also. When a rock slipped, or a tree fell, the unusual behavior suggested animation. Afterwards, when he had come to believe that he himself possessed an indwelling spirit, he probably conceived the animating entites of natural objects to be somewhat analogous, and made the gods the reflex of his own *kra*.

Objects made by human hands are not animate, and do not possess indwelling spirits, though they have ghosts, which the souls of the dead are able to make use of in deadland. There are, however, many such objects upon which the native sets great value, and as they do not possess guardian-spirits of themselves, he provides them with artificial ones. Thus, just as he kills the wives of his chief, and buries them with him, releasing their ghosts, or souls, from their bodies to enable them to continue their ministrations to their lord, so, perfectly logically, he slays a slave on the family stool, the emblem of office, or upon the great drum of the tribe, releasing the ghost from the body in order to enable it to become the guardian-spirit of the stool or drum. This is a luxury that can only be afforded by men of rank, or to ensure the safekeeping of national trophies or emblems, and hence it is only the royal stools of kings and chiefs, or paraphernalia belonging to the tribe as a whole, that are, as a rule, thus protected. The victim is decapitated upon the object so that the blood gushes over it, and on the, Gold Coast many tribal stools and drums are clotted thick with the blood of those who have been slain upon them, for it seems to be thought necessary to renew the guardian from time to time. As, when a human sacrifice is offered to a god, the victim is similarly slain upon the sacred stool or chair, it seems probable that the ghost is in this case also believed to become a guardian-spirit. No doubt the belief that all objects not made by human hands possessed indwelling, or guardian-spirits, suggested the idea of supplying artificial guardian-spirits to objects which did not come under this category. The practice is very widespread, and the custom of immolating human victims at the launching of war-canoes in the islands of the Pacific, so that the bows were sprinkled with their blood, and the Dyak practice of crushing a slave-girl to death under the first post erected at the building of a communal house, are cases in point, the sacrifice being in each case designed to provide a guardian-spirit.

With some two or three exceptions, all the gods worshipped by the Tshi tribes are purely local and have a limited area of worship. If they are nature-gods they are bound up with the natural objects they animate, if they are ghost-gods they are localised by the place of sepulture, and if they are tuletary deities, whose origin has been forgotten, their position is necessarily fixed by that of the town, village, or family they protect. In any case they are worshipped only by those who live in the neighbourbood. The exceptions are the sky-god, the earthquake-god, and the goddess of the silk-cotton trees. The vault of the heaven overhangs every town and hamlet, so that Nyankupon, [1] the god of the sky, which is believed to be solid, and the roof of the world, is universally known. Similarly, earthquakes are felt over the whole country, so that Sasabonsum, the earth-god, who is held to produce these phenomena, is also widely known. Silk-cotton trees are found everywhere, so

that Srahmantin, the goddess of these trees, is feared and worshipped everywhere. With these three exceptions there are no general gods, that is, no
gods known to the Tshi tribes as a whole; and two of them, it may be observed, in accordance with the principle that every man worships that which
is most likely to affect his lot, and which is ordinarily near at hand, though
known to all, are not paid much regard to, except when they force themselves upon the attention. Nyankupon is generally considered too distant to
have much weight in the affairs of mankind, or to take much interest therein,
but when he thunders and lightens-for to thunder, lighten, and pour out rain
are his functions and thereby reminds men that he has power to injure, they
become polite to him, and seek to propitiate him by flattery and praise.
Sasabonsum likewise is not paid much attention to, except when an earth-
quake happens, and then everybody hastens to offer sacrifices. As silk-cotton
trees are everywhere close at hand, and a great many pesrions are cushed to
death by them-for they seem particularly liable to the ravages of white ants,
and then blown down by a very moderate gale of wind-it is considered of
some importance to propitiate Srahmantin, who is the only spirit-or class of
spirits, for it is not quite clear which it is-that can be said to be generally
worshipped by the tribes as a whole.

The indwelling spirits of natural objects are held to be of human shape, but
to possess the more striking characteristics of the objects they animate.
Thus, because the silk-cotton tree has a gaunt, greyish-white trunk, which
towers high above the other trees of the forest, and often reaches to a height
of 100 feet before it throws out a branch, Srahmantin is said to be of gigantic
stature and greyish-white in color. To these characteristics native imagina-
tion has added long flowing hair, and long pendent breasts. Similarly, Tahbi,
the indwelling spirt of the huge mass of black rock on which Cape Coast Cas-
tle is built, is of immense size, and black; and Abroh-ku, the surf-god of the
landing place, is of the colour of wood ashes, and small and round, like a
breaking wave.

Among the Ewe tribes we find the smae fundamental belief that all nature
is animate, and the local nature-gods are as among the Tshi tribes, the indwelling spirits of natural objects and features; but *simulacra* are much more
common on the Slave coast than on the Gold Coast, and, as a consequence,
the tie between nature-gods and their habitiats, and between ghost-gods and
their human origin, has been more frequently weakened and lost sight of.
Hence we find a large increase in the number of tribal and general gods,
many of which have now no connection with any natural object or with manes-worship. Concurrently with the increase in the number of tribal and general gods runs the relegation of the purely local gods to an inferior position.
A god who is worshipped over a large area is naturally believed to be more
powerful than one whose area of worship is circumscribed, and the trial and
general gods, having each their special functions and attributes, monpolise
between them nearly all the phenomena and qualities which excite fear and
respect in man. The local gods are thus pushed back from the prominent po-

sition they are held among the Tshi tribes, with whom to propitiate the local gods was considered all important, and though they are worshipped by small communities and solitary families, the inhabitants of towns do not pay much attention to them. Almost every person is enrolled as a follower of one, at least, of the general and tribal gods, and when a man is secure of the favour and protection of the king, the goodwill of the court-underling is no longer of much moment to him.

Among the general deities of the Ewe tribes, Mawu, the sky-god, whose name also means to stretch over or overshadow, answers to the Nyankuopon of the Tshi tribes, and the silk-cotton tree spirits appear under the names of Huntin and Loko. The Ewes have no earthquake-god, probably because the shocks of earthquakes are rarely felt on the Slave Coast, two only being known to have occurred since 1778, whereas slight shocks are experienced on the Gold Coast every two or three years. Mawu, like Nyankupon, is considered too distant to interfere in human affairs, and as he no longer thunders and lightens, which phenomena are attributed to a new conception, Khebioso, a bird-like god, who appears to be the personified thunder-cloud, he does nothing but control the rain, and his importance has been thereby lessened. Other general deities are Aizan, protector of markets and public places, who seems to be a type generalised from the multitudinous tutelary gods of the Gold Coast; Dso, the god of fire, Legba, a phallic divinity, and Sapatan, the small-pox god. In this deification, or personification, of fire, love, and pestilence, we see a new departure. Fire is not worshipped on the Gold Coast, and there it is the local gods who inflict pestilence on their worshippers as a punishment for neglect; while love, or desire, is usually stimulated by the ghost-gods, who, as the forefathers of the ghost-gods are believed to take an interest in the propagation of their descendants, though occasionally the exciting of this passion may be found to be one out of the many attributes of a nature-god.

When we come to the Yoruba-speaking tribes we find *simulacra* in universal use, and the belief that nature-gods are the animating principles of natural objects only lingering in places remote from populous centres, and among the Jebus, who live isolated in their forests and shun intercourse with the other tribes. There are, in consequence, few local gods proper, but many tutelary deities of tribes, towns, villages, and families, and there is a very large increase in the number of general deities. Olorun, the sky god, answers to the Ewe Mawu and the Tshi Nyankupon, but he is rapidly being displaced by Obatala, a more anthropomorphic conception, and who very probably was a ghost-god whose origin has been lost sight of. The god of thunder and lightning appears under the name of Shango, and that of small-pox under the name of Shan-kpanna. Legba has become a combination of desire and evil, and Odudua, a goddess, said by the priests to be the earth, presides over the passion of love. Orisha Oko, who represents natural. fertility, Aje Shaluga, god of wealth, Shigidi, personified nightmare, and Dada, patron of vegetables, are new conceptions. A native of the Gold Coast who found his yam-crop thrive would attribute it to the fostering care of the local nature-god, and if he acquired wealth it would probably be considered due to the efforts of his tutelary deity, but here gods appear to have been made out of abstractions.

The evolution of types has been carried further than among the Ewes, and instead of each hill and mountain having its own indwelling god we have Oke, god of heights in general; while in place of the multitude of local sea-gods found on the Gold Coast and the western half of the Slave Coast, we have one general god of the sea, Olokun. Aroni, god of forests, is another example. Olosa, the lagoon, Oya, the river Niger, and the two rivers Oshun and Oba, are nature-gods, which, from being strictly local, have now become general. Ifa, god of divination, who is the benefactor of man and the unveiler of the future, was probably originally a ghost-god as no doubt was Osanhin, god of medicine. Ogun, god of iron, and hence of war, may be a personification of iron, but it is just as probable that he was the traditional discoverer of the use of iron, and hence a ghost-god, who has now been raised to the first rank. In the general tendency to regard Legba as the evil principle, we perhaps see a first step towards dualism, in which Ifa, for choice, would represent the good principle. All the gods are more anthropomorphic than was the case with the Ewe and Tshi tribes.

Looking, then, at these three groups of tribes, we find what seems to be a regular progression from the gods of hamlets and small communities, as among the Tshis, to the gods of a whole people, as among the Yorubas; and from the worship of the indwelling spirits of tangible objects, or objects believed to be tangible, as the sky, and of dead men, to the worship of personified principles. With the aggregation of peoples comes the concretion of gods. On the Gold Coast the natives dwell in small groups, isolated from one another by large tracts of forest. There are no towns, properly speaking, except on the sea-coast, and only a few large villages. Ideas percolate but slowly, and people live in the narrow circle of their own lives, knowing little or nothing of anything that transpires outside their own hamlet. To them their own surroundings are of the first importance, and the local god is the first in their estimation. There is no room here for the growth of national and general gods, for everything is narrowed down to the village circle.

Among those Ewe tribes who inhabit the western and forested portion of the Slave Coast we find much the same condition of affairs; but in the eastern Ewe districts the country is comparitively open, communities are larger, and communication is in every way freer. Here ideas circulate readily, man is constantly meeting with man, and as his mental circle widens, so do his conceptions concerning the nature of gods. Thus, among the eastern Ewe tribes we find many national and tribal gods, and several general gods, while the local gods have sunk in general estimation.

Among the Yoruba tribes this evolution has been carried still further, the county, except that inhabitated by the Jebus, being fairly open, large towns numerous, and circulation constant. Here the local god has almost disappeared, and the great majority of the gods are known to, and worshipped by, the whole of the tribes. The origin and inception of the nature-gods, as the indwelling spirits of natural objects or phenomena, being generally lost sight of, some explanation of their existence becomes necessary, and, ill consequence, we find a variety of myths dealing with the parentage and adventures of the gods.

As far as manes-worship alone is concerned-that is, the worship of spirits or gods which are known to have once been men-there is no great difference between the three lingual groups. Among the Yorubas it is, if anything, rather less developed than among the Tshis and Ewes, or rather relegated to an inferior position, in consequence of the greater power and sway of the gods generally worshipped. Whenever, however, the human origin of the ghost-god has been lost sight of, he seems to have conformed to the general rule; that is, where the circumstances have been unfavourable, he has, like the minor local nature-gods, disappeared, or been absorbed in the personality of another god, and where they have been favourable, he has acquired increased renown and area of worship, and become a national or general god.

That with the nationalisation of gods the priesthood should also become organised and developed is a natural result. Both on the Gold and Slave Coasts, and, indeed, everywhere else, the priesthood is a guild, or fraternity, the members of which require a special knowledge; and no man or woman can become a member of it without a preliminary training, or apprenticeship. On the Gold Coast, however, there are no distinct orders, or bodies, of priests. The gods being infinite in number, and local, the groups of priests are infinite in number, and local, and have no cohesion. In every village there will be found three or four priests who know the sacred dances and special ceremonies required for the worship of the gods peculiar to that village, but they know nothing of the rites and ceremonies of the gods of other towns. On the Slave Coast, on the other hand, each general god of the Ewe tribes, except Mawu, has in every town and village a considerable number of priests, whose duty it is to minister to him and to him alone. Colleges and seminaries for the instruction of novices are numerous, and to each god are attached a number of temple-women, or wives. Among the Yoruba tribes priestly organisation is carried still further, and there are three recognised orders of priests, each of which is subdivided into grades. On the Gold Coast a priest might officiate indifferently before any god of the locality for which he was, so to speak, ordained; but if a Yoruba priest of Shango were to attempt to consult Ifa there would be as great a commotion as there would be if a Roman Catholic priest were to attempt to preach in a Baptist Chapel. There is, in fact, a healthy competition between the priests of the principal gods, and each guard their own privileges very jealously.

Religion, at the stage of growth in which we find it among, these three groups of tribes, has no connection with morals, or the relations of men to one another. It consists solely of ceremonial worship, and the gods are only offended when some rite or ceremony has been neglected or omitted. If the omission be quite unintentional the result is just the same, as the gods, like uncivilised man, judge by acts and not by motives. In all ages man makes God the moral counterpart of himself, and in savage life he only revenges that which affects himself. With the wrongs of others he has nothing to do. If a man murdered his neighbour and robbed the widow and orphans, that would be a matter that would not concern the gods in the least, and, provided he paid the usual homage expected by gods from their followers, he would be as secure of their favour and protection as if he were perfectly innocent of all crime. On the other hand, years of blameless life would not save a man from punishment if he omitted some customary rite, or inadvertently gave offence. Similarly, in the Hebrew books, we find that the detestable fraud perpetrated by Jacob upon his brother Esau did not in any way lessen the favour with which he was regarded by the national god; but when the unfortunate Uzzah, with the best intentions in the world, put forth his hand and held the ark to keep it from falling, he was struck dead, because the action implied that the god was not able to protect himself. So, too, among the ancient Greeks, the gods took no cognisance of social offences, and only revenged slights offered to themselves; as, when they caused Protesilaus, the husband of Laodamia, to be the first hero slain before Troy, because she, in her eagerness to consummate her marriage, forgot to propitiate them with the usual sacrifices.

The belief that religion has no connection with morals thus seems to be inherent in man when in a certain intellectual and social condition, and it is not by any means at once got rid of by the adoption of the religion of a higher race in which the two are associated. The uneducated negroes of our colonies, for instance, who have been nominally Christian for some three generations, practically believe that the commission of grave moral offences, and even crimes, will not in the least affect their prospects of future "salvation," provided that they go to church or chapel regularly, and, in fact, pay their god all that ceremonial homage and lip-service which is, in their view, the essence of religion.

On the Gold and Slave Coasts, there is perfect liberty of thought in inatters of religion, but a man must show outward respect for the gods, because to do otherwise is to provoke calamities. A man may worship many gods, or none, just as he pleases, but he must not insult any. In fact, at this stage, man tolerates any form of religion that tolerates others and as he thinks it perfectly natural that different people should worship different gods, he does not attempt to force his own personal opinions upon anyone, or to establish conformity of ideas.

The striking resemblance which the Yoruba religious system bears to that of the ancient Greeks can scarcely have escaped notice. Olorun, the sky-god proper, now being gradually displaced by the more anthropomorphic Obatala, resembles Uranus, who was displaced by Kronos. In Greek mythology Kronos married his sister Rhea, the earth, and the Yoruba myth makes Obatala marry Odudua, who also represents the earth, though the qualities of Aphrodite appear to predominate. Olokun answers to Poseidon, Ogun, worker in iron, to Hephœstus, Orisha Oko to Priapus, Osanhin to Æsklepius, Orun, the sun, to Helios, and Oshu, the moon, to Selene. Zeus' messenger, Hermes, the lightning, was the protector of plunderers, and Shango is the god of lightning and plunder. Ifa, as the, god of prophecy, and the being who wards off evil and affords help, resembles Apollo, who, in Homer, is perfectly distinct from the sun-god, though identified with him in later times. [2]

The spirits of the trees answer to the Hama-dryads, and we have river-gods and sea-spirits. Metamorphosis to a brook, spring, or lagoon is common, and we have one example of a girl, being transformed, like Daphne, into a shrub. The gods, when consulted, gave oracular responses that differ in no essential particular from the answers given by the Oracle of Delphi. The Yorubas, like the Greeks, offer human sacrifices in time of national need. Dancing was, with the Greeks, intimately connected with worship, as Lucian says: [3] "You cannot find a single ancient mystery in which there is not dancing;" and on the Gold and Slave Coasts every god of note has his own dance, which is sacred to him, and known only to the initiated. The religion of ancient Greece has been obscured by a great deal of later poetic imagery; but, when we look into it closely, it is found to be similar to that of the Yorubas, and was no doubt produced when the Greeks were in a like intellectual condition. It is a pantheon which seems peculiar to a certain stage of culture, and is composed of nature-gods and ghost-gods. The Khonds of India have almost exactly the same objects of worship as the Yorubas, their gods being the sun-god, moon-god, earth-god, god of iron and arms, small-pox-god, god of hills, god of streams, forest-god, god of limits, god of fountains, god of rain, god of hunting, god of births, village-god, and tank-god. [4] Similar resemblances are forthcoming from almost every part of the world. In fact, the gods are everywhere much the same, because much the same phenomena and natnral objects are found everywhere, and because mankind [5] on the same plane of civilisation has much the same wants and necessities.

From a comparison of the systems of consaugainity of these lingual groups we are able to trace the order of evolution of the family, and the results go to show that Dr. Starcke's [5] theories of the priority of a system of kinship through fathers are incorrect, and that Mr. McLennin was right, in his gencral conclusions that descent through mothers was first in order.

Among the Tshi tribes of the Gold Coast descent is solely and exchisively in the female line. A family is a number of persons connected by uterine ties, all of whom bear the same clan-name. The clan-name is the test of kinship, and a family is a small circle of persons whose exact degrees of consanguinity to each other are known, within the wider circle of more distant relations, that is, the clan at large. Marriage within the clan is forbidden, and hence a father cannot be related by blood to his children, or be of the same family. Succession to property, office, or dignity follows the line of blood-descent, and a man's heir is his brother, or, failing a brother, his sister's son.

Among the Gã tribes of the Gold Coast descent is also solely and exchisively in the female line, and marriage in the mother's family is forbidden; but here the influence of the father in the household has begun to assert itself, and in some cases, chiefly where tho father is a man of some rank and power, office or dignity descends from father to son. Property is still considered to be vested in families, rather than in individuals, and succession to property remains in the female line, in the same order as among the Tshi tribes.

Among the western Ewe tribes the law of blood-descent, and of succession to office or property, is the same as with the Gã tribes; but among the eastern Ewe tribes, in Dahomi, blood-descent is on both sides of the house, and succession in the male line. This change has, however, only taken place in the royal family of Dahomi, and among what may be termed the aristocracy, who appear to have followed the lead of their sovereign. The lower orders still trace descent in the female line, and that the higher orders used also to do so is shown by the terms in use for expressing relationships. Brother and sister, for instance, can only be rendered by "mother's son" and "mother's daughter" respectively.

Among the Yoruba tribes descent is through both parents with succession in the male line, and marriage is forbidden both in the father's and mother's family so long as relationship can be traced. A man's heirs are his sons, among whom the property is equally divided. If a man have no sons, his brothers inherit. The old ideas concerning blood-descent still, however, exercise some influence, and children by the same father, but different mothers, are not generally considered proper blood-relations. Thus, going from the Tshi tribes to the Yoruba, from the least cultured to the most cultured, we find a gradual but regular change from kinship and descent through mothers only, to kinship and descent through both parents.

We are also able to trace the evolution of society from the stage in which the group, or community, as a whole, protected its own rights and exacted redress for injuries, to that in which the state protects the individual and punishes crime.

It would appear that, at first, the community or group was the social unit, and had collective rights and responsibilities, every member of the group having a, right to the protection of the group as a whole, and being in turn responsible individually for the acts or omissions of the group as a whole, or of any member of it. If we might speculate on this subject we might say that this condition dated from the time when the group was homogeneous, and had not yet been broken up into different clans by the system of blood-descent through mothers. Either no notion of blood-descent at all had been formed, or, if formed, the group-tie, the tie of association and comradeship, was considered of more moment than the blood-tie. The sole remaining trace of this condition to be found among the three lingual groups under consideration lies in the right which a creditor, whose debtor belongs to another community, has to seize the property of a third party, belonging to the same community as the person indebted, instead of recovering what is due from the latter. The group is individually and collectively responsible for debts contracted by any member.

Among the Tshi, Gã, and Ewe tribes the family, connected by uterine ties, is the social unit, and each member of a family is individually. responsible for all the others. The state, represented by the tribal or village-chief, takes no cognisance of offences unless they are such as directly concern, or are believed to concern, the interests of the community as a whole. Treason and witchcraft are almost the only offences that the state takes cognisance of. In cases of homicide, theft, rape, assault, and injury to the person or property, it is the family of the person who has suffered that alone can demand and exact satisfaction. No one else has a right to interfere, and, if the family should choose to forego all demands, no one has a right to say anything. Reparation is not sought directly from the offender, but from the family to which he belongs. It is, in fact, a case of one family arrayed against another.

Where the contending parties cannot come to mutual agreement as to the reparation, the injured party brings the case before the state, that is, the chief, who, until thus called upon to arbitrate, has no power to act. There is no fixed scale of punishments or awards; the injured family assesses its damages, and, if the injuring family does not accept the terms or effect a compromise, the dispute is referred to the chief for settlement. Murder is not necessarily, punished with death, for the family of the deceased may, if they think fit, accept a money-compensation in lieu for the loss of the services of the deceased. If the family be poor, and that of the murderer rich, they usually deem it better to exact payment than to enjoy the luxury of revenge, which the injurers would only have the effect of depriving of one of their number, without improving the position of the injured. In the contrary case the feeling of revenge is allowed to have its way; and when this occurs, the homicide is handed over to the injured family and put to death by them. In cases of theft, or injury to property, the stolen goods are returned or the amount of the damage made good, by the family to which the offender belongs; which is also liable to a fine for not having controlled the actions of the guilty member. The family itself then deals with its erring member, and punishes or pardons him, just as it thinks fit, that being a matter with which the outside public has nothing to do.

No distinction is made between crimes and accidents. Motive is never taken into account, and the harm done is always deliberated upon from the point of view of loss to the family. If a man be deliberately murdered, or killed by accident, there is equally a loss of an individual to the family, and they, can in either case take a life in exchange, or accept compensation. We saw the reflex of this condition in their religious views, the gods being likewise believed not to take motive into consideration.

Among the Yorubas, in consequence of the change in the system of blood-descents, the family has lost cohesion. It is no longer the powerful organisation it was when it rested upon the basis of the clan; for, instead of being a large group of kindred, it has become a congeries of households, each with two lines of descent, and as the family has weakened, the state has gradually usurped its privileges. The state here takes cognisance of serious crimes, and only minor injuries to the person or property are left to the initiative of the family. The restoration of the stolen property, and the imposition of a fine on the family, is no longer considered a sufficient reparation for theft. Theft has come to be regarded as all offence against social order, in which the whole community is interested, and lience a first offence is punished by flogging or fine, a second by mutilation, and a third by death. The family, being no longer collectively responsible for the actions of its several members, is not allowed to deal with the guilty member as it thinks fit. The state motes out justice; every man is responsible for his own conduct, and punishment falls upon the guilty individual instead of upon the group of kindred.

We are also able to trace to some extent the evolution of ideas concerning property. In those groups of tribes which trace descent through mothers only, property is vested in families rather than in individuals. There is, of course, individual property, but it usually is limited to minor articles, such as utensils, weapons, &c. Houses, the family gold ornaments, insignia, stools, and properties that have been handed down from bygone generations, are vested in the head of the family, and cannot be alienated without the consent of the family as a whole. At the demise of the head of the family the next of kin who succeeds has the usufruct of the family property in his turn, and is responsible for its safe custody. Among the Yorubas, in consequence of the change in the system of descents, property is vested in households, that is, in a smaller group of kindred, and divided among the heirs, who are the sons, or, in default of sons, brothers. As here, equally with the tribes who trace descent solely in the female line, the order of succession is unalterable; property in all cases remains in the family, the only difference being that among the Yorubas it is distributed with each succeeding generation, instead of being kept together; but the tendency of the Yoruba custom undoubtedly is to destroy the notion that property belongs to the group of kindred, and to make it individual.

In the case of all the tribes land is held in common, and there is no individual property in land, though the notion that land can be the property of the individual, instead of the community, has, as has been said, begun to appear among the Yorubas. Probably, in early times, moveable as well as immoveable property was once common. It still is, to a large extent, common to the family, and, at all earlier stages when the group was homogeneous, it was no doubt common to the group or community; for the custom which allows a creditor to seize the property of a third party belonging to the same community as the debtor, seems to point to a notion that the community as a whole must have benefited by what the debtor received. If all property were once common to the group, as land is now, then the following changes probably occurred. When the homogeneous group became heterogeneous, and broke up into clans in consequence of the system of female descents, property became common to the clan. Then, when the clan became divided into uterine families, property became common to the uterine family, as it still is on the Gold Coast; and, when the uterine families came to an end, owing to the recognition of the blood-tie between father and child, property became vested in households, as it is with the Yorubas. In other words, as the units of, which society was originally composed became subdivided into smaller and smaller groups, so did property become vested in a gradually decreasing number of persons, until it finally became individual.

[1] Nyankupon. *Nyan* means "to awake," but seems primarily to have meant "to stretch," or "to extend." *Pon* is anything flat, as "door, table-top "; *po*, "ocean," is from the same root. *Ku* seems to be a euphonic change from *kru*, "rounded, curved." The word Nyankupon would thus mean "the stretched-out, curved, flat surface," or shortly "the outspread vault."

[2] In the Roman mythology Air married Earth, and the marriage was renewed every year in spring. (Virgil, Georg. ii., 325.) Here, Air (Orungan) marries Water (Yemaja).

[3] On "Dancing," c. 15.

[4] Latham, "Ethnology of the British Colonies," p. 140.]

[5] "The Primitive Family."

www.ingramcontent.com/pod-product-compliance
Lightning Source LLC
Chambersburg PA
CBHW051828040426

42447CB00006B/428